salton sea

atlas

REDLANDS INSTITUTE

UNIVERSITY OF REDLANDS

REDLANDS, CALIFORNIA

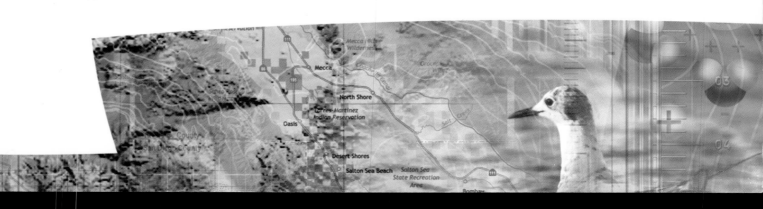

ISBN: 1-58948-043-0

Library of Congress Cataloging-in-Publication Data
Redlands Institute (Redlands, Calif.)
Salton Sea atlas / Redlands Institute, University of Redlands.
    p. cm.
   Includes bibliographical references and index.
   ISBN 1-58948-043-0 (hc)
   1. Salton Sea (Calif.)—Maps. 2. Salton Sea (Calif.)—Environmental conditions—Maps.
3. Hydrology—California—Salton Sea—Maps. 4. Physical geography—California—Salton Sea—Maps.
5. Limnology—California—Salton Sea—Maps. 6. Ecology—California—Salton Sea—Maps.
7. California—Salton Sea—History—Maps. I. Title.
G1527.S15 R3 2002
912.794'99—dc21   2002031020

Printed and bound in the United States of America.
Published by ESRI Press.

Redlands Institute Web site: www.institute.redlands.edu
ESRI Press Web site: www.esri.com/esripress

salton sea

atlas

THE REDLANDS
INSTITUTE
UNIVERSITY OF REDLANDS

ESRI Press
REDLANDS, CALIFORNIA

Enlightened
decision making
through geographic
information
systems

We are at a crossroads. The decisions that we make today, not just as citizens of the United States or North America or the West, but of the world, about our environment will have repercussions far beyond our own lives.

Our ability to understand the infinitely complex processes of nature is imperfect at best, yet our ability, and willingness, to manipulate or impact those processes is greater than it has ever been in history. What is absolutely paramount now is that we balance our understanding and power with care and patience—with better understanding of the past, the present, and the future.

The Salton Sea is in many ways a microcosm. It, too, is at a crossroads. The issues at the center of the restoration effort are the same ones affecting literally thousands of other plant, animal, and human communities around the world. There are tough problems to be dealt with, many important societal values at stake, and far-reaching consequences of both action and inaction. Sound management and effective policy decisions can only be built on good information and clear-headed, clean-handed scientific investigation. To say we need the right tools to work these complex problems and devise the best solutions is only to underscore what every good mechanic, gardener, carpenter, or chef knows. It's only common sense.

One of the right tools for this job is a geographic information system. Its utility can be felt at every point along the spectrum of investigation, analysis, debate, and action. By connecting large amounts of information in databases to clear, visually compelling maps, satellite photographs, 3-D models, and other kinds of images, GIS not only augments the data with a spatial component and the image with information, it makes the sharing of it all possible on an unprecedentedly broad scale.

The Salton Sea Database Program at the University of Redlands has been using GIS technology to provide the Salton Sea community with data and analytical tools to build a better understanding of the complex issues involved, at many levels of interest and concern. The *Salton Sea Atlas* is one important and particularly compelling outcome of that work. It provides comprehensive and vividly presented information that will help the community of stakeholders better understand the issues involved, and what is to be gained or lost by our decisions over the coming years.

"GIS technology... provide[s] the Salton Sea community with data and analytical tools to build a better understanding of the complex issues involved."

Jack Dangermond
President, ESRI

the Salton Sea landscape in change

We regard all landscapes as symbolic, as expressions of cultural values, social behavior, and individual actions worked upon particular localities over a span of time. Every landscape is an accumulation, and its study may be undertaken as formal history. (Meinig 1979)

Meinig's statement from *The Interpretation of Ordinary Landscapes* is especially salient for the Salton Sea. Landscape transformation is a continuum of change associated with the endless journey of humans throughout time. The rich history associated with the transformation of the Salton Basin to its present state involves an epic saga of great vision, pioneering spirit, tragedies, successes, and failures. This history reflects how human ingenuity, perseverance and technology have overcome extreme environmental conditions over time.

A permanent waterbody in the Salton Trough formed during 1905–7 has replaced the transient large lakes of the past. Human settlement in this area has also changed, bringing additional interest and values to be accommodated in the vision for the future of the Salton Sea. Thus, the historic record for the twenty-first century will reflect the vision, "pioneering spirit," and ingenuity of current society for: "A society can rightly be judged by the dreams of its people. Every dream is a story about the future, a vision of how things should be" (de Buys and Myers 1999).

Although the Salton Sea is largely sustained by irrigation drainwater, it provides major recreation opportunities for humans and is California's crown jewel of avian biodiversity. Therefore, the choices we make regarding the Salton Sea have major implications, not only for human society but also for other species. Our stewardship responsibilities extend beyond the interests and values of our generation: "We do not inherit the Earth from our parents, we borrow it from our children" (Anonymous).

Therefore, it is imperative that we make wise choices in selecting the path to be followed at the Salton Sea. The water issues of the Salton Sea are contemporary issues of global scope for which there are no easy solutions. The *Salton Sea Atlas* provides a wealth of information for enhancing understanding of this dynamic ecosystem and the factors that influence environmental outcomes. The choices we make have long-term consequences that will not only impact the future for the Salton Sea but will also impact local and regional communities and speak loudly of the level of commitment we do or do not have towards the stewardship of North American bird populations.

Milton Friend
Chief Scientist
Salton Sea Office

"Landscape transformation is a continuum of change associated with the endless journey of humans throughout time."

We have learned a great deal about the Salton Sea in the past four years. Under the direction of Dr. Milton Friend and the Salton Sea Science Office, baseline reconnaissance studies have been completed characterizing the hydrodynamics, chemical and biological limnology, salinity, eutrophication, sediments, vegetation, and fish and bird populations of the Salton Sea.

> "Issues facing the Salton Sea embody a changing paradigm..."

We learned that the Sea was not polluted. Pesticides, selenium, and other toxic chemicals are all below federal health standards in the Sea. In fact, the Sea is a natural sink for many of these substances, locking them away in the deeper, anoxic waters, away from fish and wildlife. Scientists described more than 400 species of microscopic plankton—one-tenth of them new to science. Contrary to bad press over the past few years, we learned that the Sea hosts one of the most productive fisheries in the world, with perhaps 100 million fish thriving in its nutrient rich waters; and we learned that the Sea is even more important for migratory birds than anyone imagined. Hosting two-thirds of all of the species in the United States and Canada combined, the Sea provides an essential stopover for millions of migratory birds—not just for the Pacific Coast flyway, but for birds all across the United States and Canada, extending from Russia and the north slope of the Arctic tundra to Central America and Peru.

The purpose of the *Salton Sea Atlas* is to make this information available to decision makers, regulatory agencies, environmental organizations, stakeholders, and the concerned public, as they deliberate over alternatives to restore or attempt to stabilize salinity, eutrophication, and wildlife habitats. We have attempted to do this in a graphically compelling way, combining the latest in geographic information science with graphic arts and illustration, and I am very proud of the work produced by our many talented staff members, contractors, and contributing scientists.

Issues facing the Salton Sea embody a changing paradigm: can the Sea be maintained in the long-term? Can we, as a society, manage this rich part of our natural heritage in the face of continuing growth and demand for water? Decision makers must have good information in order to evaluate the potential impacts of water transfers, restoration and clean-up activities, or understand the consequences of not doing anything at all and letting the Sea become a dead sea.

In any case, there remains the need for access to the best and most recent information available in order to arrive at an alternative that meets the needs of our rapidly growing region, while maintaining environmental resources for fish, wildlife, and humanity—and to this end, the University of Redlands Salton Sea Database Program will continue in its efforts to provide this information to anyone and everyone concerned with the Salton Sea.

Dr. Timothy P. Krantz,
Salton Sea Database Program Director

contents

area information steward

adaptive management

community outreach

monitoring and evaluation

Awareness of environmental change has increased dramatically throughout the world, and these changes are happening at an unprecedented scale and pace. Equally unprecedented is our increasing ability to collect and distribute data and information. Opportunities exist for applying this information and bringing information management tools to bear on the monumental task of environmental management and problem solving.

The concept of an Area Information Steward evolved from these two trends, to collect as much information as possible about a rapidly changing world, and to ensure accurate management, organization, and analysis of that information.

The structure for Area Information Stewardship is straightforward: an infrastructure for the collection and analysis of spatial data that not only brings all manner of data together geographically, but organizes and—more importantly—integrates it and facilitates its movement to and use by interested parties both within the geographic area of concern, and to stakeholders distributed around the globe. The Salton Sea Database Program at the University of Redlands works in just such a way.

Effective environmental management requires ongoing monitoring and adaptation to change. An Area Information Steward supports adaptive management by facilitating communication between stakeholders to build common understanding and share information. This type of informed dialog is essential in evaluating both past efforts and future priorities. The wide range of people involved in planning, researching, and championing management alternatives necessitates a wide range of credible and authoritative information resources, as well as appropriate levels of synthesis.

Transformation of Knowledge

Understanding how to address an issue is as critical as understanding why. While data serves a vital role in informing a decision process, community dialog is essential to common understanding among stakeholders. While disagreements may persist, this dialog ensures that participants not only apply the best information at hand, but also understand differing viewpoints and the values behind them.

Baseline Reconnaissance

Scientific consensus must inform policy and management intervention. A baseline scientific assessment to identify and resolve knowledge gaps forms the basis for recommending and evaluating change.

Ongoing Studies and Legacy Data

Study and analysis of previous data collection efforts often provides context for investigating current and future trends and understanding change. Techniques such as data mining and knowledge management provide new insights into legacy data and past studies.

Pure and Applied Research

Basic research and understanding of natural systems remain critical to effective problem solving. Traditional scientific research is increasingly integrated into policy and management activities. Further, communication of scientific knowledge to a diverse audience is essential.

Science

GEOgraphic Context

Geography unifies information and provides a framework for addressing interrelated issues. Many of the most pressing issues in the world today have a geographic component. They have a place of origin, area of effect, and even connections to other places. Geographic context is critical when addressing interrelated issues in a comprehensive way.

Hierarchy of Scale

Places are innately linked to one another: watersheds within continents; continents within the world. Further, complexity increases when addressing regional problems in the context of their larger geographic relationships. Applying a scale of analysis appropriate to the scale of a single issue is a common approach. But the variety of social, economic, and environmental issues and their interrelationships, necessitates multiple scales of analysis. Comprehensively addressing the diversity of issues facing a region with an integrated approach requires consistent information at a variety of scales.

Salton Sea Watershed

North America

Salton Sea Region

POLICY

Policy and Regulations

Targets, goals, and guidelines must not only respond to the expressed needs of constituents, but also be based on realistic data and adequate understanding of the proposed impacts of new policy.

Priority Setting

Constituents at multiple levels—local, state, and federal—influence political priorities. This process benefits greatly from an informed public. Politicians themselves need access to comprehensive information at the appropriate level of synthesis to weigh and prioritize the diverse needs of their constituents.

Budget and Funding

Most policy-level decisions become rationalized on the basis of economic cost and perceived benefits. Setting expectations of performance and evaluating progress are essential for funding long-term and continued programs.

Project Implementation

Management intervention in a region takes many forms. Enforcing regulations, implementing programs, or even construction of large-scale projects, all require extensive planning and evaluation.

Monitoring

Through coordination and communication between ongoing monitoring efforts not otherwise mandated to share information and resources, these programs can take advantage of increased efficiency in the region, including: standardizing methods, data formats, and field data collection; and clarifying overlapping mandates.

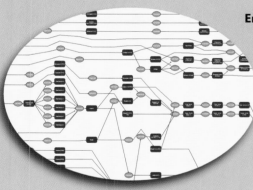

Environmental Design

Effective management intervention requires a planning approach that addresses diverse public interests, weighing economic, environmental, and social factors. Principles of environmental design, first applied in design disciplines such as urban planning and architecture, have seen increasing use in fields such as conservation biology and systems engineering.

Management

Information Empowers Communities

While geography itself is a unifying element, access to shared information builds communities across geographic boundaries. Experts on saline lakes, bird migration, or even arid farming might share an interest with Salton region communities, regardless of geographic relationship. Shared topical interests make region-specific data applicable in a much larger geographic context. The benefits of wide distribution of data and information underscore the need for data standards and increased accessibility.

Information Networks: a New Infrastructure

Information partnerships facilitate multidisciplinary geography-based problem solving. Even basic information necessary for resolving many issues such as political boundaries and land ownership (historically two very contentious issues) can require extensive dialog between governments and organizations. Internationally, the notion of an information infrastructure—data resources that are integrated and shared across multiple sectors—is an emerging concept. In the United States, government data made available by mandate, has greatly enriched private sector projects, local government, and academic research. Increasingly, standards for cataloging and distributing geographic information, under the guidance of the Federal Geographic Data Committee, have greatly improved accessibility as well.

Current efforts to extend the Spatial Data Infrastructure concept to regions, nations, and international collaborators with widely differing social, economic, and legal systems may revolutionize global partnerships in characterizing and addressing complex problems.

salton sea database program

The University of Redlands has been collecting and archiving data on the Salton Sea since 1998, leading a cooperative effort involving dozens of organizations, public agencies, and researchers. The University's Salton Sea Database Program (SSDP) is now considered a foremost source for geospatial data, bibliographic references, and other information about the Sea and its environment.

Many consider the Salton Sea an ecosystem in peril. Claimed by some to be an artificial and naturally intermittent water body destined to waste away (the Salton Sea was created by an inundation of the Colorado River in 1905), ecological change at the Salton Sea and its eventual fate is a source of controversy. Public attention revolves around the question: "Do we save the Salton Sea?", followed closely by the question of "how?" Informing the decision-making process is crucial for any restoration, which could ultimately cost hundreds of millions of dollars over several decades, and lead to extensive habitat change or loss.

The SSDP houses an infrastructure of data management and analysis tools to support multidisciplinary and coordinated decision making across all the scientific teams and stakeholders involved in the restoration project. It also provides tools for communicating issues and alternatives in informative, graphically compelling, and understandable forms that can be readily provided to both technical and nontechnical audiences, including: public representatives and policy makers, community decision makers, scientists, government and non-government organizations, commercial interests, private landowners, and the general public.

Information Providers, Area Information Stewards, & The Salton Sea Database Program
This network of collaborators provides data and information to a wide range of communities.

Stakeholders
Stakeholders are communities of people collecting and evaluating diverse information in the context of decision making.

Salton Sea Watershed
North America
Salton Sea Region

Request for Information
Supporting an adaptive management process requires the ability to respond to changing concerns and needs. While standard informational products satisfy most stakeholders, responding to specialized and changing needs of a diverse stakeholder group is a key strategic goal for the SSDP. Since 1998, hundreds of requests have been fielded, ranging from simple questions about the region to custom map products, presentations, and analyses.

what is GIS

A geographic information system is a set of tools and methods for capturing, managing, and analyzing geographically referenced information. A GIS integrates location-based data, such as an address or map coordinate. This integration allows for display, exploration, and analysis of complex relationships. A GIS is comprised of several components: data; equipment, including computers; software; methods; output, including maps, reports, and other visualizations or synthesis; and the people who use it.

data
output
people
methods
software
hardware

Data
Data exists in many forms. In the past, GIS data was an extremely expensive component of a GIS (as much as 80 or even 90 percent of the cost for a typical local government GIS budget). Data costs have declined significantly. This is due in large part to an economy of scale as more businesses and public agencies require and develop data. A great deal of attention focuses on developing data standards to facilitate storage, retrieval, and cataloging

The concept of metadata—or data about data—which describes source, method, and appropriate uses, among other things, is a growing priority. Data integration—the combination and reconciliation of disparate data sources—as well as automation of legacy data, are growing efforts.

Community Presentations

SSDP staff have made dozens of presentations to community groups, schools and other venues to provide information about the Salton Sea and the restoration planning issues and activities. A diverse stakeholder audience is represented, including congressional representatives and other local and regional public leaders, resource managers, local and tribal government representatives, the interested public, and school children.

Atlas

While extensive, most of the information and data on the Salton Sea is often inaccessible to the general public. Appropriate levels of synthesis are required to effectively inform the entire stakeholder community. This atlas is a tool to assist in understanding complex natural and cultural processes to inform management and policy decisions.

Environmental Assessment

In the United States, environmental regulations require impact assessments for most new developments and projects. With any ongoing restoration project planning, environmental assessment and reporting is a major undertaking. The SSDP provided a variety of data and map exhibits to the consultants preparing an Environmental Impact Statement and Report for the restoration alternatives considered by the Salton Sea Authority and Bureau of Reclamation.

Cross-Media Database

Online access to information is one of the core tools developed by SSDP to support regional collaboration and research. Basic scientific data from reconnaissance studies, current and historical published scientific reports, geographic data, remotely sensed data from satellites, photographs, Web sites, events, organizations, and people all represent sources of useful information. Based on existing and emerging library and information science standards and research, as well as geographic information science, the SSDP designed and implemented a cross-media database to integrate information by topic, time, and location.

Reconnaissance Data

Baseline reconnaissance studies were commissioned by various restoration project participants to help fill data gaps associated with the ecological assessment activities of the Science Subcommittee (SSC). SSDP supported these studies by providing collateral information, establishing GIS-related standards and guidelines, establishing frameworks for management, and sharing baseline information among the project's science team.

Wildlife Health

Students and staff assisted the Salton Sea Authority and the Salton Sea Science Office in the design of a data collection system to help record observations concerning fish and bird health at the Sea. This comprehensive program, designed to aid evaluation and response to wildlife health issues facing the Sea and its surroundings, required collaboration between federal and state resource managers across multiple agencies.

Enhanced Evaporation System

Controlling rising salinity levels at the Sea is a primary goal for restoration projects. Evaluating the effectiveness and implications of various management interventions is a continuing process. Evaporation of Salton Sea water to remove salt is one of several alternatives being evaluated. Students and staff worked with the Salton Sea Authority, the Bureau of Reclamation, and a consulting engineering company to perform siting analysis for evaporation ponds that would remove salt from the Sea.

Water-Quality Data Coordination

Based upon stakeholder interviews, it was determined that an inventory and assessment of water-quality monitoring activities in the Salton Basin was needed to improve future data collection efforts. In response, the SSDP, together with the State Regional Water Quality Control Board, began a comprehensive inventory and characterization  of 18 federal, state, and local government agencies involved with water quality data collection. Today, the project is helping to strengthen region-wide water quality monitoring and collaboration efforts.

Bird Banding Analysis

University of Redlands students and staff assisted the Salton Sea Science Office in analyzing bird banding data from the USGS to help determine the significance of the Salton Sea to migratory birds along the Pacific Flyway. This 30-year data set, widely used for managing bird populations throughout North America, revealed not only a high degree of bird use at the Salton Sea, as expected, but also connections across North America.

Output

The science and art of graphic and cartographic communication is essential to effective application of GIS. Without useful synthesis and meaningful output, no benefits will be realized from the results. From statistical reports and traditional maps to interactive digital maps, GIS can aid in visualization of complex ideas and even simulation of real-world issues.

Methods

In the present Information Age, an increasing number of tools are available to manage and analyze information. Like any tool, the real power behind its use is effective application.

From project and workflow management to statistical analyses, the effective use of GIS relies on careful design and methods. Even so, formalizing methods in the GIS realm is a complex issue. Ideas and techniques developed in one context may be inappropriate in others. This is especially true where economic, social, and political circumstances alter those contexts on several levels at once.

However, access to appropriate techniques is only one facet of an effective methodology. To be an effective practitioner, familiarity with the tools is not enough. Increasingly, creative, properly-

Equipment

The earliest GIS produced only very elementary analyses and rudimentary cartography. Today, computers perform increasingly complex analyses. Computers, digital storage space, as well as data gathering equipment such as satellites and Global Positioning Systems are all examples of equipment used to support GIS activities. Perhaps the most significant component of a GIS today is digital data networks. The use of GIS across the Internet now facilitates a global network of collaborators, offering GIS data, services, and presentation for a wide audience.

Software

New software tools are making GIS both more capable and more accessible. Previously seen as an esoteric niche apart from mainstream information technology practices, GIS has become an increasingly visible and essential tool in our lives. GIS software enables us to examine and understand our data in new ways. Applications range from the specialized to the mundane: retailers can target consumers, governments can evaluate their level of service and community needs, and the public can get driving directions from Web sites, all through GIS.

People

Like any tool, the use of GIS is only limited by the imagination and capability of its users. Traditionally, GIS required a very specialized skill set. As the ease of use in computer technology and the pervasiveness of digital devices have increased, so has use of GIS. Even with the ease of use of GIS, geographic knowledge and spatial thinking are still essential to addressing geographic problems. The GIS practitioner must not only be a technology expert, but must apply their expertise appropriately in new and increasingly effective ways in a changing world

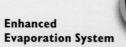

making the atlas

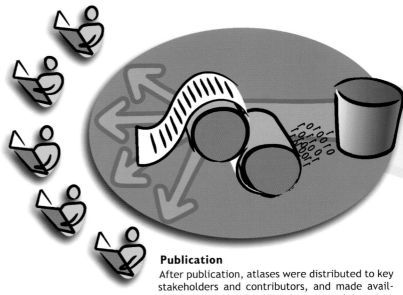

Primer and Contributor Identification

Collaboration between key stakeholders and SSDP staff provided the foundation for preliminary atlas development. An "atlas primer" was circulated among recognized experts involved in Salton Sea science and policy. The primer introduced potential collaborators to the concept of an atlas as a new tool for communicating their expertise to the public.

Publication

After publication, atlases were distributed to key stakeholders and contributors, and made available to the general public. Content and data generated in the process of creating the atlas further enhanced the SSDP digital library holdings.

This atlas is part of a series of products designed to serve the informational and educational needs of a broad stakeholder group. At the Salton Sea, the wide range of people involved in planning, researching, and championing management alternatives required an information resource that was not only authoritative, but also accessible. By developing greater common understanding about the relationships between the natural environment, cultural context, and social values, a broader range of people can participate in environmental planning. Management and policy decisions can be more effective and socially relevant.

The atlas was developed over a two-year period, involving University of Redlands staff and researchers, as well as key experts concerned with science, management, and planning at the Salton Sea. A highly collaborative process was developed to: identify key concerns and points of contention; solicit and encourage expert-level input; integrate topics across scientific disciplines where possible; and communicate complex issues.

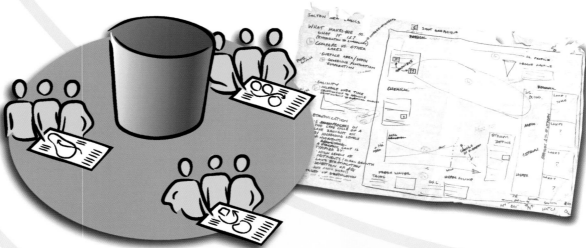

Storyboarding

Expert contributors—specialists in each of their disciplines—collaborated with the SSDP to develop a "story" to explain their topic. Collaboration ensured accuracy of content and preserved important linkages to atlas topics. Often, this dialog surfaced common interests and concerns among experts. It is hoped that interdisciplinary collaboration among experts in the region will continue in the future.

Information Collection

Using the storyboard as an outline, data was collected to develop maps, graphics, diagrams, figures, and text. Much of the data and research required to produce the atlas existed in published sources. The SSDP cross-media database—a digital library about the Salton Sea—provided a starting point for research. A wide variety of sources, including federal and local agencies, provided further research material.

GIS
Geographic Information Systems

Maps are key for communicating complex issues. A GIS provides tools for managing and analyzing complex information and producing digital representations of the landscape. These graphic representations of reality can greatly enhance our understanding. In addition to providing compelling images, much of GIS

Needs Assessment

Each story was assessed to identify specific data requirements. Geographic data can be described in many ways. Themes, or topics, describe the type of information represented by a piece of data. Scale, accuracy, precision, and extent describe spatial characteristics of data. Attributes are tabular data that describe characteristics of locations. The time frame and currency of data was also important. Each story in the atlas required specific themes, attributes, time frame, and spatial characteristics.

Data Inventory and Evaluation

Data needs, as assessed for each atlas story, were compared against existing data in the SSDP libra and other sources. For each stor in the atlas, a wide variety of da sources might exist—or sometim none at all. Where multiple sourc existed, each data source was eval ated and compared to determine su

Draft Atlas Review
The newly revised atlas pages were assembled into a draft atlas. At this stage the atlas was in near-final form. Key stakeholders, seeing the assembled atlas for the first time, once again reviewed the compiled pages for consistency and story flow.

Spread Review and Refinement
Atlas sections were sent to their original expert contributors for review. Key stakeholders also participated, identifying inaccuracies and providing specific suggestions for improvements. Atlas revisions responded to a wide variety of input.

Spread Development
Individual pages took shape as teams of cartographers, graphic designers, and writers began the production process. Teams worked closely with each other to maintain a cohesive story and consistent style. Each page received several rounds of revision and evaluation before it was considered for external review.

Cartography
Maps that addressed each story's r... generated from digital data. Using dat... lytical products, maps were designed to c... the atlas. Teams of data specialists, cartogra... graphic designers collaborated on each ma... used to create products ranging from three-d... representations to simple location reference

Spatial Analysis
Envisioning complex information often requires data analysis and synthesis. Each atlas story required a different level and approach of spatial analysis.

Data Refinement and Quality Control
A quality-control process was used for each of the data created for the atlas. To ensure accuracy, SSDP staff and expert contributors reviewed and refined new data.

Building the Database
GIS specialists worked with data sources to acquire existing digital information. Where data did not exist, an "automation" plan was developed to take source information and convert it to a digital representation. Data were then integrated to

E very land has a story. The story of the Salton Sea begins millions of years ago, at the convergence of three massive tectonic plates. Mountains and valleys emerged from the intersection of the Pacific Plate, Farallon Plate, and North American Plate.

Over the past few million years, changing global climate and the flow of water has shaped the Salton Basin and its environs. Today, the Basin is one of the most topographically diverse regions in the world, and is home to an extraordinarily diverse range of plants and animals.

physical geography

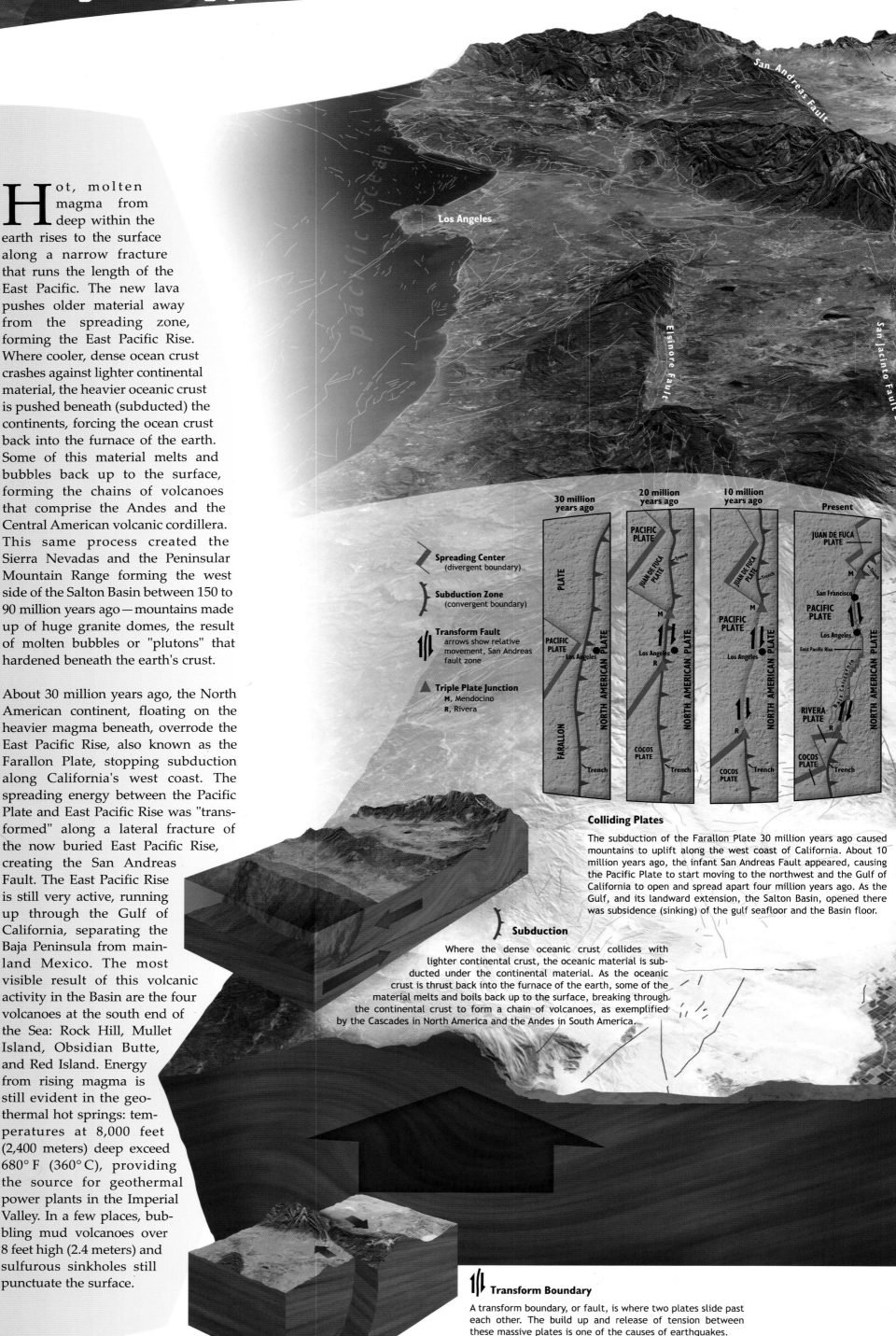

Hot, molten magma from deep within the earth rises to the surface along a narrow fracture that runs the length of the East Pacific. The new lava pushes older material away from the spreading zone, forming the East Pacific Rise. Where cooler, dense ocean crust crashes against lighter continental material, the heavier oceanic crust is pushed beneath (subducted) the continents, forcing the ocean crust back into the furnace of the earth. Some of this material melts and bubbles back up to the surface, forming the chains of volcanoes that comprise the Andes and the Central American volcanic cordillera. This same process created the Sierra Nevadas and the Peninsular Mountain Range forming the west side of the Salton Basin between 150 to 90 million years ago—mountains made up of huge granite domes, the result of molten bubbles or "plutons" that hardened beneath the earth's crust.

About 30 million years ago, the North American continent, floating on the heavier magma beneath, overrode the East Pacific Rise, also known as the Farallon Plate, stopping subduction along California's west coast. The spreading energy between the Pacific Plate and East Pacific Rise was "transformed" along a lateral fracture of the now buried East Pacific Rise, creating the San Andreas Fault. The East Pacific Rise is still very active, running up through the Gulf of California, separating the Baja Peninsula from mainland Mexico. The most visible result of this volcanic activity in the Basin are the four volcanoes at the south end of the Sea: Rock Hill, Mullet Island, Obsidian Butte, and Red Island. Energy from rising magma is still evident in the geothermal hot springs: temperatures at 8,000 feet (2,400 meters) deep exceed 680° F (360°C), providing the source for geothermal power plants in the Imperial Valley. In a few places, bubbling mud volcanoes over 8 feet high (2.4 meters) and sulfurous sinkholes still punctuate the surface.

San Andreas Fault

Los Angeles

Elsinore Fault

San Jacinto Fault Zone

pacific ocean

30 million years ago

20 million years ago

10 million years ago

Present

Spreading Center
(divergent boundary)

Subduction Zone
(convergent boundary)

Transform Fault
arrows show relative
movement, San Andreas
fault zone

Triple Plate Junction
M, Mendocino
R, Rivera

PACIFIC PLATE

NORTH AMERICAN PLATE

FARALLON

Trench

Los Angeles

PACIFIC PLATE

JUAN DE FUCA PLATE

M

Los Angeles
R

COCOS PLATE

Trench

JUAN DE FUCA PLATE

Trench

M

PACIFIC PLATE

Los Angeles

R

COCOS PLATE

Trench

JUAN DE FUCA PLATE

M

Trench

San Francisco

PACIFIC PLATE

Los Angeles

East Pacific Rise

Baja California

RIVERA PLATE

R

COCOS PLATE

Trench

NORTH AMERICAN PLATE

Colliding Plates

The subduction of the Farallon Plate 30 million years ago caused mountains to uplift along the west coast of California. About 10 million years ago, the infant San Andreas Fault appeared, causing the Pacific Plate to start moving to the northwest and the Gulf of California to open and spread apart four million years ago. As the Gulf, and its landward extension, the Salton Basin, opened there was subsidence (sinking) of the gulf seafloor and the Basin floor.

Subduction

Where the dense oceanic crust collides with lighter continental crust, the oceanic material is subducted under the continental material. As the oceanic crust is thrust back into the furnace of the earth, some of the material melts and boils back up to the surface, breaking through the continental crust to form a chain of volcanoes, as exemplified by the Cascades in North America and the Andes in South America.

Transform Boundary

A transform boundary, or fault, is where two plates slide past each other. The build up and release of tension between these massive plates is one of the causes of earthquakes.

Plate Tectonics

Inspired by the "fit" of the Americas with Europe and Africa, the theory of plate tectonics was first postulated by Alfred Wegener in 1915, stating that the continents "drift" like rafts on denser oceanic crust. Lacking evidence of the causal mechanisms behind continental drift, however, the theory was debated and debunked at the time. Now, thanks to deep oceanographic mapping and high-resolution satellite imagery, scientists can not only explain the mechanics of plate tectonics, but can measure the relative movements of the continental plates in millimeters per year.

North American Plate
Eurasian Plate
Pacific Plate
Arabian Plate
Philippine Plate
Pacific Plate
Cocos Plate
Caribbean Plate
African Plate
Nazca Plate
South American Plate
Indo-Australian Plate
Antarctic Plate

Washington
Colombia Plateau
Rocky Mountain System
Montana
Oregon
Idaho
Great Plains Province
Columbia Plateau
Wyoming
Pacific Mountain System
Basin and Range
California
Nevada
Utah
Colorado
Pacific ocean
Colorado Plateau
Arizona
New Mexico
Mexico
Texas

San Andreas Fault

Salton Sea

Red Island
Mullet Island
Rock Hill
Obsidian Butte

Brawley Fault Zone

Imperial Fault Zone

Sand Hills Fault

Geomorphic Provinces

Within North America, mountain ranges, plateaus, plains, and basins owe their formation to various geologic processes. These diverse regions are called "geomorphic provinces." For example, subduction of the East Pacific Rise under the North American Plate pushed up volcanic mountains to create the Pacific Mountain System. Similar means formed the much older Great Basin and Range, but rain, wind, and massive prehistoric water bodies further shaped this region over millions of years. Geomorphic settings greatly influence today's climate patterns, vegetation, and even human settlement.

Spreading Center

Rising molten magma from deep within the earth reaches the surface and spreads out in either direction along the East Pacific Rise, creating new oceanic crust. Older material pushes steadily outward and away from the spreading center, becoming cooler and denser as it rides on this crustal conveyor belt.

Current Vegetation Land Cover

Map labels: steppe-like · polar alpine desert · open boreal woodlands · ice sheet permanent ice · sparse tundra · dense tundra · mid taiga · southern taiga · open boreal woodlands · cold temperate giant coniferous rainforests · semi-arid temperate woodlands · mid taiga · temperate deciduous broad-leaved forest · sparse short grass steppe · Mojave Desert · Victorville, CA · Yuma, AZ · Sonoran Desert · temperate semi-desert · broad-leaved temperate evergreen forest · savanna · semi-arid temperate scrub · dense tall grass steppe · sparse short grass steppe · tropical rainforest · monsoon/dry forest

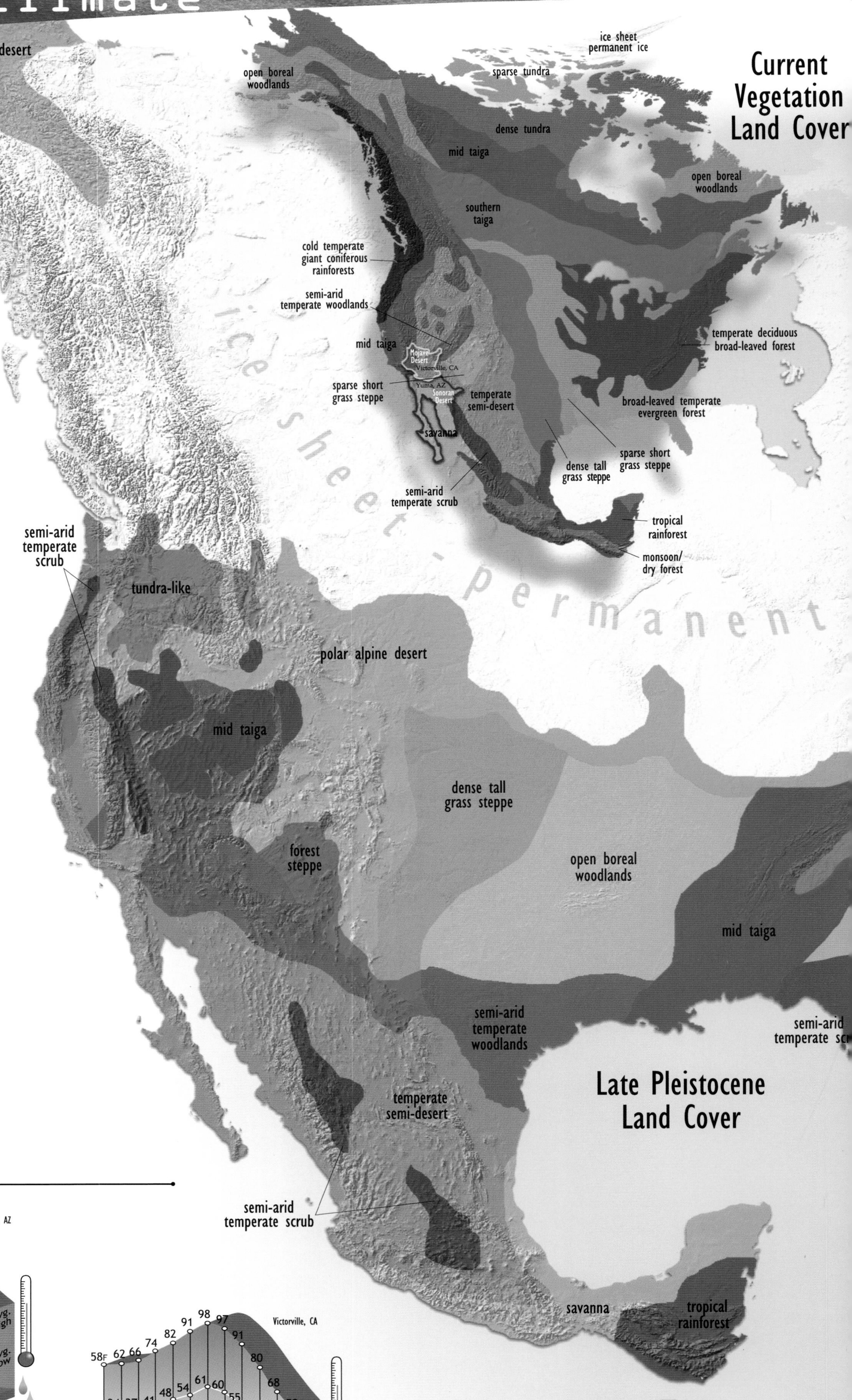

The Salton Sea Basin lies at the intersection of two great deserts, the Mojave to the north, and the Sonoran to the south and west. While both are sparsely vegetated, these deserts experienced profound changes in climate and vegetation over the past two to three million years. During the Pleistocene geologic era, global climate shifted back and forth between Ice Age conditions and warmer temperatures similar to modern ones. Average global temperature was as much as 14.4°F (8°C) cooler than today. Glacial ice covered much of North America, and temperate forests extended far south of their current range. For the past 10,000 years, the Holocene era, warmer temperatures have prevailed.

Though also an arid region during the Pleistocene era, vegetation typical of a wetter, cooler, desert climate thrived in the Salton Basin. As the climate warmed, the range and diversity of vegetation species changed throughout North America and the world. Today, while both the Mojave and Sonoran deserts are relatively arid and hot, the Sonoran Desert is warmer. Some plants thrived or adapted to this new climate, while others now grow only in the temperate Mojave, where temperatures often reach freezing.

Late Pleistocene Land Cover map labels: ice sheet - permanent · semi-arid temperate scrub · tundra-like · polar alpine desert · mid taiga · forest steppe · dense tall grass steppe · open boreal woodlands · mid taiga · semi-arid temperate scrub · semi-arid temperate woodlands · temperate semi-desert · semi-arid temperate scrub · savanna · tropical rainforest

Desert Climate Today

Yuma Valley, AZ: 69, 74, 79, 86, 93, 101, 105, 104, 100, 90, 76, 69 (Avg. High); 40, 42, 46, 51, 58, 65, 74, 74, 67, 56, 45, 40 (Avg. Low); .3in, .3, .2, .1, .03, .02, .5, .2, .2, .2, .4, .4

Victorville, CA: 58, 62, 66, 74, 82, 91, 98, 97, 91, 80, 68, 59 (Avg. High); 30, 34, 37, 41, 48, 54, 61, 60, 55, 45, 35, 30 (Avg. Low); 1in, .9, .8, .3, .1, .05, .2, .3, .2, .5, .5, .7

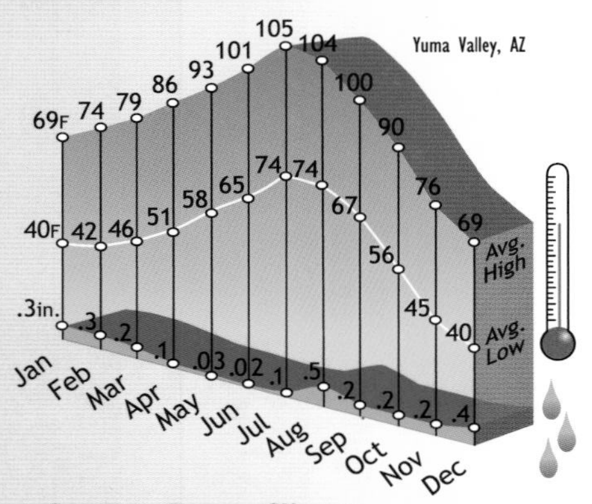

Sonoran Desert Climate

Because the Sonoran Desert is a sub-tropical desert, much of its moisture comes during the summer monsoon season, which is from July through September. Precipitation varies between 4.7 to 11.8 inches each year (120 to 300 mm), and average monthly temperatures range from 61 to 92°F (16 to 24°C). During the summer, daytime and nighttime temperatures vary, with temperatures exceeding 100°F (37.7°C) during the day and dropping to 65°F (18°C) at night. In the winter months, daytime and nighttime temperatures range between 70 and 40°F (21°C and 4°C).

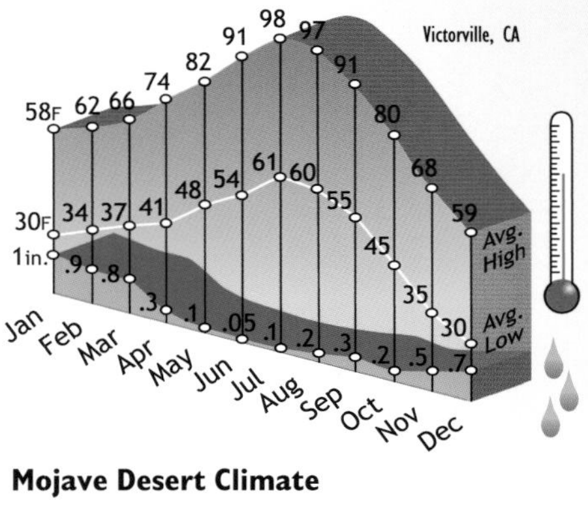

Mojave Desert Climate

Less arid than the Sonoran desert, the Mojave still receives very little rain — some in the form of winter snow. Most places receive less than 6 inches of annual rain, and deep in the desert rainfall is only 2 to 4 inches a year. Usually warm throughout the year, temperature varies more than in the Sonoran Desert. Day and night temperatures have a wider range with winter temperatures often dropping to below freezing.

Packrat Middens

Packrats (*Neotoma lepida*) are small desert rodents that forage for plants, leaves, and seeds. True to their names, packrat nests are full of discarded refuse known as middens. From these middens, scientists have reconstructed 40,000 years of climate and vegetation history. Aided by dry desert conditions, plant material is preserved in a crystalline substance formed from solidified packrat urine—called amberat due to its amber-like color and texture.

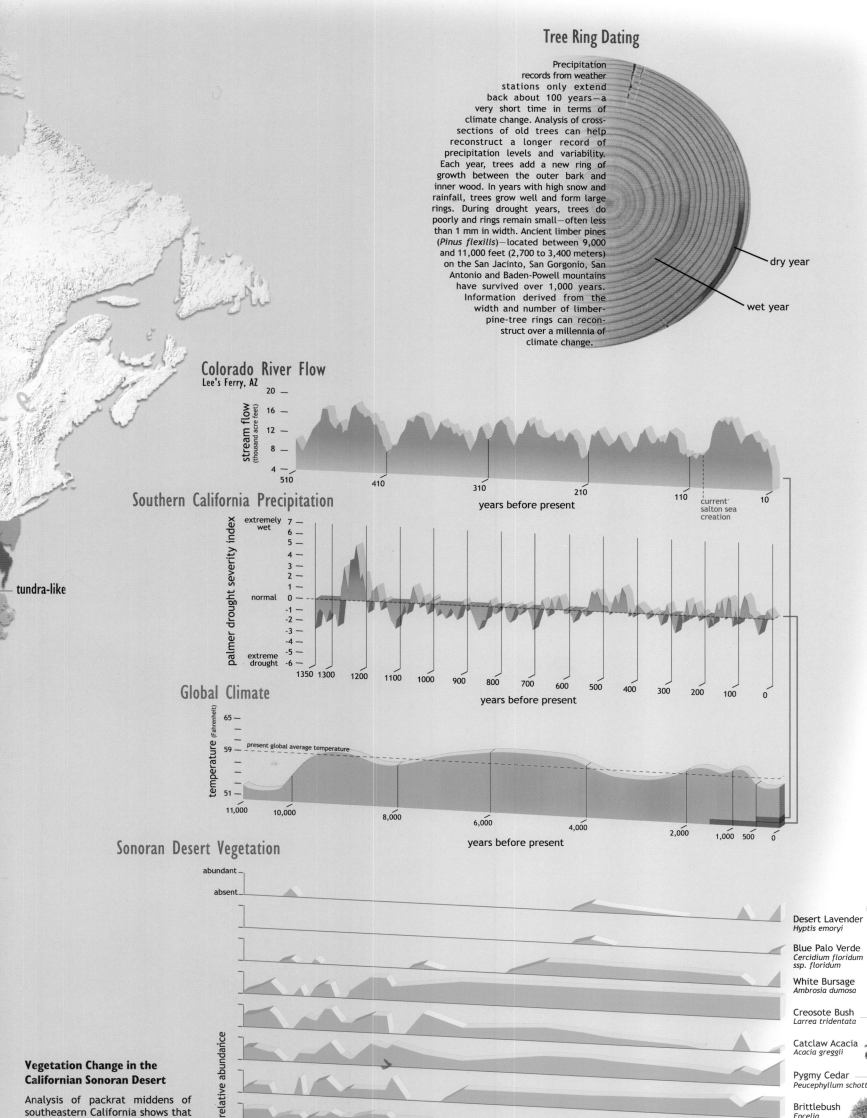

Tree Ring Dating

Precipitation records from weather stations only extend back about 100 years—a very short time in terms of climate change. Analysis of cross-sections of old trees can help reconstruct a longer record of precipitation levels and variability. Each year, trees add a new ring of growth between the outer bark and inner wood. In years with high snow and rainfall, trees grow well and form large rings. During drought years, trees do poorly and rings remain small—often less than 1 mm in width. Ancient limber pines (*Pinus flexilis*)—located between 9,000 and 11,000 feet (2,700 to 3,400 meters) on the San Jacinto, San Gorgonio, San Antonio and Baden-Powell mountains have survived over 1,000 years. Information derived from the width and number of limber-pine-tree rings can reconstruct over a millennia of climate change.

dry year

wet year

Colorado River Flow

Lee's Ferry, AZ

stream flow (thousand acre feet)

20
16
12
8
4

510   410   310   210   110   current   10
                                                        salton sea
                                                        creation

years before present

Southern California Precipitation

palmer drought severity index

extremely wet 7
6
5
4
3
2
1
normal 0
-1
-2
-3
-4
extreme -5
drought -6

1350 1300 1200 1100 1000 900 800 700 600 500 400 300 200 100 0

years before present

tundra-like

Global Climate

temperature (Fahrenheit)

65
59 present global average temperature
51

11,000 10,000   8,000   6,000   4,000   2,000 1,000 500 0

years before present

Sonoran Desert Vegetation

abundant
absent

relative abundance

Vegetation Change in the Californian Sonoran Desert

Analysis of packrat middens of southeastern California shows that the Californian Sonoran Desert was more humid 13,000 to 10,000 years ago, with precipitation nearly 50 percent higher than today. Joshua trees, no longer present in the Sonoran Desert, are now found farther north in the Mojave Desert. Vegetation typical of the eastern Sonoran, species such as creosote bush, brittlebush and catclaw acacia, replaced historic species 9,000 to 10,000 years ago. Today, Joshua trees do not grow any closer than 60 to 90 miles (100 to 150 km) to the northwest of the Salton Sea.

11,000 10,000   8,000   6,000   4,000   2,000 1,000 500 0

years before present

Desert Lavender
Hyptis emoryi

Blue Palo Verde
Cercidium floridum ssp. floridum

White Bursage
Ambrosia dumosa

Creosote Bush
Larrea tridentata

Catclaw Acacia
Acacia greggii

Pygmy Cedar
Peucephyllum schottii

Brittlebush
Encelia californica

Mojave Sage
Salvia mohavensis

Mormon Tea
Ephedra viridis

Bigelow Beargrass
Xerophyllum tenax

California Juniper
Juniperus californica

Ragged Rock Flower
Crossosoma bigelovii

Whipple Yucca
Yucca whipplei var. parishii

Joshua Tree
Yucca brevifolia

The Salton Basin is a land of physical extremes. The tallest mountain peaks in Southern California rise to the northwest—Mt. San Gorgonio (11,502 feet / 3,506 meters) and Mt. San Jacinto (10,804 feet / 3,292 meters), with cool temperatures, ample rainfall, and alpine vegetation. Winter persists on the higher peaks for eight months out of the year, with snow accumulations of over 60 feet on north slopes of Mt. San Gorgonio. Yet just 50 miles to the south lies the Salton Sea at -227 feet below sea level. A balmy and warm winter contrasts the even hotter summer months, with average July temperatures of 92°F. Some areas average only 2.5 inches of rainfall per year, making the Salton Basin one of the driest places in the Western Hemisphere.

Mountains surrounding the Basin greatly influence the local climate. Cool, moist, westerly winds waft in from the Pacific Ocean across the coastal plains. The air masses are forced upwards as they collide with the San Bernardino and San Jacinto Mountains. As rising air masses cool and condense, their moisture falls on the western slopes and mountain high country. Prevailing winds squeeze through the Banning Pass, driving wind farms in the Coachella Valley. As the air descends into the Basin, it heats up on its way down to the desert floor. Once over the ridges, the now dry air flows down the mountain slopes into the Salton Basin, compressing and warming further as it descends.

In summer months, warm, moist tropical air moves from the Gulf of California and Mexico into the Colorado Desert with the Sonoran monsoon, bringing occasional thundershowers to the Basin from July through October. Occasionally, tropical cyclones develop over the warm waters of the Upper Gulf of California, spawning hurricane-strength winds and torrential rains, causing flash floods as the runoff rushes from the desert mountains toward the Salton Sea.

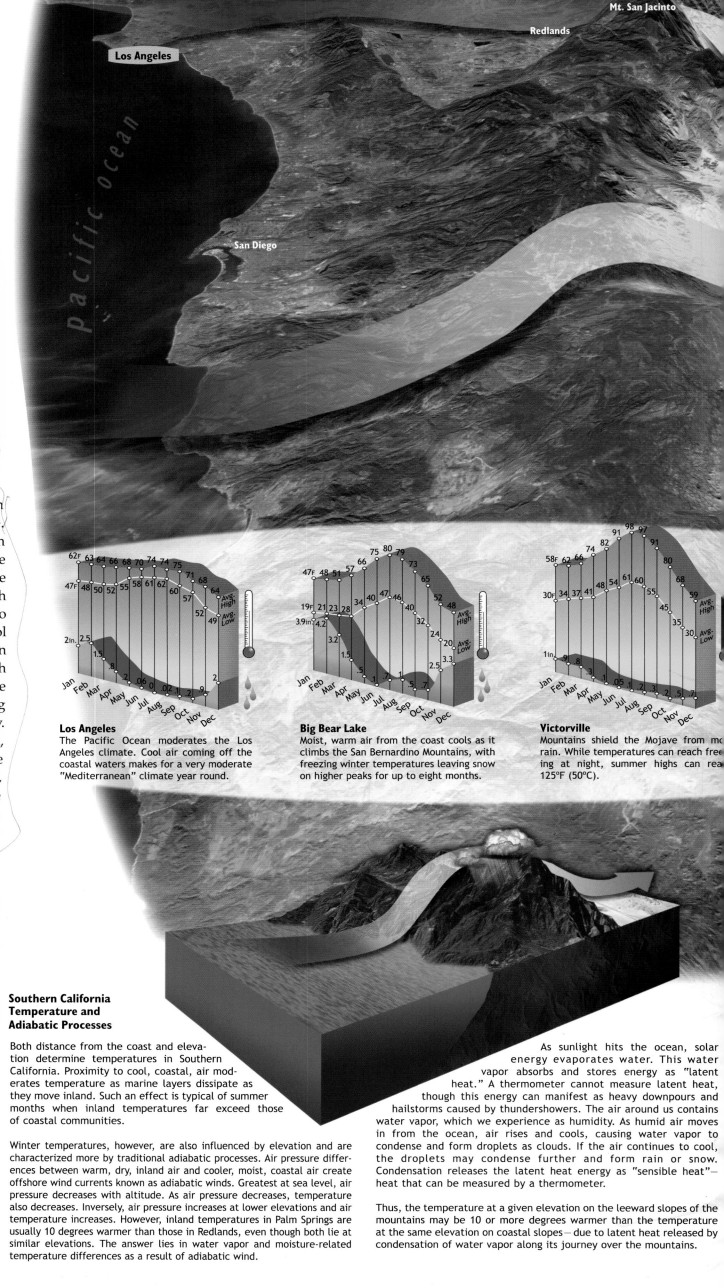

Los Angeles
The Pacific Ocean moderates the Los Angeles climate. Cool air coming off the coastal waters makes for a very moderate "Mediterranean" climate year round.

Big Bear Lake
Moist, warm air from the coast cools as it climbs the San Bernardino Mountains, with freezing winter temperatures leaving snow on higher peaks for up to eight months.

Victorville
Mountains shield the Mojave from mo rain. While temperatures can reach free ing at night, summer highs can rea 125°F (50°C).

Southern California Temperature and Adiabatic Processes

Both distance from the coast and elevation determine temperatures in Southern California. Proximity to cool, coastal, air moderates temperature as marine layers dissipate as they move inland. Such an effect is typical of summer months when inland temperatures far exceed those of coastal communities.

Winter temperatures, however, are also influenced by elevation and are characterized more by traditional adiabatic processes. Air pressure differences between warm, dry, inland air and cooler, moist, coastal air create offshore wind currents known as adiabatic winds. Greatest at sea level, air pressure decreases with altitude. As air pressure decreases, temperature also decreases. Inversely, air pressure increases at lower elevations and air temperature increases. However, inland temperatures in Palm Springs are usually 10 degrees warmer than those in Redlands, even though both lie at similar elevations. The answer lies in water vapor and moisture-related temperature differences as a result of adiabatic wind.

As sunlight hits the ocean, solar energy evaporates water. This water vapor absorbs and stores energy as "latent heat." A thermometer cannot measure latent heat, though this energy can manifest as heavy downpours and hailstorms caused by thundershowers. The air around us contains water vapor, which we experience as humidity. As humid air moves in from the ocean, air rises and cools, causing water vapor to condense and form droplets as clouds. If the air continues to cool, the droplets may condense further and form rain or snow. Condensation releases the latent heat energy as "sensible heat"— heat that can be measured by a thermometer.

Thus, the temperature at a given elevation on the leeward slopes of the mountains may be 10 or more degrees warmer than the temperature at the same elevation on coastal slopes—due to latent heat released by condensation of water vapor along its journey over the mountains.

Mojave Desert

Great Basin Extent

Salton Sea

Im Springs

Coachella Valley

Salton Sea

Global Climate

Climate is a function of precipitation and temperature over time. Latitude influences precipitation and temperature on a global scale. Warmer climates tend to lie nearer the equator, whereas cooler climates occur at higher latitudes. Warm, dry deserts in the Northern Hemisphere, like the Sonoran Desert, tend to fall between 25° and 40° latitude. Other factors such as topography and water bodies also influence climate locally.

global climate ⊕   ⬡ great basin climate

Tropical Rainy Climates: Characterized by monthly average temperatures above 64.4° F (18°C) and the absence of winter seasons. Rainfall exceeds evaporation.

Dry Climates: Evaporation exceeds precipitation levels; consequently, no natural permanent streams originate in dry climates.

Steppe Climate: Typified by grasslands and considered a transition climate between desert and more humid climates.

Desert Climate: Characterized by an arid climate and meager rainfall levels usually fewer than 15 inches (40 cm).

Mild/Humid Climates: Characterized by the occurrence of both summer and winter seasons, mild/humid climates have average temperatures above 50°F (10°C) and lows under 64.4°F (18°C) but above 26.6°F (-3°C).

Mild Humid Climate/Dry Summer: Less than 1.2 inches (3 cm) of rain falls in the driest months but total precipitation levels top three times that amount.

Mild Humid Climate/No Dry Season: In the driest month, precipitation tops 1.2 inches (3 cm).

Snowy-forest (microthermal) Climates: Average temperatures for the coldest month are below 26.6°F (-3°C) and 50°F (10°C) in the warmest.

Snowy-forest Climate/Dry Season: Dry seasons fall within the summer months.

Snowy-forest Climate/Moist Winters: Snowy climates with the absence of dry seasons.

Polar Climates: Average temperatures in the warmest months fall short of 50°F (10°C) and are without summer seasons.

Highland Climates: Temperature and moisture vary in highland climates with more pole-like conditions in higher latitudes.

Salton Sea
Warmer than the Mojave, the Salton Basin receives infrequent, but occasionally torrential, summer rains.

Great Basin States

Wyoming

Nevada

Utah

Colorado

California

Salton Sea

Arizona

New Mexico

gulf of california

Mexican-Pacific Tropical Cyclone

Warm waters collect in the Gulf of California in the summer, approaching temperatures of 85 to 90°F. The blazing desert sun on the warm Gulf waters contributes huge volumes of water vapor to the atmosphere. The hot desert landscape heats the air like a pot in an oven, causing the air to rise. The rising air mass picks up latent heat energy from the Gulf, creating huge thunderheads and occasionally a tropical cyclone. High winds of near hurricane strength pick up sand and debris ahead of the impending storm, sometimes followed by torrential rain. Although these storms only come into the Salton Basin once every five to ten years, they can drench the Sea with three or four years' worth of average precipitation in just a few hours.

Salton Sea

Pacific Ocean

Baja California

Gulf of California

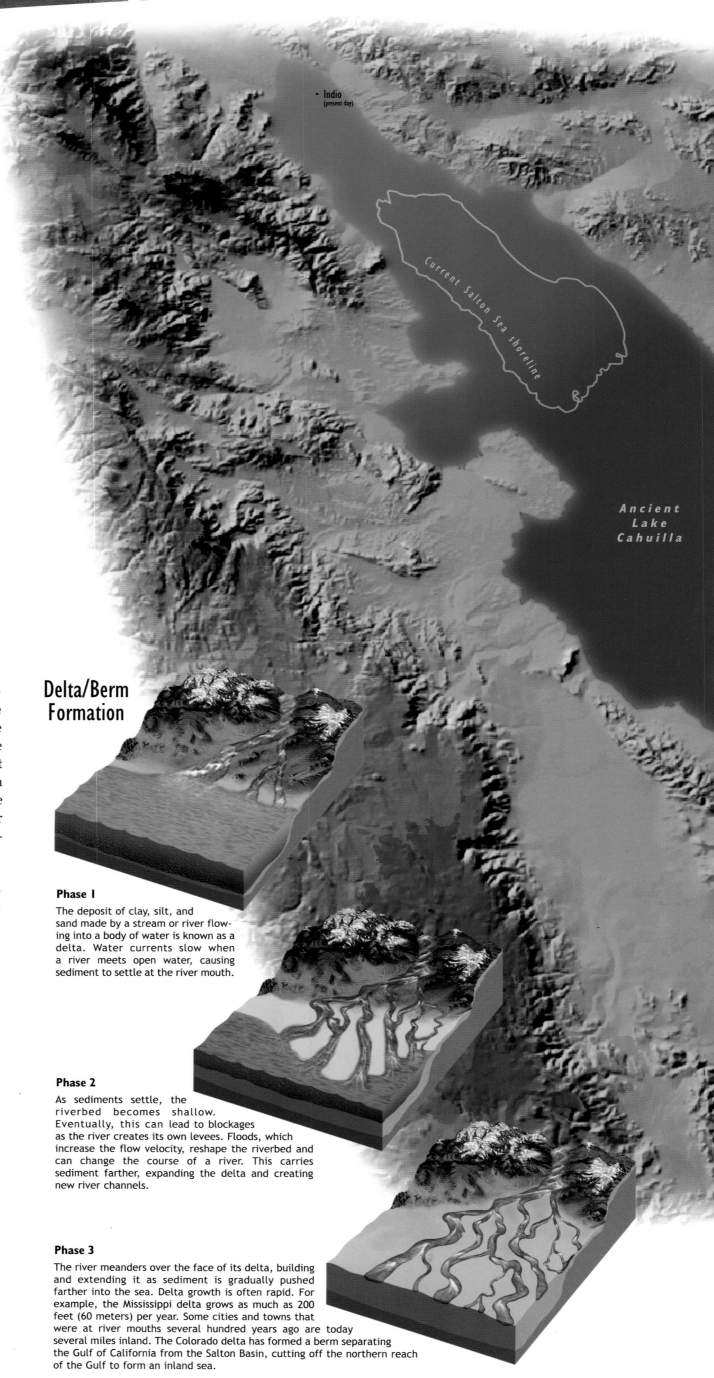

The Lower Colorado River has changed its course many times in the past. At the end of its journey in the Gulf of California, the river fans out and deposits sediment, building a massive delta many miles wide. Bearing mud and sand borne of the torrential flows that cut the Grand Canyon over several million years, sediment fills the lower reaches of the Colorado River. Periodic floods transform the sediment-choked riverbed, carrying its muddy issue ever farther and expanding the delta.

Before becoming part of the current extent of the delta, the Salton Basin was part of the Gulf of California, reaching as far north as present day Indio. The river intersected the Gulf near Yuma, forming a delta that extended ever wider and farther west into the narrow Gulf. Continued sediment deposits established a massive natural dam, or berm, across the Gulf, isolating the arm of the Sea to the north as a new lake. The isolated lake soon evaporated in the arid desert climate, leaving a barren depression below sea level — the Salton Basin. The Gulf to the south was pushed further and further south as build up of sediment continued.

In the several million years that followed, the Lower Colorado River changed course, driven by sediment deposits and periodic floods, sometimes flowing south through the large berm to the Gulf, and sometimes to the north, filling the Salton Basin, or even to the Gulf via the Salton Basin. Ancient Lake Cahuilla, created 400 years ago, took about 18 years to fill and covered approximately three times the surface area of the current Salton Sea. Today, agricultural runoff fed by the Colorado River largely maintains the Sea.

Indio
(present day)

Current Salton Sea shoreline

Ancient
Lake
Cahuilla

Delta/Berm Formation

Phase 1

The deposit of clay, silt, and sand made by a stream or river flowing into a body of water is known as a delta. Water currents slow when a river meets open water, causing sediment to settle at the river mouth.

Phase 2

As sediments settle, the riverbed becomes shallow. Eventually, this can lead to blockages as the river creates its own levees. Floods, which increase the flow velocity, reshape the riverbed and can change the course of a river. This carries sediment farther, expanding the delta and creating new river channels.

Phase 3

The river meanders over the face of its delta, building and extending it as sediment is gradually pushed farther into the sea. Delta growth is often rapid. For example, the Mississippi delta grows as much as 200 feet (60 meters) per year. Some cities and towns that were at river mouths several hundred years ago are today several miles inland. The Colorado delta has formed a berm separating the Gulf of California from the Salton Basin, cutting off the northern reach of the Gulf to form an inland sea.

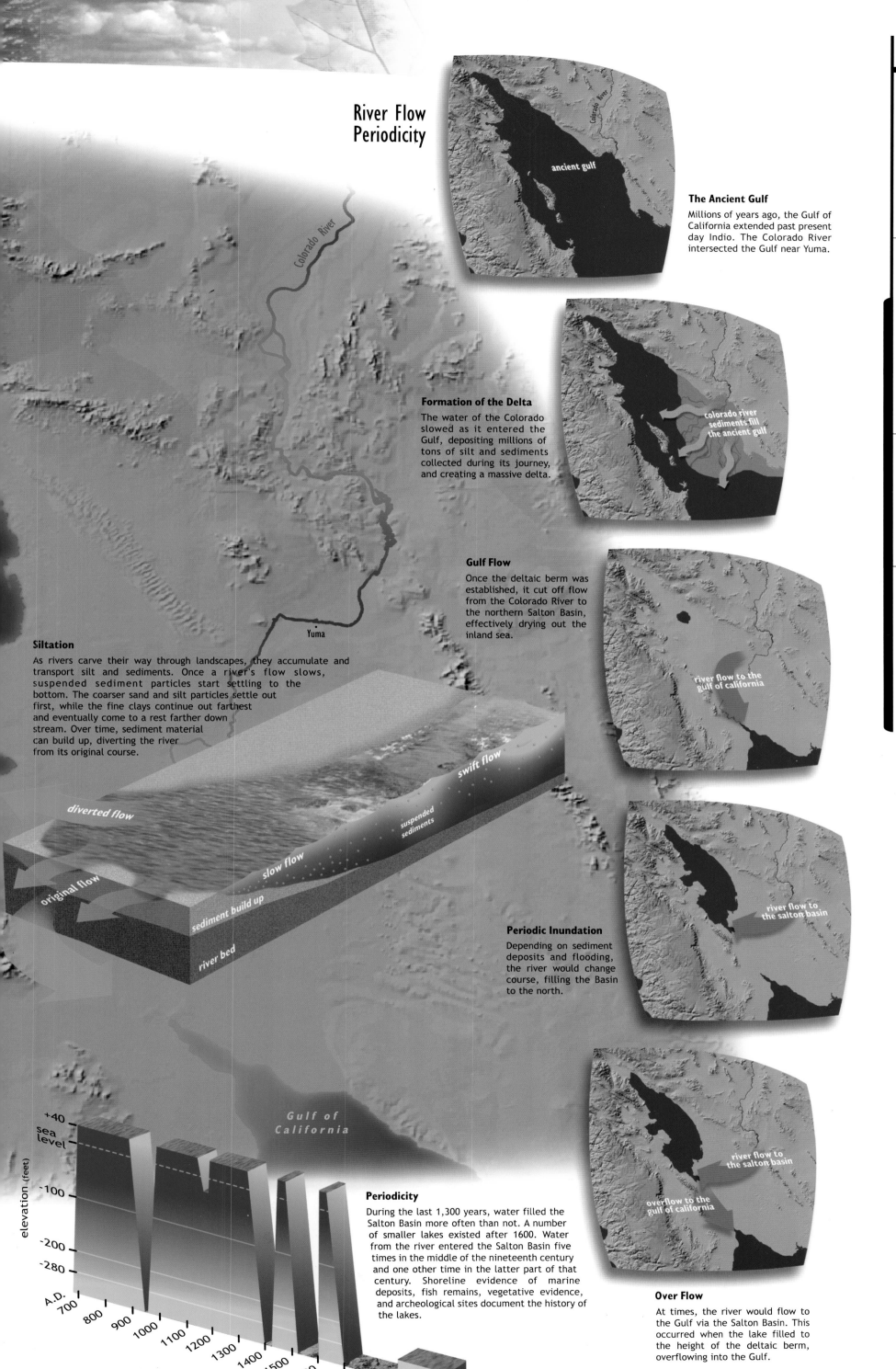

River Flow Periodicity

The Ancient Gulf

Millions of years ago, the Gulf of California extended past present day Indio. The Colorado River intersected the Gulf near Yuma.

Formation of the Delta

The water of the Colorado slowed as it entered the Gulf, depositing millions of tons of silt and sediments collected during its journey, and creating a massive delta.

Gulf Flow

Once the deltaic berm was established, it cut off flow from the Colorado River to the northern Salton Basin, effectively drying out the inland sea.

Siltation

As rivers carve their way through landscapes, they accumulate and transport silt and sediments. Once a river's flow slows, suspended sediment particles start settling to the bottom. The coarser sand and silt particles settle out first, while the fine clays continue out farthest and eventually come to a rest farther down stream. Over time, sediment material can build up, diverting the river from its original course.

Periodic Inundation

Depending on sediment deposits and flooding, the river would change course, filling the Basin to the north.

Periodicity

During the last 1,300 years, water filled the Salton Basin more often than not. A number of smaller lakes existed after 1600. Water from the river entered the Salton Basin five times in the middle of the nineteenth century and one other time in the latter part of that century. Shoreline evidence of marine deposits, fish remains, vegetative evidence, and archeological sites document the history of the lakes.

Over Flow

At times, the river would flow to the Gulf via the Salton Basin. This occurred when the lake filled to the height of the deltaic berm, overflowing into the Gulf.

The Salton Basin comprises one of the most diverse assemblages of plants and animals in North America, principally due to its extreme topography and climates. From searing tropical desert bajadas to icy, alpine summits, habitats change dramatically in very short distances. As elevation increases, the cooler temperatures support different species. These steep slopes support remarkably diverse plant and animal communities. From lower Sonoran creosote bush scrub to Canadian/Hudsonian lodgepole and limber pines, one ascends through four "life zones"—series of vegetation types that are encountered with increasing elevation.

Cooler climates lie at higher elevations *and* latitudes. In the Basin, elevation affects climate the same as traveling some 40 degrees of latitude —from subtropical desert in the valleys, to Arctic alpine tundra at the top of San Gorgonio. From the lowest elevations in the Salton Basin to the highest peaks of San Jacinto, life zones range from lower Sonoran Desert to Canadian life zone in just several miles. This is the most abrupt range of life zones in such a short horizontal distance in North America.

Since the beginning of the Pleistocene era, two to three million years ago, world climate has experienced a half dozen Ice Ages and warmer interglacial periods. As climate changed, plants and animals adapted to the new climate, migrated, or died out. As a result of the diverse elevation-driven life zones, the Basin is a veritable floristic crossroads. Many species reach their northernmost limits on the hot, south-facing slopes of the Basin, such as the California fan palm (*Washingtonia filifera*), miserable spurge (*Euphorbia misera*), and elephant tree (*Bursera microphylla*). Others attain their southernmost limits as Ice Age relicts on the peaks of San Jacinto (*Oxyria digyna* and *Ranunculus eschscholzii*) and San Gorgonio (*Phyllodoce breweri*).

Arctic Alpine Life Zone

With snow-mantled peaks, winter lasts up to eight months a year on the summit of San Gorgonio. This harsh landscape is the cold extreme of Salton Basin climates. Above the tree line, plants and animals hunker close to the ground to eke out a meager existence on the wind-swept peaks. However, more than 40 species of plants thrive here, including several unique varieties.

Clark's nutcracker
Nucifraga columbiana

Baird's swallowtail
Papilio bairdii bgirdii

Golden-mantled ground squirrel
Callospermophilus lateralis

Rayless daisy
Erigeron aphanactis

Mt. San Jacinto

Black bear
Euarctos americanus

Long-tailed weasel
Mystek frenate

Williamson's sapsucker
Sphyrapicus thyroideus

Lemon lily
Lillium parryi

Limber pine
Pinus flexilis

Canadian/Hudsonian Life Zone

Lodgepole (*Pinus contorta ssp. murrayana*) and limber pine (*Pinus flexilis*) replace the ponderosa pine as the common tree species. As tall as 80 feet in places, the trees become dwarfed and gnarled krummholz (crooked wood), deformed by the wind near the timberline. Bighorn sheep (*Ovis canadensis*) traverse the whole range of life zones, generally keeping to the steep slopes that afford quick escape from mountain lions (*Felis concolor*).

Lodgepole pine
Pinus contorta ssp.murrayana

Western pine elfin
Callophry's eryphon

Peninsular bighorn
Ovis canadensis

Utah juniper
Juniperus osteosperma

Bobcat
Lynx rufus

White-headed woodpecker
Picoides albolarvatus

Mule deer
Odocoileus hemionus

Transition iris
Iris hartwegii

Steller's jay
Cyanocitta stelleri

Snow plant
Sarcodes sanguinea

Western azalea
Rhododendron occident

Western skink
Eumeces skiltonianus

Mountain king snake
Lampropeltis zonata

Transition Life Zone

Increased density of woodlands and forests typify this montane landscape. The characteristic ponderosa pine (*Pinus ponderosa*) marks a transition from desert to more temperate alpine climates. Animals in this life zone include the mule deer (*Odocoileus hemionus*) and bobcat (*Lynx rufus*).

Temperature/Rainfall
elevation in feet above sea level
(approximates)

35 in.
40°F
Arctic/Alpine
10,000 and above

22 in.
60°F
Canadian/Hudsonian
7,000-10,000

Transition
5,000-7,000

3 in.
90°F
Rainfall
Temperature

Upper Sonoran
3,300-5,000

Lower Sonoran
(includes dunes)
3,300 and below

Watershed Biomes

Mt. San Gorgonio
Mt. San Jacinto

Arctic Alpine life zone

Canadian/Hudsonian life zone

Transition life zone

Upper Sonoran life zone

Lower Sonoran life zone

an Gorgonio

POINT OF VIEW

Salton Sea

salton sea watershed

Floristic Provinces

Cucumboreal region/
Vancouverian province

North American Atlantic region/
North American prairie province

Rocky Mountain region/
Rocky Mountain province

pacific ocean

Madrean region/
Great basin province

Madrean region/
California province

Salton Sea

Madrean region/
Sonoran province

Floristic Provinces

The flora of the Salton Basin is part of the Colorado Desert subdivision of the Sonoran Desert Floristic Province. The desert biome is perhaps best represented in Anza Borrego State Park, with numerous species, including the spindly ocotillo (*Fouquieria splendens*) and several species of cacti. Following winter rains or summer thundershowers, the desert floor springs to life with brilliant carpets of wildflowers, including sand verbena (*Abronia villosa*), evening primrose (*Oenothera deltoides*), and desert lilies (*Hesperocallis undulata*).

Pancake cactus
Opuntia chlorotica

Chuparosa
Beloperone californica

Ladder-backed woodpecker
Picoides scalaris

Red diamondback
Crotalus ruber

Brittle bush
Encelia farinosa

Joshua tree
Yucca brevifolia

Gray fox
Urocyon cinereoargenteus

Desert dandelions
Malacothrix glabrata

Ringtail
Bassariscus astutus

Great purple hairstreak
Mitoura spinetorum

Sidewinder
Crotalus cerastes

Upper Sonoran Life Zone

Evidence of moister and cooler temperatures, pine and oak woodlands include evergreen oaks (*Quercus spp.*), pinyon pine (*Pinus monophylla*), and California juniper (*Juniperus californica*). Greater amounts of vegetation support greater animal populations and larger predators, such as the gray fox (*Urocyon cinereoargenteus*).

California patch
Chlosyne californica

Dune sunflower
Helianthus niveus ssp. canescens

Greater roadrunner
Geococcyx californicus

Sagebrush lizard
Sceloporus graciosus

Calliope hummingbird
Stellula calliope

Sand verbena
Abronia villosa

Verdin
Auriparus flaviceps

Barrel cactus
Ferocactus acanthodes

Birdcage evening primrose
Oenothera deltoides

Badger
Taxidea taxus

Coyote
Canis latrans

Pacific diamondback
Crotalus viridis helleri

Fringe-toed lizard
Uma notata

Banded gecko
Coleonyx variegatus

Desert kangaroo rat
Dipodomys deserti

Desert hairy scorpion
Hadrurus arizonesis

Lower Sonoran Life Zone

With blistering heat and minimal precipitation, plants and animals adapt to hot days and cooler nights, and survive on scarce moisture and ground water. Succulents, such as cacti, store water in their prickly flesh. California fan palms (*Washingtonia filifera*) cluster around oases, where ground water is close to the surface. The palo verde (*Cercidium floridum*) sends deep roots to tap distant ground water. Many animals seek shelter during the day, and forage in the balmy night air.

Ocotillo
Fouquieria splendens

Desert agave
Agave deserti

Desert tarantula
Aphonopelma chalcodes

Saltbush Scrub and Sand Dunes

Part of the Lower Sonoran life zone, dune formations stretch across the valley floor. The Algodones Dunes along the southeast side of the Basin are the largest dune ecosystem in North America. Formed by the marine origin of the valley and the accumulation of salts from runoff, highly saline soils in some areas inhibit all but the most highly salt-tolerant plants. Saltbush (*Atriplex spp.*), iodine bush (*Allenrolfea occidentalis*), and saltgrass (*Distichlis spicata*) survive and thrive along the Salton Sea shore.

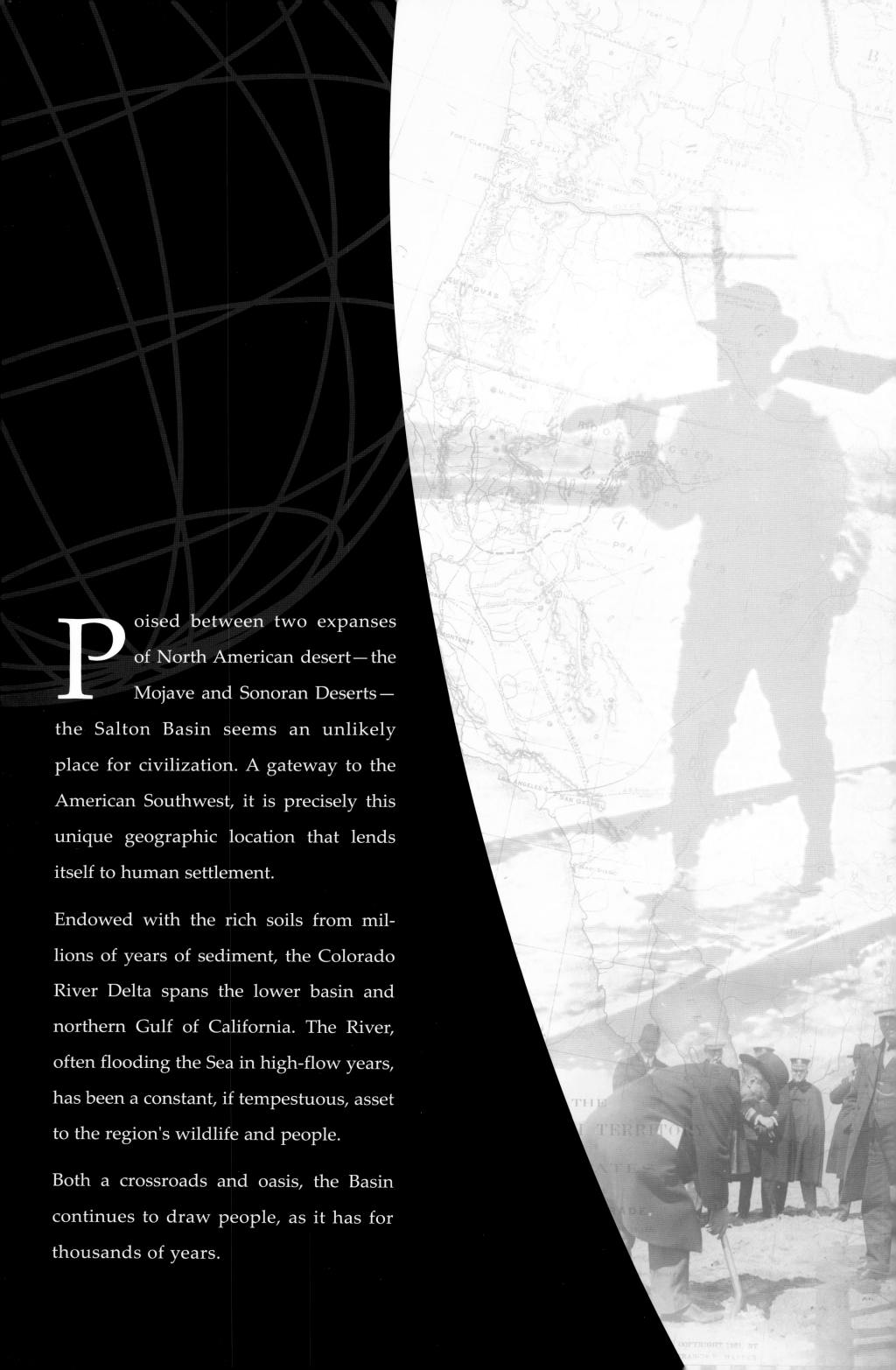

Poised between two expanses of North American desert—the Mojave and Sonoran Deserts—the Salton Basin seems an unlikely place for civilization. A gateway to the American Southwest, it is precisely this unique geographic location that lends itself to human settlement.

Endowed with the rich soils from millions of years of sediment, the Colorado River Delta spans the lower basin and northern Gulf of California. The River, often flooding the Sea in high-flow years, has been a constant, if tempestuous, asset to the region's wildlife and people.

Both a crossroads and oasis, the Basin continues to draw people, as it has for thousands of years.

cultural
history

Serrano

The Serrano were hunters and gatherers in the Mojave Desert and San Bernardino Mountains. They traded acorns, deerskins, and seed foods.

Mojave Desert

Prior to European exploration and settlement, as many as 300,000 Native Americans lived in various tribes throughout what is now California. With 300 regional dialects of 100 language groups, the California peoples were extraordinarily diverse—each tribe's history and culture influenced by their local climate, natural resources, and neighbors. In Southern California, various tribes flourished, from the coastal Gabrieleño to the Cahuilla of the arid Salton Basin. Intertribal trade for local goods, crafts, and foodstuffs extended throughout the region.

The Cahuilla are a Takic-speaking group of people who occupied an area generally within what is now Imperial and Riverside Counties, including San Gorgonio Pass, the San Jacinto and Santa Rosa mountains, the Coachella Valley, and the northern end of the Imperial Valley. More than a dozen independent and politically autonomous clans each owned land, extending from the desert valley floor to the mountain areas. Within the larger clan holdings, family lineages comprised independent communities and controlled different resource areas.

San Bernardino Mou

Mt. San Gorgonio

Tongva

A wealthy and politically complex coastal tribe, the Tongva (Gabrieleños) used clam shell beads as currency and traded extensively with inland tribes. Their resources included shells, sea otter pelts, dried fish and seatite vessels.

Cahuilla

The Cahuilla lifestyle was well adapted to take advantage of local resources and climate. They traded with other tribes, fished Lake Cahuilla when it was present, and were known for their basket making.

Population estimates of the Cahuilla people before Spanish contact in 1774 were at 10,000 people within seven or more distinct groups, inhabiting 2,400 square miles. Today, there are only about 1,000 Cahuilla in the Salton Basin.

Coachel Valle

Mt. San Jacinto

Pacific Ocean

Luiseño

A fishing culture on the coast hunting in the inland areas, the Luiseño used shells for trade and currency.

Cupeño

The Cupeño were evicted from their land in 1903 due to a U[...] Supreme Court decision in favo[...] local land owners.

The Cahuilla House

The round or oblong shape of the Cahuilla house (*kish*), set halfway below ground, minimized sun exposure and provided optimal shelter from the hot, desert climate. Usually constructed of nearby materials, including oak, greasewood, or manzanita, the frame was covered by willow or mesquite branches, or yucca or palm fronds and roofed with bulrush.

Ipai

The Ipai fished in coastal zones and hunted in the inland areas. The Ipai used shells for trade and currency. They also traded tobacco, sandals, and fishing nets.

Tipai

Acorns were a staple food source for the Tipai, along with farming and fishing. The Tipai traded salt, tobacco, and food. The tribe extended into Baja California.

Basket Making

Basket making was an important industry for Cahuilla women. Older women and young girls made close-weaved baskets, often adorned with elaborate designs, such as rattlesnakes, eagles, whirlwinds, and important plants. While used commonly for daily work and storage, baskets also served an important role in rituals and ceremonies, often being burned as offerings or given as gifts. Gift baskets symbolized great wealth and were treasured possessions. When a basket maker died, the community burned her baskets and never used her designs again.

Fish Trap

This hypothetical reconstruction of a fish trap [...] based on ethnographic data on Lower Colorado Rive[...] fishing technology. Instead of fishing nets, inter[...] woven arrowweed fences also may have been used[...] Either end may have been opened to catch fish. Hov[...] the traps actually worked remains a mystery.

Pottery

The Cahuilla made pots from coils of clay, then shaped, smoothed, and finally fired them in an earthen pit. Pottery included large vessels (*kow-a-mal-em*) for cooking and water storage, and shallow serving dishes (*wa-yi-mail*).

Obsidian

Obsidian, a volcanic glass, forms from fast-cooling lava flows. The molecular structure of this glassy substance creates razor sharp edges. Obsidian fractures easily, making it ideal for arrowheads and blades. The volcanic origin of the Salton Basin made obsidian relatively abundant, and trade with other tribes in the region thrived.

Modern Indian Reservations

The federal government established reservations throughout the United States in the late 1800s. Western practices of agriculture, largely already in place, became the norm. Today, Cahuilla livelihood is chiefly based on farming, cattle ranching, tourism, and, recently, gambling casinos. Regarded as a dying language, with only older people speaking the Cahuilla dialect with fluency, some communities and families continue to teach the language to their children.

Cahuilla dancers

The Modern Cahuilla People

The Cahuilla became familiar with Europeans as early as 1797. Those in western Cahuilla areas were baptized and worked among the Spanish. In the following three decades, Spaniards, Mexicans, and Americans each made contact with the Cahuilla, exposing them to new people, new ways, and disease. In 1852, the Toro leader, Chungil, along with other Cahuilla and Luiseño leaders, signed a treaty with the United States government, although Congress never ratified it.

Ancient Lake Cahuilla

For thousands of years, the Colorado River would overflow its banks and flow into the Salton Basin. This cycle occurred approximately every 100 to 150 years, taking up to 20 years to fill the Basin and 60 years to recede. Surveys along the relic shoreline have found hundreds of fishing camps and villages.

William P. Blake, a geologist for the 1853 U.S. government exploration for a transcontinental railroad, asked the Cahuilla about the shoreline evidence of the ancient lake, and heard accounts of a great water which covered the whole valley. Cahuilla ancestors lived in the mountains, coming down to fish and hunt geese and ducks. As the waters subsided, they moved their villages down from the mountains, following the shore. The waters suddenly returned, overwhelming villagers, driving them back to the mountains.

Parallel lines of stone fish traps indicate that camps were relocated to follow the receding shoreline. Excavations have yielded fish bones from at least four species of fish native to the Colorado River and the Gulf of California, including the razorback sucker and the bonytail chub.

Agave Harvest

Agave, a succulent desert plant, stores much of its energy as a starchy heart, protected from animals by its spiny and tough leaves. Stored energy peaks just before the plant blooms. Since agave flowers at the end of the winter months, it emerged as a vital food source during lean winters. The agave harvest, still practiced today, was an important community event. Some varieties farther south are made into the alcoholic beverage tequila.

Halchidhoma

Driven off their land in the 1830s by the Mojave tribe, the Halchidhoma were absorbed by the Maricopa on the Gila River and their land given to the Chemehuevi.

Quechan

The Quechan have a highly developed agriculture. They raised and traded corn, beans, pumpkins, and gourd rattles. They fished in the Colorado River. The Quechan hunted and gathered in the upland area, and are well known for their pottery.

Canadian-Hudsonian

This zone, the smallest proportion of Cahuilla territory, was largely used for hunting deer, sheep, and other smaller animals.

Transitional

Coniferous forests and meadows provided a cool summer climate for hunting and foraging.

Upper Sonoran

The Cahuilla gathered the majority of their diet from this zone, a more temperate climate than the desert and valley floors.

Lower Sonoran

The largest portion of Cahuilla territory, this zone hosted many important food staples, including agave, yucca, and screwbean.

Lodgepole Pine
(wexet)

Manzanita
(kelel)

Black Oak
(qwinyily)

Pinyon Pine
(tevat)

Juniper
(yuyily)

Chamise
(u ut)

Agave
(amul)

Catclaw
(sichingily)

Buckthorn
(mutal)

Palo Verde
(u uwet)

California Fan Palm
(maul)

Barrel Cactus
(kupash)

Screwbean Mesquite
(qwinyal)

Yucca
(hunuvat)

Ocotillo
(utush)

Creosote
(atukul)

Goat Nut
(gawnaxal)

Cahuilla name

Cahuilla Annual Harvest Cycle

FALL

Late Fall
The harvest is an important occasion, with most of the village gathering black-oak acorns, seeds, berries, and goat nuts for winter storage.

Late Summer/Early Fall
Grass seeds, chia, saltbush seeds, pinyon nuts, palm tree fruit, thimbleberry, juniper berries, and chokecherry are harvested during this time.

SUMMER

Summer
Screwbean are harvested in great quantities; also harvested are honey mesquite, manzanita, various berries, yucca, and various cacti.

WINTER

Early Winter
Early winter was the time for ceremonies and religious observances, including celebration of renewal for the year ahead.

Late Winter
During late winter agave becomes the primary staple, in addition to hunting in mountain regions; there is also a greater reliance on food stores.

SPRING

Spring
Yucca, wild onion, barrel cactus, tuna cactus, goosefoot, catclaw, and ocotillo are harvested.

Resource Distribution

Tribal Land Use

Canadian-Hudsonian
Transitional
Upper Sonoran
Lower Sonoran

8% 2%
30%
60%

Food Use

Canadian-Hudsonian
Transitional
Upper Sonoran
Lower Sonoran

20% 5% 15%
60%

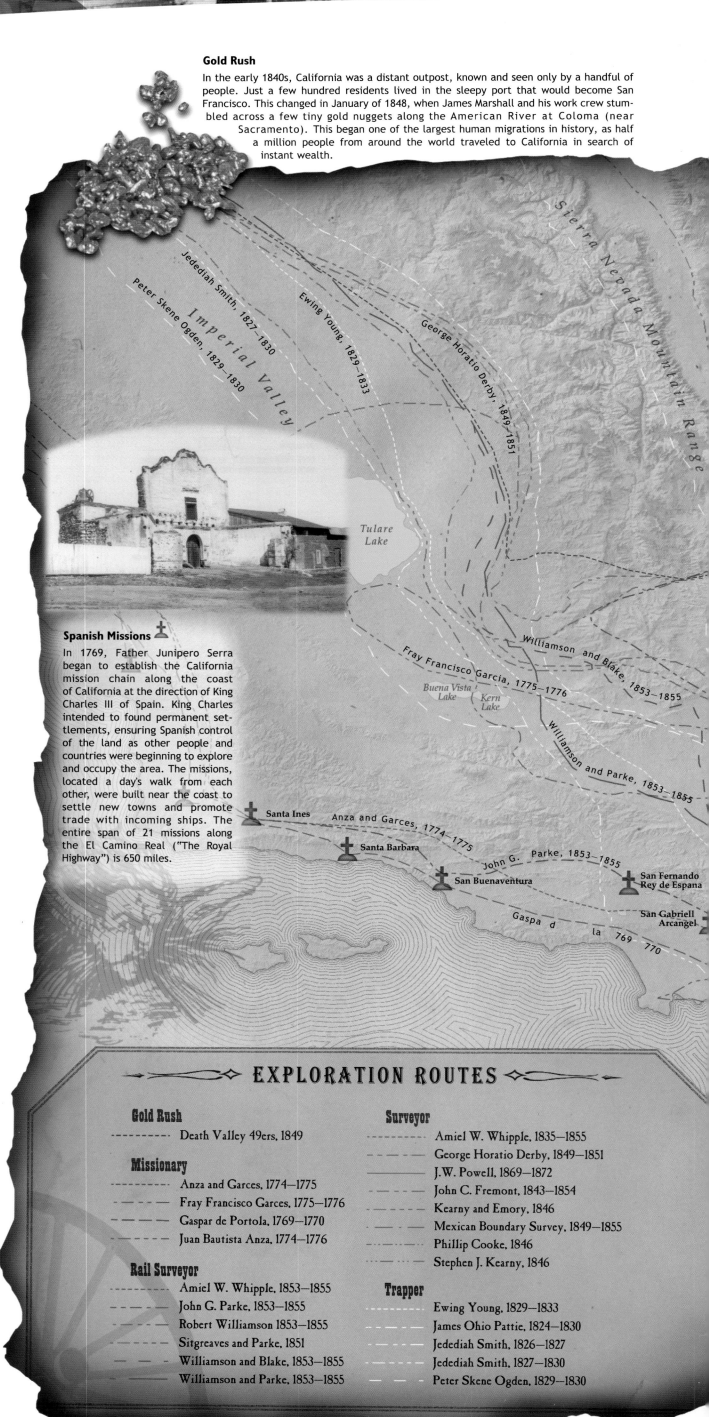

Gold Rush
In the early 1840s, California was a distant outpost, known and seen only by a handful of people. Just a few hundred residents lived in the sleepy port that would become San Francisco. This changed in January of 1848, when James Marshall and his work crew stumbled across a few tiny gold nuggets along the American River at Coloma (near Sacramento). This began one of the largest human migrations in history, as half a million people from around the world traveled to California in search of instant wealth.

Spanish Missions ⚓
In 1769, Father Junipero Serra began to establish the California mission chain along the coast of California at the direction of King Charles III of Spain. King Charles intended to found permanent settlements, ensuring Spanish control of the land as other people and countries were beginning to explore and occupy the area. The missions, located a day's walk from each other, were built near the coast to settle new towns and promote trade with incoming ships. The entire span of 21 missions along the El Camino Real ("The Royal Highway") is 650 miles.

Conquest of the American Southwest by the Spaniards in the sixteenth and seventeenth centuries led to extensive exploration of the Colorado River region. One of the first Europeans to explore the lower Colorado River, Francisco Vasquez de Coronado quested for Cibola— the fabled "Seven Cities of Gold" —in 1539. A member of his party, Melchior Diaz, crossed the river into the Salton Basin, but did not find any gold. It was not until the establishment of missions along the California coast, starting in 1769, that the Spanish again searched for an overland route to promote trade and expand their territory. Father Francisco Garces crossed the Basin from San Diego to Yuma in 1771, calling the trail "El Camino de Diablo" (The Devil's Pathway).

The first travelers from the eastern United States were trappers and fur traders. They arrived in the 1840s and established new commercial centers along the trade routes between California and other states. The discovery of gold at the sawmill of John Sutter — a Swiss pioneer trader — on the south fork of the American River started the gold rush in 1849. It is estimated that over eight thousand emigrants crossed the desert on their way to the California gold fields, avoiding the snow and high mountain passes of the northern routes.

In 1853, Congress authorized a series of explorations for the discovery of a practical railroad route to the Pacific Coast — especially a southern route not interrupted by winter snows. One of the survey geologists, William R. Blake, was the first to explain the origin of the Salton Sink and to trace its ancient history. Blake also recognized the potential of irrigation in the valley with water brought in from the Colorado River — a bold and original idea in 1857. Forty years later, the web of irrigation canals was practically identical with the plans recommended by Blake's engineer, Ebenezer Hadley.

EXPLORATION ROUTES

Gold Rush
- - - - - - - - - Death Valley 49ers, 1849

Missionary
- - - - - - - - - Anza and Garces, 1774—1775
- - - - - Fray Francisco Garces, 1775—1776
- - - - - Gaspar de Portola, 1769—1770
- - - - - Juan Bautista Anza, 1774—1776

Rail Surveyor
- - - - - - - - - Amiel W. Whipple, 1853—1855
- - - - - John G. Parke, 1853—1855
- - - - - Robert Williamson 1853—1855
- - - - - Sitgreaves and Parke, 1851
- - - - - Williamson and Blake, 1853—1855
- - - - - Williamson and Parke, 1853—1855

Surveyor
- - - - - - - - - Amiel W. Whipple, 1835—1855
- - - - - George Horatio Derby, 1849—1851
- - - - - J.W. Powell, 1869—1872
- - - - - John C. Fremont, 1843—1854
- - - - - Kearny and Emory, 1846
- - - - - Mexican Boundary Survey, 1849—1855
- - - - - Phillip Cooke, 1846
- - - - - Stephen J. Kearny, 1846

Trapper
- - - - - - - - - Ewing Young, 1829—1833
- - - - - James Ohio Pattie, 1824—1830
- - - - - Jedediah Smith, 1826—1827
- - - - - Jedediah Smith, 1827—1830
- - - - - Peter Skene Ogden, 1829—1830

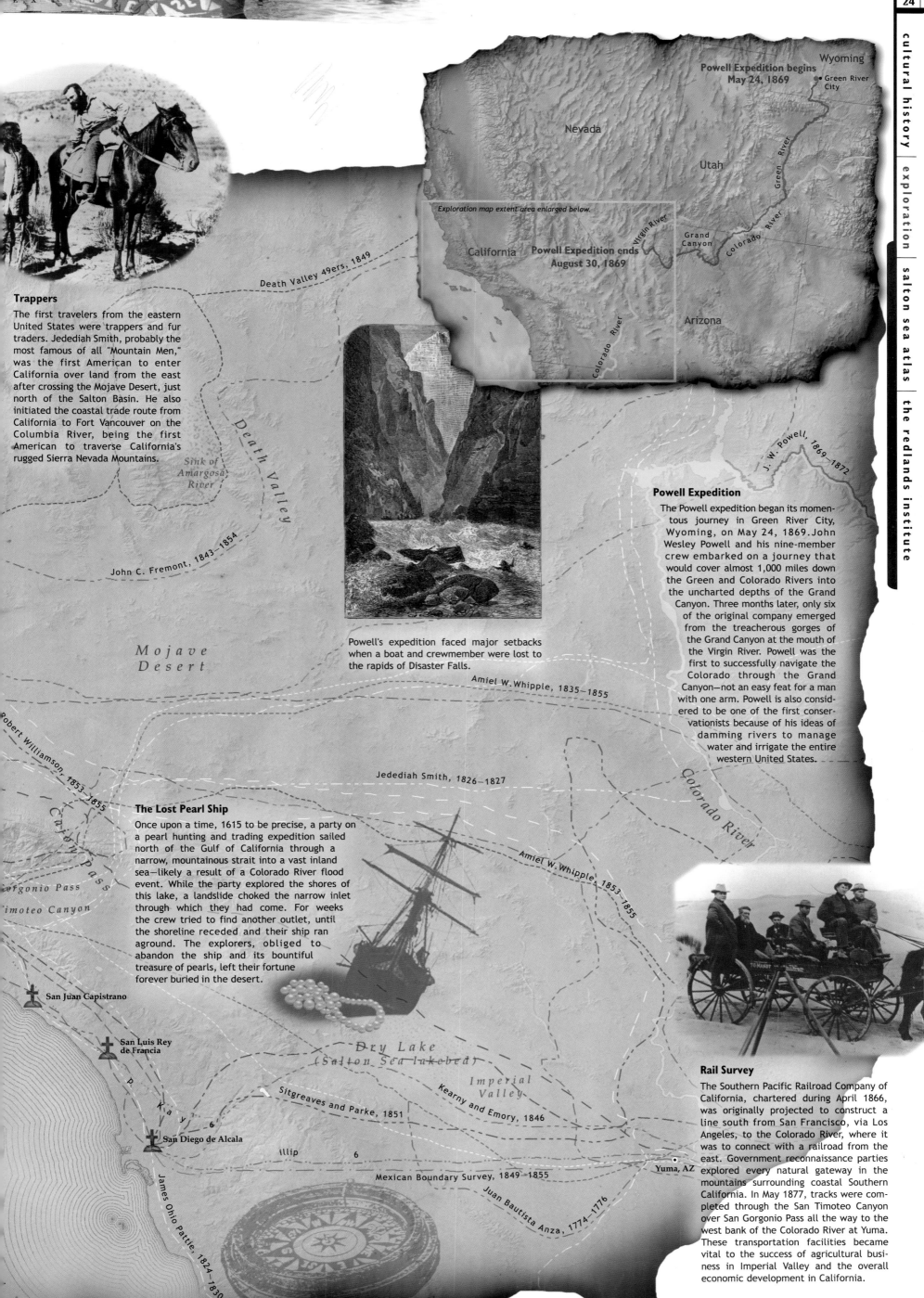

Trappers

The first travelers from the eastern United States were trappers and fur traders. Jedediah Smith, probably the most famous of all "Mountain Men," was the first American to enter California over land from the east after crossing the Mojave Desert, just north of the Salton Basin. He also initiated the coastal trade route from California to Fort Vancouver on the Columbia River, being the first American to traverse California's rugged Sierra Nevada Mountains.

Powell's expedition faced major setbacks when a boat and crewmember were lost to the rapids of Disaster Falls.

Powell Expedition

The Powell expedition began its momentous journey in Green River City, Wyoming, on May 24, 1869. John Wesley Powell and his nine-member crew embarked on a journey that would cover almost 1,000 miles down the Green and Colorado Rivers into the uncharted depths of the Grand Canyon. Three months later, only six of the original company emerged from the treacherous gorges of the Grand Canyon at the mouth of the Virgin River. Powell was the first to successfully navigate the Colorado through the Grand Canyon—not an easy feat for a man with one arm. Powell is also considered to be one of the first conservationists because of his ideas of damming rivers to manage water and irrigate the entire western United States.

The Lost Pearl Ship

Once upon a time, 1615 to be precise, a party on a pearl hunting and trading expedition sailed north of the Gulf of California through a narrow, mountainous strait into a vast inland sea—likely a result of a Colorado River flood event. While the party explored the shores of this lake, a landslide choked the narrow inlet through which they had come. For weeks the crew tried to find another outlet, until the shoreline receded and their ship ran aground. The explorers, obliged to abandon the ship and its bountiful treasure of pearls, left their fortune forever buried in the desert.

Rail Survey

The Southern Pacific Railroad Company of California, chartered during April 1866, was originally projected to construct a line south from San Francisco, via Los Angeles, to the Colorado River, where it was to connect with a railroad from the east. Government reconnaissance parties explored every natural gateway in the mountains surrounding coastal Southern California. In May 1877, tracks were completed through the San Timoteo Canyon over San Gorgonio Pass all the way to the west bank of the Colorado River at Yuma. These transportation facilities became vital to the success of agricultural business in Imperial Valley and the overall economic development in California.

Powell Expedition begins
May 24, 1869

Wyoming

Green River City

Nevada

Utah

Green River

Exploration map extent area enlarged below.

California

Powell Expedition ends
August 30, 1869

Virgin River

Grand Canyon

Colorado River

Arizona

Colorado River

J. W. Powell, 1869–1872

Death Valley 49ers, 1849

Death Valley

Sink of Amargosa River

John C. Fremont, 1843–1854

Mojave Desert

Robert Williamson, 1853–1855

Amiel W. Whipple, 1835–1855

Jedediah Smith, 1826–1827

Colorado River

Amiel W. Whipple, 1853–1855

Cajon Pass

Gorgonio Pass

Timoteo Canyon

San Juan Capistrano

San Luis Rey de Francia

San Diego de Alcala

Dry Lake
(Salton Sea lakebed)

Imperial Valley

Sitgreaves and Parke, 1851

Kearny and Emory, 1846

Yuma, AZ

James Ohio Pattie, 1824–1830

Mexican Boundary Survey, 1849–1855

Juan Bautista Anza, 1774–1776

Historic Rail Maps

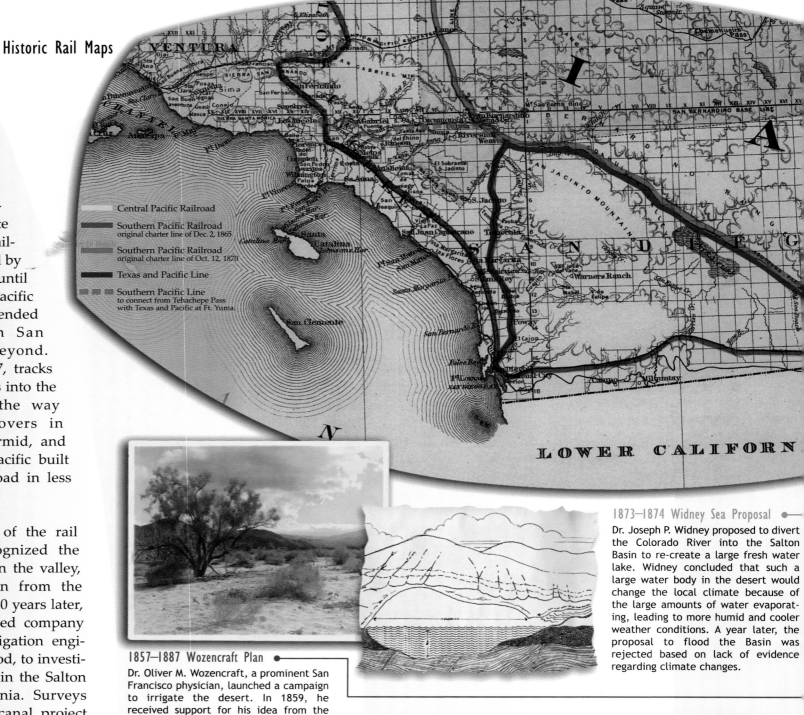

Central Pacific Railroad

Southern Pacific Railroad
original charter line of Dec. 2, 1865

Southern Pacific Railroad
original charter line of Oct. 12, 1870

Texas and Pacific Line

Southern Pacific Line
to connect from Tehachepe Pass
with Texas and Pacific at Ft. Yuma.

In 1853, government reconnaissance parties began exploration for a southern route of the transcontinental railroad—one uninterrupted by winter snows. It was not until 1875 that the Southern Pacific Railroad Company extended their route through San Gorgonio Pass and beyond. Two years later, in 1877, tracks descended from the pass into the Colorado Desert all the way to Yuma, with stopovers in Whitewater, Indio, Durmid, and Pilot Knob. Southern Pacific built over 200 miles of railroad in less than two years.

William R. Blake, one of the rail survey geologists, recognized the potential for irrigation in the valley, using water brought in from the Colorado River. Nearly 40 years later, in 1892, a Colorado-based company sent an experienced irrigation engineer, Charles R. Rockwood, to investigate irrigation potential in the Salton Basin and Baja California. Surveys revealed that a single canal project could irrigate two million acres in the desert, with the Salton Sink serving as a drainage area. The California Development Company, an investment group formed in 1896, began construction in August of 1900. The company dug 400 miles of irrigation ditches by early 1902, making water available for up to 100,000 acres.

With readily available water and rail access, the Imperial Valley flourished. In 1904, the population boomed with residents numbering 10,000 in the newly formed towns of Brawley, Holtville, Heber and Calexico. By 1905, 120,000 acres of reclaimed land were under cultivation. Easy access to a major cross-country rail corridor tapped national markets. With readily available water, the Basin was ripe for lucrative opportunities.

1857–1887 Wozencraft Plan

Dr. Oliver M. Wozencraft, a prominent San Francisco physician, launched a campaign to irrigate the desert. In 1859, he received support for his idea from the State Legislature of California, granting him rights to the land he planned to supply with water. Congress showed some interest in his proposal, but diverted its attention to the Civil War in 1861. Up until his death in 1887, Wozencraft worked diligently to realize his unfulfilled dream of prosperity in the Salton Basin.

1873–1874 Widney Sea Proposal

Dr. Joseph P. Widney proposed to divert the Colorado River into the Salton Basin to re-create a large fresh water lake. Widney concluded that such a large water body in the desert would change the local climate because of the large amounts of water evaporating, leading to more humid and cooler weather conditions. A year later, the proposal to flood the Basin was rejected based on lack of evidence regarding climate changes.

1853 Rail Survey

William R. Blake, a survey geologist, explored the Salton Basin for a southern railroad route to avoid the northern winter snows. Blake recognized the potential for irrigation in the valley with water brought in from the Colorado River, a bold and original idea at the time. Forty years later, the web of irrigation canals was practically identical with the plans recommended by Blake's engineer, Ebenezer Hadley.

1875 Southern Pacific Railroad (SPRR) Extension

Contracts were signed to extend the Southern Pacific Railroad through the San Gorgonio Pass. Laborers worked on grading the railroad through San Timoteo Canyon and over San Gorgonio Pass— many perishing from the intense heat in the Cabazon Valley.

Rail

1850

1860

1870

California Population (millions)

400,000

550,000

Water

1901 Imperial Valley is born

In March 1901, the Imperial Land Company was formed to promote settlement, attracting colonists, planning towns, and bringing land into cultivation. George Chaffey and his associates called the land "Imperial Valley," which was more inviting to settlers and small investors than using ominous words like "desert" and "sink." That same year, water flowed through the Pilot Knob head gate, and irrigation of the Salton Basin became a certainty.

1884–1905 New Liverpool Salt Company

Over centuries, frequent inundation left behind large amounts of salt in the Basin. In 1884, the New Liverpool Salt Company began the first large-scale salt extraction. Connected with the railroad at the Salton Sea, the company shipped over 1,500 tons of salt per year to San Francisco. Most of the salt was scraped from the playa crust with plows. The flood of 1905 destroyed the New Liverpool Salt Company's works.

1902 Imperial and Gulf Railway Company

Anthony Heber and William Holt established the Imperial and Gulf Railway Company in 1902 to extend the railroad route south to Mexico. Work began at Imperial Junction on October 16, 1902, and the 41-mile section from Imperial Junction to Calexico opened on June 29, 1904. Southern Pacific organized the Inter-California Railway on June 18, 1904, which continued the work beyond Calexico into the Republic of Mexico.

1896–1912 California Development Company

Rockwood formed a new investment group in 1896. The company contracted George Chaffey, a civil engineer, in 1900 to lead the canal construction projects. Chaffey went on to build canals that would carry 400,000 acre-feet of water per year to the Basin. Chaffey also founded the border town of Calexico as a tent city for workers on the Alamo Canal.

People

1876 SPRR Extension

In January 1876, regular train service extended to Whitewater; in May, the 70-mile section from Colton to Indian Wells (Indio) was completed and opened for traffic in late July.

1877 SPRR Extension

Flowermid was reached on March 8, 1877, Pilot Knob on April 29, and on May 23, 1877, tracks were laid to the west bank of the Colorado River at Yuma.

1891–1893 California Irrigation Company

John C. Beatty formed the California Irrigation Company to transfer Colorado River water to the Salton Basin. In 1892, Beatty engaged Charles R. Rockwood, an experienced irrigation engineer, to investigate irrigation opportunities in the Basin and adjacent areas. Attributing lack of public confidence in reclamation experiments, Beatty and his associates were unable to secure enough capital; bankruptcy followed two years later.

1902–1905 Imperial Valley Flourishes

More settlers arrived in the area and formed new water companies. Before April 3, 1902, 400 miles of irrigation ditches had been dug. Population increased from 2,000 settlers at the end of 1902, to 7,000 in 1903, and to 10,000 in 1904. In early 1905, 120,000 acres of reclaimed land were under cultivation.

1880

1890

1900

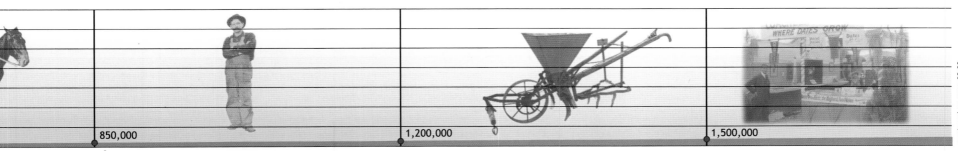

850,000

1,200,000

1,500,000

continued on page 32-33

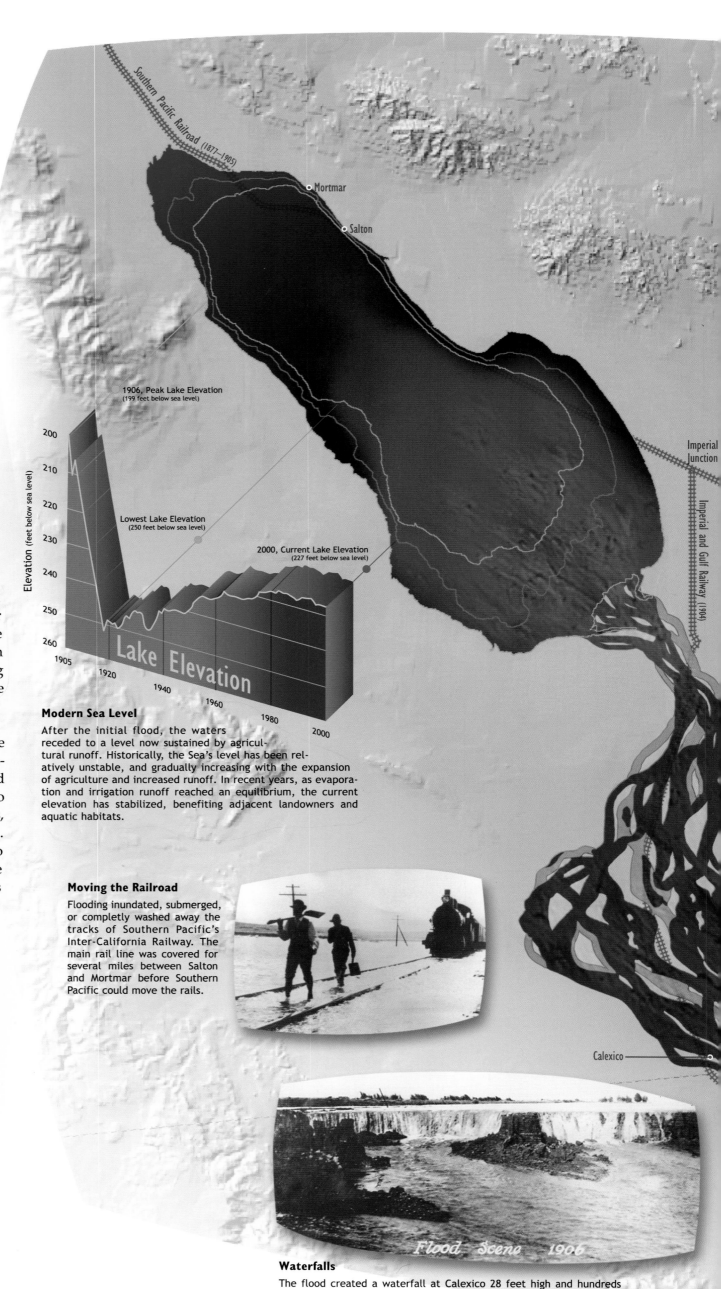

In nine months, the runaway waters of the Colorado had eroded from the New and Alamo River channels and carried down into the Salton Sea a yardage almost four times as great as that of the entire Panama Canal …Very rarely, if ever before, has it been possible to see … in a few months a change which usually requires centuries.

- H.T. Cory, Chief Engineer, California Development Company, 1906

In the first few years of the 1900s, the Imperial Valley blossomed into fertile farmland courtesy of the Colorado River. But the Colorado proved a fickle benefactor, first filling the main canal feeding the valley with silt, then breaking through a new channel constructed to relieve the shortage. The flood of 1905 widened the channel to more than a half-mile, all that was necessary for the entire Colorado River to come rushing through, spreading over an area 10 miles wide before flowing down into the Basin and forming the Salton Sea.

Once it had breached its bounds, the river was unstoppable, flooding thousands of acres of farmland and destroying large portions of Calexico and Mexicali. Rail lines, salt works, fields, and houses were submerged. The floods of June 1906 poured so much water into the Basin that the Salton Sea rose as much as 7 inches a day, covering upwards of 400 square miles.

By the end of 1906, the California Development Company ran out of money. At the request of the federal government, the Southern Pacific Railroad finally filled the breach in 1907.

1906, Peak Lake Elevation (199 feet below sea level)

Lowest Lake Elevation (250 feet below sea level)

2000, Current Lake Elevation (227 feet below sea level)

Elevation (feet below sea level)

200 · 210 · 220 · 230 · 240 · 250 · 260

Lake Elevation

1905 · 1920 · 1940 · 1960 · 1980 · 2000

Modern Sea Level

After the initial flood, the waters receded to a level now sustained by agricultural runoff. Historically, the Sea's level has been relatively unstable, and gradually increasing with the expansion of agriculture and increased runoff. In recent years, as evaporation and irrigation runoff reached an equilibrium, the current elevation has stabilized, benefiting adjacent landowners and aquatic habitats.

Moving the Railroad

Flooding inundated, submerged, or completly washed away the tracks of Southern Pacific's Inter-California Railway. The main rail line was covered for several miles between Salton and Mortmar before Southern Pacific could move the rails.

Southern Pacific Railroad (1877–1905)

Mortmar

Salton

Imperial Junction

Imperial and Gulf Railway (1904)

Calexico

Waterfalls

The flood created a waterfall at Calexico 28 feet high and hundreds of yards across, cutting away massive amounts of sediment.

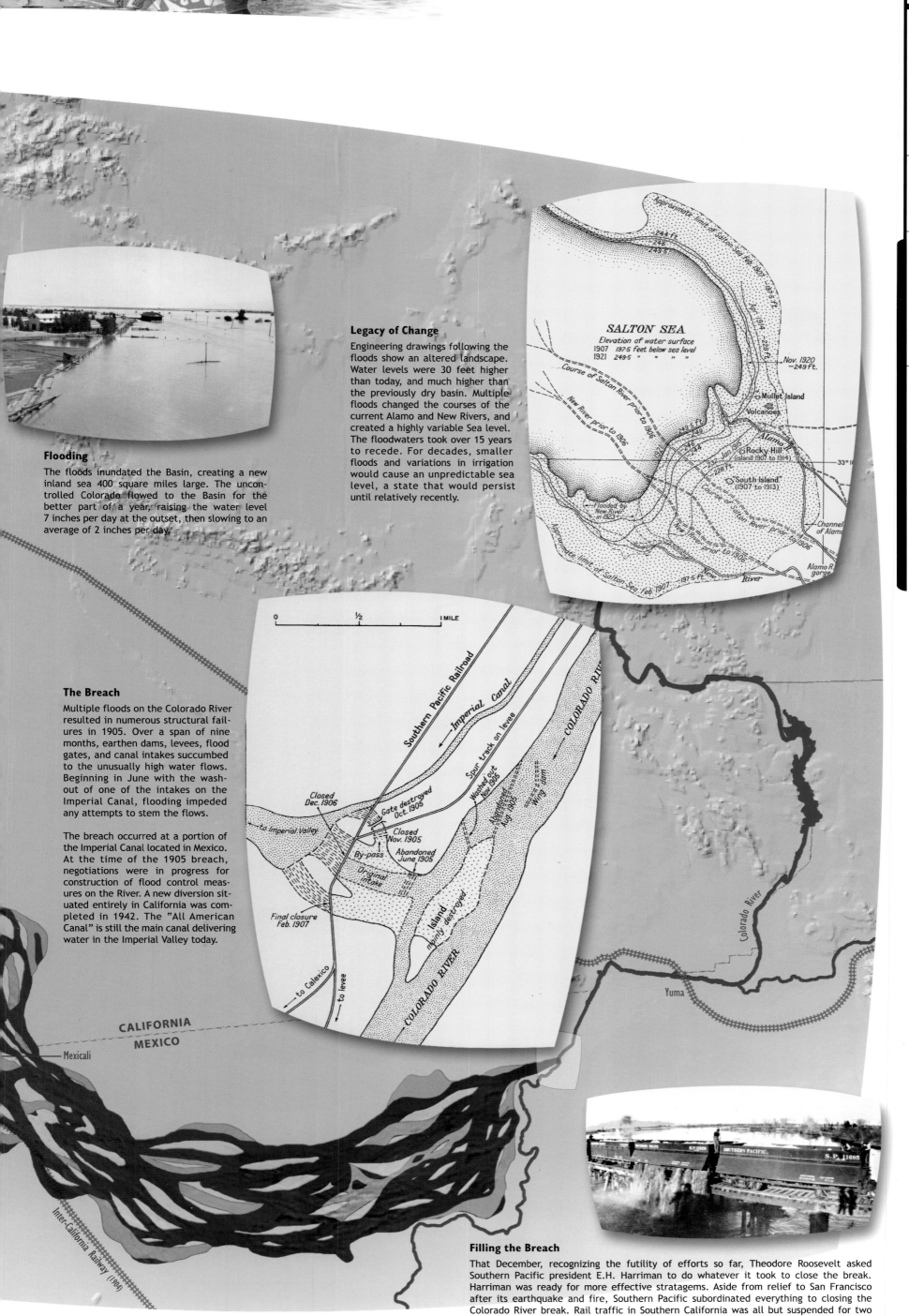

Flooding

The floods inundated the Basin, creating a new inland sea 400 square miles large. The uncontrolled Colorado flowed to the Basin for the better part of a year, raising the water level 7 inches per day at the outset, then slowing to an average of 2 inches per day.

Legacy of Change

Engineering drawings following the floods show an altered landscape. Water levels were 30 feet higher than today, and much higher than the previously dry basin. Multiple floods changed the courses of the current Alamo and New Rivers, and created a highly variable Sea level. The floodwaters took over 15 years to recede. For decades, smaller floods and variations in irrigation would cause an unpredictable sea level, a state that would persist until relatively recently.

SALTON SEA
Elevation of water surface
1907 197·5 feet below sea level
1921 249·5 "   "   "   "

The Breach

Multiple floods on the Colorado River resulted in numerous structural failures in 1905. Over a span of nine months, earthen dams, levees, flood gates, and canal intakes succumbed to the unusually high water flows. Beginning in June with the washout of one of the intakes on the Imperial Canal, flooding impeded any attempts to stem the flows.

The breach occurred at a portion of the Imperial Canal located in Mexico. At the time of the 1905 breach, negotiations were in progress for construction of flood control measures on the River. A new diversion situated entirely in California was completed in 1942. The "All American Canal" is still the main canal delivering water in the Imperial Valley today.

Filling the Breach

That December, recognizing the futility of efforts so far, Theodore Roosevelt asked Southern Pacific president E.H. Harriman to do whatever it took to close the break. Harriman was ready for more effective stratagems. Aside from relief to San Francisco after its earthquake and fire, Southern Pacific subordinated everything to closing the Colorado River break. Rail traffic in Southern California was all but suspended for two months as Southern Pacific routed 700 rail cars of gravel to the Salton Basin. On February 10, 1907, two million cubic feet of rock and three million dollars later, Southern Pacific closed the breach, and the River once again headed toward the Gulf of California.

In the past, melting snows transformed the Colorado River into a rampaging giant, flooding low-lying lands and destroying crops, property and lives. During the hot, dry summer months the Colorado turned into a placid trickle of water. With increased western migrations, settlers turned their energy towards taming the River in an effort to assure a stable year-round water supply and reclaim the arid desert.

At the earliest stages of development along the Colorado River, few recognized the contentious issue its waters would become. While supporting a growing population and enabling intensive agriculture, Colorado River water allocations have become a source of prolonged dispute. Today, one of the most controlled rivers in the world, a myriad of legislation and institutions govern its use. Resulting from decades of legal debate, this multitude of legal documents — known collectively as the "Law of the River"— affect every aspect of its management and operation.

Establishing the basis for today's geographic divisions for water allocation, the Colorado River Compact of 1922 divided the River into upper and lower basins. The responsibility of dividing each basin's annual 7.5 million-acre-feet share of Colorado River water fell to the states. Major federal and state water projects followed, including the massive Boulder (now Hoover) and Glen Canyon Dams. People came in droves to reap the bounty of the cheap water in the desert. Today, the River supplies water and power to nearly 30 million people across the arid west and remains a central issue for future growth and resource management.

In the Imperial Valley, a labyrinth of canals delivering Colorado water transformed the desert landscape into a flourishing oasis. Of California's allocation of lower basin water, agriculture in the Imperial Valley claims the lion's share. Today, Imperial Valley is considered one of the most productive agricultural regions in the world, a billion dollar annual industry nurtured and sustained by Colorado River water.

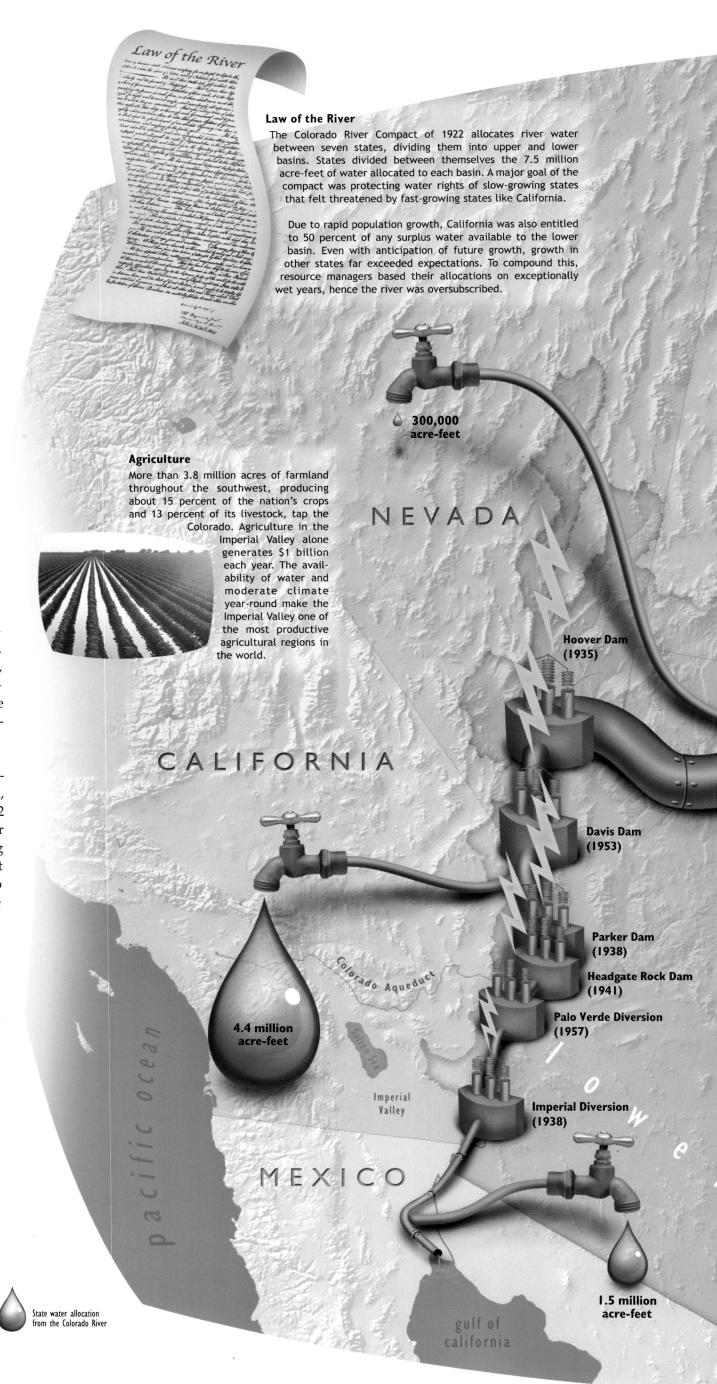

Law of the River
The Colorado River Compact of 1922 allocates river water between seven states, dividing them into upper and lower basins. States divided between themselves the 7.5 million acre-feet of water allocated to each basin. A major goal of the compact was protecting water rights of slow-growing states that felt threatened by fast-growing states like California.

Due to rapid population growth, California was also entitled to 50 percent of any surplus water available to the lower basin. Even with anticipation of future growth, growth in other states far exceeded expectations. To compound this, resource managers based their allocations on exceptionally wet years, hence the river was oversubscribed.

Agriculture
More than 3.8 million acres of farmland throughout the southwest, producing about 15 percent of the nation's crops and 13 percent of its livestock, tap the Colorado. Agriculture in the Imperial Valley alone generates $1 billion each year. The availability of water and moderate climate year-round make the Imperial Valley one of the most productive agricultural regions in the world.

300,000 acre-feet

NEVADA

Hoover Dam (1935)

CALIFORNIA

Davis Dam (1953)

Parker Dam (1938)

Headgate Rock Dam (1941)

Colorado Aqueduct

Palo Verde Diversion (1957)

4.4 million acre-feet

Salton Sea

Imperial Valley

Imperial Diversion (1938)

pacific ocean

MEXICO

State water allocation from the Colorado River

1.5 million acre-feet

gulf of california

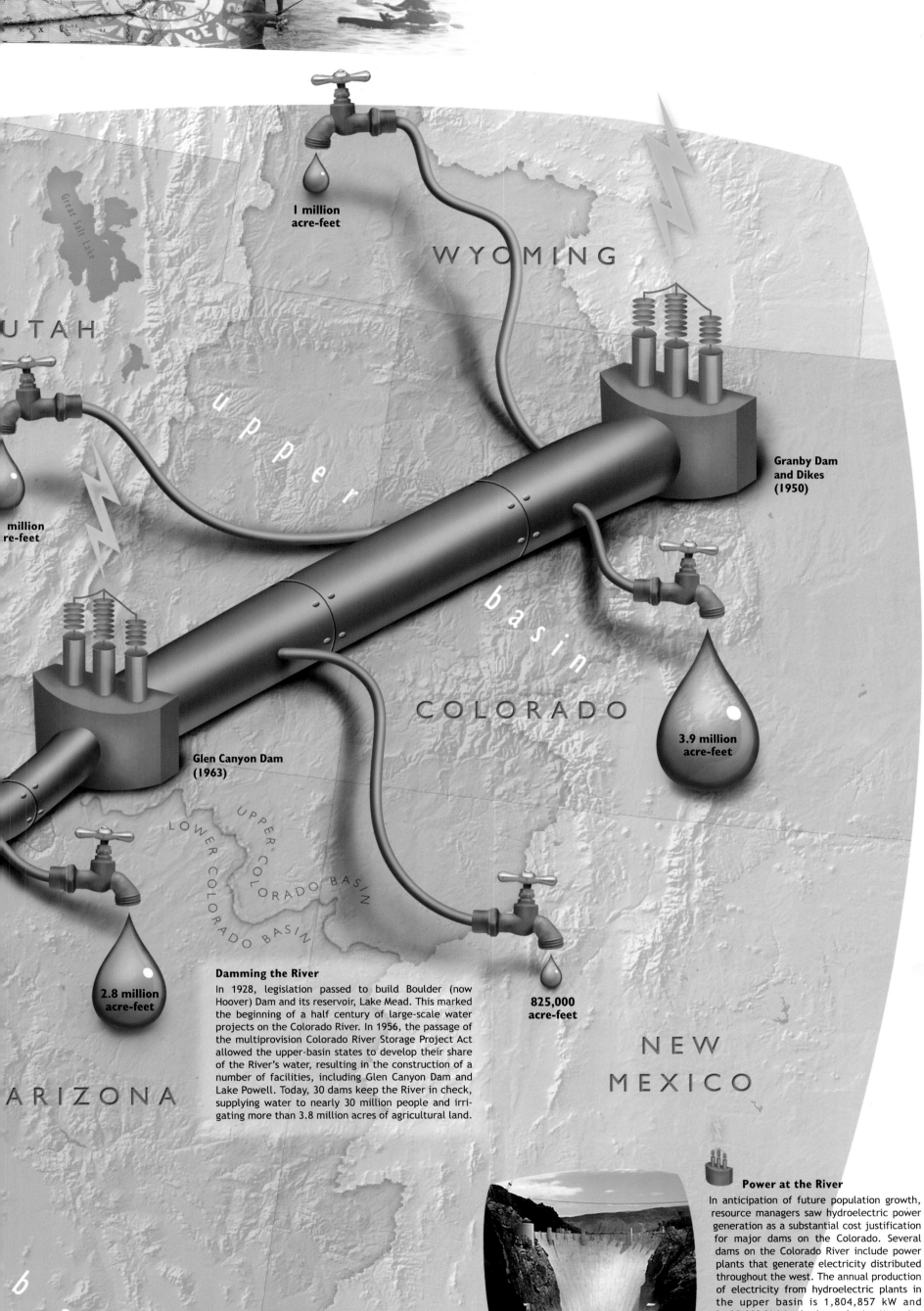

I million
acre-feet

WYOMING

UTAH

u p p e r

Granby Dam
and Dikes
(1950)

million
re-feet

b a s i n

COLORADO

3.9 million
acre-feet

Glen Canyon Dam
(1963)

UPPER COLORADO BASIN

LOWER COLORADO BASIN

Damming the River

In 1928, legislation passed to build Boulder (now Hoover) Dam and its reservoir, Lake Mead. This marked the beginning of a half century of large-scale water projects on the Colorado River. In 1956, the passage of the multiprovision Colorado River Storage Project Act allowed the upper-basin states to develop their share of the River's water, resulting in the construction of a number of facilities, including Glen Canyon Dam and Lake Powell. Today, 30 dams keep the River in check, supplying water to nearly 30 million people and irrigating more than 3.8 million acres of agricultural land.

2.8 million
acre-feet

825,000
acre-feet

NEW
MEXICO

ARIZONA

b a s i n

Power at the River

In anticipation of future population growth, resource managers saw hydroelectric power generation as a substantial cost justification for major dams on the Colorado. Several dams on the Colorado River include power plants that generate electricity distributed throughout the west. The annual production of electricity from hydroelectric plants in the upper basin is 1,804,857 kW and 2,438,800 kW in the lower basin. Managing power generation and water flow has become increasingly difficult, as resource managers try to balance the needs of electricity, recreation, and habitat along the river.

Historic United States Geological Survey Maps

1908

1950s

In the twentieth century, life at the Salton Sea saw many changes. A booming agricultural industry, supported by Colorado River water and a transcontinental railhead, transformed the barren desert. The ancient lake, once a bountiful resource for the native peoples, was reborn as the Salton Sea, created by natural disaster and sustained by irrigation runoff. Today, the Sea is still a bountiful oasis, supporting a diverse ecology and one of the most productive fisheries in the world.

After the devastating floods of 1905–7, the agriculture industry in the Imperial Valley continued to grow, expanding the web of irrigation canals and providing settlers with more water for their new farmlands. By 1931, the Imperial Valley was home to over 5,000 farms with a population of almost 60,000 people. With the completion of the All American and Coachella Canals in the late forties, the agricultural industry matured into a billion dollar commerce. Today, the Imperial and Coachella Valleys export fruit and vegetables year-round, serving winter produce markets nationally and abroad.

Since the formation of the Sea, agriculture has had a more constant presence than recreation. As early as the 1920s, the Salton Sea attracted visitors from throughout Southern California, even becoming a trendy Hollywood film destination. Visitation declined following negative perceptions of environmental change at the Sea during the 1960s and 1970s, coincident with increasing national awareness of environmental issues. This national awareness culminated in landmark legislation such as the National Environmental Protection Act, Endangered Species Act, and Clean Water Acts. In recent years, the Sea's diverse wildlife, particularly migratory birds and sport fish, has created a resurgent tourism industry.

1900s Imperial Valley Blooms
At the turn of the century, with the installation of hundreds of miles of canals and promising crop results, the colonization and development of the valley proceeded rapidly. Grapes, melons, and garden vegetables matured in the Valley earlier than in any other part of California. Barley was a profitable crop; alfalfa could be cut five or six times a year, and the finest quality Egyptian cotton yielded more than a bale (500 pounds) to the acre. Experiments also proved that the climate and soils were well adapted to the culture of grapefruit, oranges, lemons, olives, figs, dates, apricots, pomegranates, peaches, and pears.

About 8,000 acres of land were prepared for cultivation by the end of 1901. Before April 3, 1902, 400 miles of irrigation ditches had been dug, making water available for more than 100,000 acres of land. By 1905, over 10,000 people had settled in the Basin, and cultivated land had grown to 120,000 acres. From 1905 to 1907, the Colorado River flooded and destroyed settlements, farms, and thousands of acres of prime land in the Imperial Valley.

Boom Era: 1920s–1930s Hollywood at the Sea
Organized recreation launched at the Salton Sea in the mid-1920s. The movie industry saw the Sea as a premiere location to film pictures.

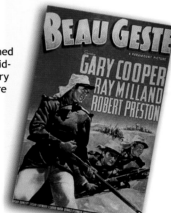

Recreation

1930s–1940s All American and Coachella Canals:
Imperial Valley recovered from the floods, and 11 years later, in 1915, the number of acres covered in crop reached a remarkable 300,000. In 1934, construction started on the All American Canal and was completed in 1942. The Coachella Canal broke ground in 1938 and was finalized 10 years later. With the completion of these two canals, water could now be distributed to farmers all over the Valley, leading to an explosion in agriculture acreage and value.

Agriculture

Continued from page 27

California Population (millions)	Salton Sea Valley Agriculture Dollars (millions)	Salton Sea Visitation (thousands)	1910	1920	1930	1940
35	1500	661				
30	1285	567				
25	1071	472				
20	857	378				
15	642	283				
10	428	189				
5	214	94				

A Changing Landscape

2000

The Salton Basin has changed dramatically over the past century. This satellite image, recorded in 2000 at nearly 300 miles above the earth, shows reflected infrared light—the deep red areas representing the productive agriculture of the Coachella and Imperial valleys.

Boom Era: 1930s–1940s Racing Takes Off

In 1929, boat races took place at the Sea, with over 2,000 people witnessing the setting of five world records. The first major regatta took place in 1942 and became a popular annual event where boaters tested for horsepower and new racing techniques. Normally held at Newport Marina, the regatta was moved to the Salton Sea because Newport became overcrowded with wartime vessels. In 1951, the Salton Sea regatta set an unprecedented 21 world records.

The Salton City "500"
World's Richest Power Boat Race

Hurricane IV   G-2

The Salton Sea is known as the fastest boat-racing lake in the nation for two reasons: the Sea has a high salt content, making boats more buoyant; and, at 227 feet below sea level, the higher atmospheric density makes engine performance more powerful.

Bust: 1950s The Salton Riviera

California in the 1950s witnessed a growing population and large-scale land development. One of the most successful developers at the time—Penn Phillips—saw the Salton Basin as the "Salton Riviera" and was determined to establish its shining jewel: Salton City. Endowed with marinas, a country club, championship golf courses, shopping centers, a private airstrip, and luxury resort hotels, Phillips planned to invest approximately $20 million in roads, sewers, water mains, telephone lines, and other infrastructure. Toward the end of 1960, Phillips bailed out on the Salton City project, selling all interest. Several years later, the Texas-based Holly Corporation bought the Salton City project and tried to accelerate the pace of construction without much success.

LEASE SALE

Boom Era: 1950s More Fish in the Sea

In the 1950s, the California Department of Fish and Game stocked a variety of fish species including sargo, corvina, and croaker, in a successful attempt to create a sport fishery. For decades, the Sea was a noted destination for anglers and became a major tourist attraction. With up to 400,000 boats and 16 campgrounds, the Sea was one of the most popular recreation destinations in California. People throughout Southern California came to the Sea for various activities such as camping, water skiing, fishing, hiking, bird watching, and boating. Even sea lions were introduced (unsuccessfully) in 1951 as the Sea was established as a state park and recreation area. Bird watching and hunting revenues brought in 3.1 million dollars annually.

Boom Era: 1960s The Glamorous Salton Sea

The North Shore was developed in the late 1950s and saw the completion of the North Shore Motel and Yacht Club. In 1962, the expansion of the North Shore Yacht Club made it the largest marina in Southern California. Celebrities flocked to the Sea, including Bing Crosby, Sonny Bono, The Beach Boys, Jerry Lewis, and the Marx Brothers. Championship golf courses were built in 1963 and attracted celebrities like Desi Arnaz, Tommy Bolt, and Harry James.

2000 Resurgence

The Salton Sea is within a 90-minute drive of 20 million people in Southern and Baja California. In the past four years, visitation at the Salton Sea has increased to an average of 250,000 a year. New fishing jetties, a boat launch, harbor facilities, upgraded campgrounds, day-use areas, more parking areas, expanded trails and visitor centers are planned. State park visitor centers offer educational seminars, interpretive programs, and kayak and jet boat trips. The Sonny Bono National Wildlife Refuge offers another visitor center, trails, and some of the best birding opportunities at the Sea. Several private and public facilities are available for waterfowl hunting, including managed wetland habitats.

People

Las Vegas
Lake Mead
Los Angeles to Lake Mead 289 highway miles
San Diego to Lake Mead 355 mi.
Lake Mohave
Topock Marsh
Los Angeles to Lake Havasu 299 mi.
Lake Havasu
Silverwood Lake
Big Bear Lake
Alamo Lake
Los Angeles to Salton Sea 150 mi.
San Diego to Lake Havasu 366 mi.
Los Angeles
Lake Matthews
Anaheim
San Diego to CS 118 mi.
Long Beach
Lake Elsinore
Santa Ana
Lake Hemet
Colorado River
Pacific Ocean
Vail Lake
Lake Henshaw
Clark Lake
Sutherland Lake
Salton Sea
Lake Hodges
Ferguson Lake
San Diego
Barrett Lake

Bust: 1960s–1990s A New Low

The mid-1960s saw park attendance average over 500,000 visitors per year, rivaling Yosemite National Park. Seen as a promising desert oasis, speculators flocked to buy a piece of the dream. Unfortunately, the dreams and promises of the Salton Sea came to an abrupt end when lake elevations became unstable, inundating local businesses, homes, and marinas. Many developers cancelled their contracts due to the Sea's unpredictable shoreline. With the creation of local freshwater lakes like Lake Perris and Lake Silverwood, tourism at the Sea dropped rapidly. Reports of pollution, pictures of massive fish and bird die-offs, and occasional malodors, led to a broad public misconception of the Sea's condition. In 1995, the Sea hit its lowest point in 50 years with only 87,000 visitors.

2000 Winter Breadbasket of the United States

Today, Imperial Valley's agricultural lands include over 572,286 acres; farmland in Coachella Valley covers about 56,600 acres. Control of the Colorado River and construction of the All American and Coachella Canals made expansion of agricultural land possible, creating a billion-dollar industry in the Basin. A frost-free climate with temperate seasons and dry summers allows for year-round crops, making the Valleys' farmlands some of the most productive in the world. While most farming in the midwestern corn belt of the United State comes to a halt during the winter, the Salton Basin continues to supply the nation with plentiful fruits and vegetables.

1950   1960   1970   1980   1990   2000

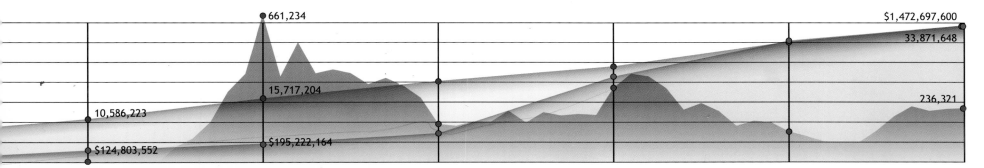

661,234 · $1,472,697,600

15,717,204 · 33,871,648

10,586,223 · 236,321

$124,803,552 · $195,222,164

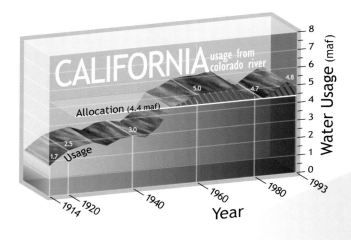

Population growth in the American west over the past century has created ever more demand for water. Essential to the settlement and prosperity of the region, management of Colorado River water allocations has become a daunting challenge. Surplus water, the unused portion of a state's yearly allocation, is increasingly rare. The era of surplus water is now threatened by deficit use. California, once dependent on surplus water from other states, must now meet the needs of their growing population with less water. Once using up to 5.2 million acre-feet, including the surplus from other states, California must find new ways to decrease use to 4.4 million acre-feet.

Population growth rates in the Southwest are among the highest in the nation. Southern California alone is projected to add nearly eight million people by the year 2020. To quench the thirst of these millions of people, municipalities and resource managers have speculated on all manner of water projects. The lion's share of water use in California supports a vital and highly productive agricultural industry. Rather than invest in large infrastructure to import water from even longer distances, in recent years, cities searching for nearby water for growing populations have proposed paying farmers to line their ditches and canals, and install other water saving devices. In return, the cities can purchase the salvaged or "conserved" water.

Conservation measures, such as reclaiming irrigation tailwater and drainage water, and construction of reservoirs and interceptor canals would likely result in reduced inflows to the Salton Sea. The potential environmental, economic, and social consequences of reduced inflow to the Salton Sea are a source of concern in managing water in the region.

Colorado River Water in California

As demand has increased, California has relied on unused surplus river water from Arizona and Nevada to augment its allocation. California's current use of Colorado River water is approximately 5.2 million acre-feet per year, while its apportionment is 4.4 million acre-feet per year. In July 1996, Secretary of Interior Bruce Babbitt called upon California to reduce its reliance on surplus water and to develop a plan to live within its 4.4 million acre-feet entitlement. California's stakeholders have been in negotiations to come up with a plan for reduction in use —the California 4.4 plan. California water officials are outlining projects to improve water conservation, while continuing to use the River's surpluses until 2016.

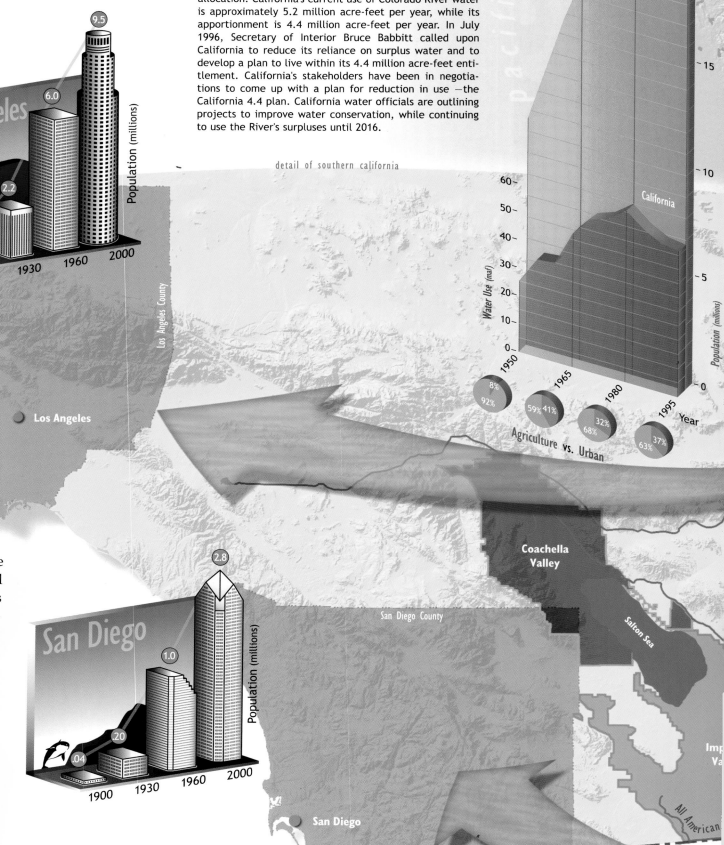

detail of southern california

Los Angeles, San Diego, Coachella Valley, and Imperial Valley Water Use

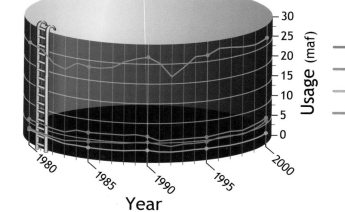

— City of San Diego
— City of Los Angeles
— Coachella Valley Water District
— Imperial Irrigation District

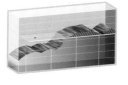

State-wide population and water usage

Water usage from the Colorado River

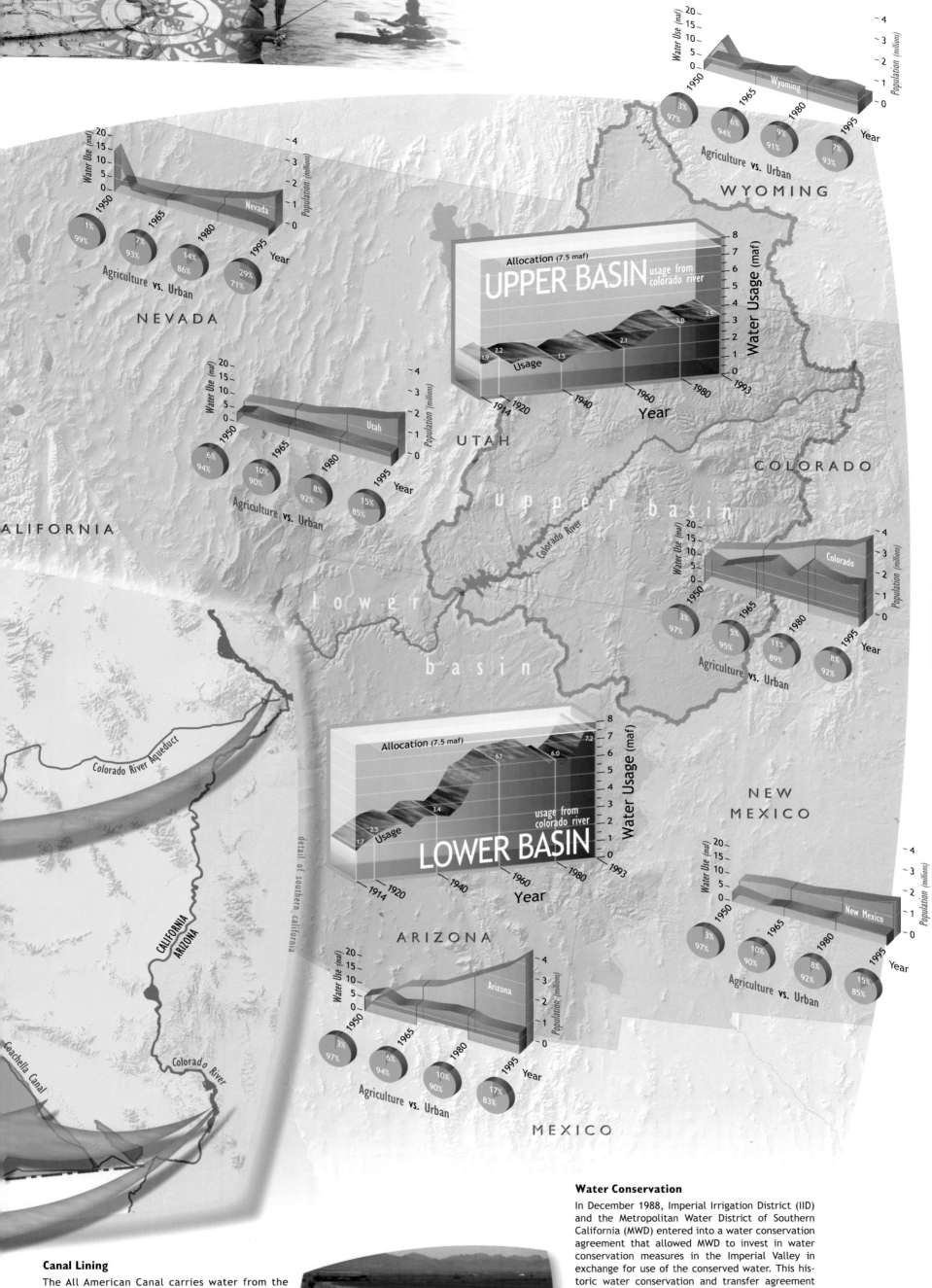

Wyoming
Water Use (maf): 20, 15, 10, 5, 0
Population (millions): 4, 3, 2, 1, 0
Year: 1950, 1965, 1980, 1995
Agriculture vs. Urban: 3% / 97%, 6% / 94%, 9% / 91%, 7% / 93%

WYOMING

Nevada
Water Use (maf): 20, 15, 10, 5, 0
Population (millions): 4, 3, 2, 1, 0
Year: 1950, 1965, 1980, 1995
Agriculture vs. Urban: 1% / 99%, 7% / 93%, 14% / 86%, 29% / 71%

NEVADA

UPPER BASIN usage from colorado river
Allocation (7.5 maf)
Water Usage (maf): 8, 7, 6, 5, 4, 3, 2, 1, 0
Usage: 1.9, 2.2, 1.5, 2.1, 3.0, 3.5
Year: 1914, 1920, 1940, 1960, 1980, 1993

UTAH

COLORADO

upper basin

Colorado River

Utah
Water Use (maf): 20, 15, 10, 5, 0
Population (millions): 4, 3, 2, 1, 0
Year: 1950, 1965, 1980, 1995
Agriculture vs. Urban: 6% / 94%, 10% / 90%, 8% / 92%, 15% / 85%

CALIFORNIA

lower

basin

Colorado
Water Use (maf): 20, 15, 10, 5, 0
Population (millions): 4, 3, 2, 1, 0
Year: 1950, 1965, 1980, 1995
Agriculture vs. Urban: 3% / 97%, 5% / 95%, 11% / 89%, 8% / 92%

NEW MEXICO

Colorado River Aqueduct

LOWER BASIN usage from colorado river
Allocation (7.5 maf)
Water Usage (maf): 8, 7, 6, 5, 4, 3, 2, 1, 0
Usage: 1.7, 2.5, 3.4, 6.1, 6.0, 7.2
Year: 1914, 1920, 1940, 1960, 1980, 1993

detail of southern california

CALIFORNIA / ARIZONA

Colorado River

ARIZONA

New Mexico
Water Use (maf): 20, 15, 10, 5, 0
Population (millions): 4, 3, 2, 1, 0
Year: 1950, 1965, 1980, 1995
Agriculture vs. Urban: 3% / 97%, 10% / 90%, 8% / 92%, 15% / 85%

Arizona
Water Use (maf): 20, 15, 10, 5, 0
Population (millions): 4, 3, 2, 1, 0
Year: 1950, 1965, 1980, 1995
Agriculture vs. Urban: 3% / 97%, 6% / 94%, 10% / 90%, 17% / 83%

Coachella Canal

MEXICO

Water Conservation

In December 1988, Imperial Irrigation District (IID) and the Metropolitan Water District of Southern California (MWD) entered into a water conservation agreement that allowed MWD to invest in water conservation measures in the Imperial Valley in exchange for use of the conserved water. This historic water conservation and transfer agreement between IID and MWD has been praised as a model of cooperation between agriculture and urban centers to stretch California's limited water resources. The program included structural and nonstructural conservation measures, such as lining canals with concrete, implementing reservoirs, and building on-farm irrigation water management. These conservation projects in Imperial Valley will save approximately 106,110 acre-feet of water annually, making water available to MWD.

Canal Lining

The All American Canal carries water from the southernmost reaches of the River on the U.S. side of the border to fields in Imperial Valley 80 miles to the west. In a continuing effort to stretch limited water supplies as far as possible, Congress authorized lining portions of the All American and Coachella canals in 1988. An estimated 70,000 acre-feet of water is lost through seepage into the desert sands each year. Ground water from canal seepage accounts for some inflow to the Sea each year and is a significant water source for Mexico.

The Sea is full of life. One of the most productive fish habitats in the world, the combination of physical environment, water chemistry, and biological systems supports a delicate ecological balance. As a terminal lake (one with no natural water outlet), high evaporation rates and intensive neighboring human activity has led to accelerated environmental change at the Sea.

Rapid environmental change has led to increased stresses on wildlife. The stress brought on by this environmental change, rather than simply environmental quality, has led to wildlife disease and die-offs. An integral stopover for international bird migration, local change and the stress it causes has far-reaching impacts throughout the Western Hemisphere.

limnology
the sea today

The Salton Sea has no outflow. The Sea lies at the bottom of a 7,851 sq. mi. (20,333 km²) watershed collecting all drainage within this closed Basin. Over 90 percent of all water entering the Sea results from agricultural runoff, with the remaining coming from natural precipitation, ground water, or urban use. Irrigation water, diverted from the Colorado River to a complex system of canals and drains, flows through the agriculture fields of the Imperial and Coachella valleys before draining to the Sea.

The Colorado River drains 17 percent of the land in the United States on its 1000-mile journey to Mexico and the Gulf of California. On the way, the natural runoff feeding the river accumulates various sediments and minerals. Before the construction of dams in the twentieth century, these sediments, including various soluble minerals and salts, were carried the entire course of the river—all the way to the Gulf. The large sediment loads often turned the River chocolate brown as it churned southward, picking up more sediment and minerals.

Once diverted to the Salton Basin, urban and agricultural practices concentrate salts and minerals already in the water. Agriculture and urban uses in the watershed further add more nutrients, salts, and chemicals. Several million tons of salt are added to the Salton Sea every year. Water entering the Sea can be as much as five times saltier than the Colorado River.

An enormous amount of water— 1.36 million acre-feet, over 15 percent of the total volume of the Sea— evaporates each year, leaving behind millions of tons of salts, minerals, and nutrients. Over its 100-year history, salinity has increased from the very low levels found in the Colorado River to 25 percent more than ocean water—more than a 40-fold increase.

Evaporation

The large surface area of the Sea and the hot, arid desert environment cause a large amount of water to evaporate. Each year, 1.36 million acre-feet evaporate. Evaporation concentrates various chemicals in the Salton Sea, including salts.

Closed Basin

All water bodies have a watershed, the catchment area where natural precipitation falls before flowing to the lake or river. Unlike many watersheds, the Salton Basin has no outlet, since no streams or rivers flow from the Sea. This geography influences the chemical, physical, and biological processes of the Sea. Usually, an outlet can serve to stabilize water quality by constantly flushing the system.

In-Basin Precipitation

Like many deserts in the American Southwest, periodic downpours characterize the Basin, including thunderstorms and flash floods. This brief rainfall can turn the Desert into a colorful scene of blooming wildflowers. Anza Borrego State Park, just west of the Sea, is renowned for spectacular spring wildflowers. Slightly more than 3 percent of the water entering the Sea comes from natural precipitation.

Ground Water

Fresh-water aquifers under the Salton Bas are the smallest contributors of wat entering the Sea. Less than 100,000 acr feet enter the Sea from ground water ea year. Historically a lifeline for Nati Americans during dry periods, plants an animals rely on natural springs fed by the aquifers. Increased pumping of grou water resources has lowered the grou water level in some areas.

44 ppt
Salton Sea

5 ppt
New River and Alamo River

35 ppt
Ocean water

1 ppt

reat Basin Precipitation

ne of the largest rivers in North America, the
olorado River drains 17 percent of the United
ates. Spring rains and winter snow fill the river
ch year, sustaining a complex ecology of temper-
e forests, arid deserts, and riparian areas. Much
this water is stored in immense reservoirs behind
assive dams constructed in the early twentieth
ntury, and is used to quench the thirst of millions
people and agriculture throughout the western
ates and Mexico.

Colorado River Water

Like any river, the natural runoff feeding the Colorado accumulates various
sediments and minerals. As the River
churns its way southward, it picks up
more sediment—sometimes turning it
chocolate brown. Before damming the
Colorado, the River carried sediments
along its entire course. Some naturally occurring elements, like salts
and selenium, become concentrated
as the River progresses.

Inflow Sources

Ground water
Rainfall — Other Sources (1%)
hitewater
River

4%
3%

7%

8%

45%

32%

gricultural
Drains

New River

Alamo River

Agriculture Runoff

Just as evaporation at the Sea
concentrates things in the water,
evaporation of irrigation water similarly
can concentrate these same substances.
Irrigation water collects salts and other minerals
naturally occurring in soils. Fertilizers and pesticides can
also accumulate in drain water. Most of the nutrients
feeding the Sea originate as fertilizers on agricultural fields. Pesticide levels in the Sea
however are currently lower than federal
drinking water standards.

Urban Runoff

A relatively small portion of water entering the Sea
results from urban uses. Wastewater from urban
areas, primarily the city of Mexicali, Mexico, but also
from smaller communities in Imperial Valley, carries
nutrients and urban pollutants. Much of these urban
pollutants are sequestered in riparian vegetation
and sediments before they reach the Sea.

Salinity Levels

Water entering the Sea is about five times
saltier than the Colorado River. Salt,
naturally occurring in the River, concentrates as it progresses. Evaporation at the
Sea further concentrates salts. Over the
100-year history of the Sea, salinity has
increased from low levels found in the
Colorado River to 25 percent more than
ocean water—more than a 40-fold increase.

50
40
30
20
0 ppt
10
5

Fresh water

Salt

s per thousand)

Physical Limnology

The remarkably shallow profile and large surface area of the Sea greatly affect its physical, chemical, and biological environment. The Salton Sea is a little over 35 miles (56 kilometers) long and 15 (24 kilometers) wide, but only 51 feet (16 meters) deep. If compared to a puddle 301 feet (11 meters) long, the length of a football field, it would be 1 inch deep (2.5 cm)—a puddle which would evaporate in minutes in the hot desert. Absent of current inflows, the Sea would dry up in about 10 years. But rivers replace one-sixth of the Sea each year—an equal amount evaporates each year. Shallow waters, external air temperature, sun, and wind each contribute to a highly volatile environment.

With the accumulation of salts and minerals over the past century, the Salton Sea has become a veritable chemical reservoir. Because the Sea has no outflow, water leaves the Sea only through evaporation, leaving behind salts, minerals, and other substances—millions of tons over the past 100 years. This accumulation of substances creates an ever-changing chemistry. For example, as oxygen solubility decreases, many chemical processes change. Previously oxidized compounds may be altered, some dissolving in water or capturing others in bottom sediment.

Since the formation of the Sea, the amount of nutrients and organic material entering the Sea has increased with intensified urbanization and agriculture. In recent decades, inflow of nutrients has exceeded the capacity of the Sea to provide a stable environment. Increased nutrients in the lake stimulate algae growth. Often short-lived, these algae blooms settle to the bottom and decompose. Organisms that break down organic material use oxygen. More growth leads to more decomposition and consumption of oxygen. Stress on aquatic life from low oxygen levels leads to greater mortality, and may contribute to massive fish die-offs.

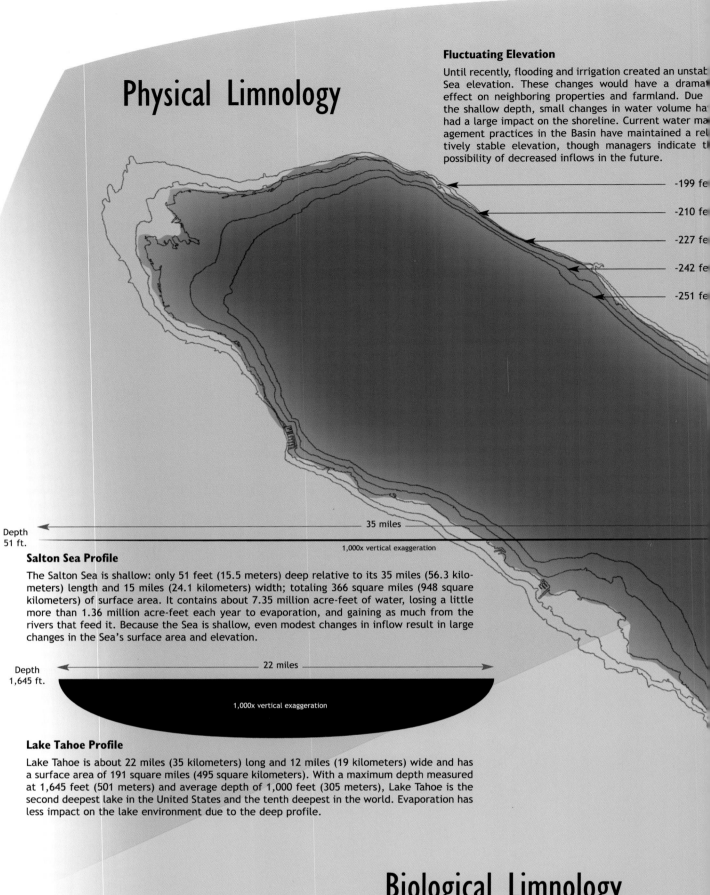

Fluctuating Elevation

Until recently, flooding and irrigation created an unstab Sea elevation. These changes would have a drama effect on neighboring properties and farmland. Due the shallow depth, small changes in water volume ha had a large impact on the shoreline. Current water ma agement practices in the Basin have maintained a rel tively stable elevation, though managers indicate t possibility of decreased inflows in the future.

-199 fe
-210 fe
-227 fe
-242 fe
-251 fe

Depth 51 ft.

35 miles

1,000x vertical exaggeration

Salton Sea Profile

The Salton Sea is shallow: only 51 feet (15.5 meters) deep relative to its 35 miles (56.3 kilometers) length and 15 miles (24.1 kilometers) width; totaling 366 square miles (948 square kilometers) of surface area. It contains about 7.35 million acre-feet of water, losing a little more than 1.36 million acre-feet each year to evaporation, and gaining as much from the rivers that feed it. Because the Sea is shallow, even modest changes in inflow result in large changes in the Sea's surface area and elevation.

Depth 1,645 ft.

22 miles

1,000x vertical exaggeration

Lake Tahoe Profile

Lake Tahoe is about 22 miles (35 kilometers) long and 12 miles (19 kilometers) wide and has a surface area of 191 square miles (495 square kilometers). With a maximum depth measured at 1,645 feet (501 meters) and average depth of 1,000 feet (305 meters), Lake Tahoe is the second deepest lake in the United States and the tenth deepest in the world. Evaporation has less impact on the lake environment due to the deep profile.

Biological Limnology

Oligotrophic

Oligotrophic lakes tend to have clear waters due to lack of nutrients, limiting algal growth and fish populations. Relatively sterile soils surround Lake Tahoe, and minimal amounts of nutrients and minerals enter the lake.

Mesotrophic

A mesotrophic lake's rich inflow of nutrients, especially phosphorus and nitrogen, create an environment in which an abundance of species may flourish. Balanced population growth is a characteristic of mesotrophic lakes, and is considered ideal for fisheries.

Lake Tahoe

35 miles

Lake Erie

210 miles

Oxygen

Nutrients

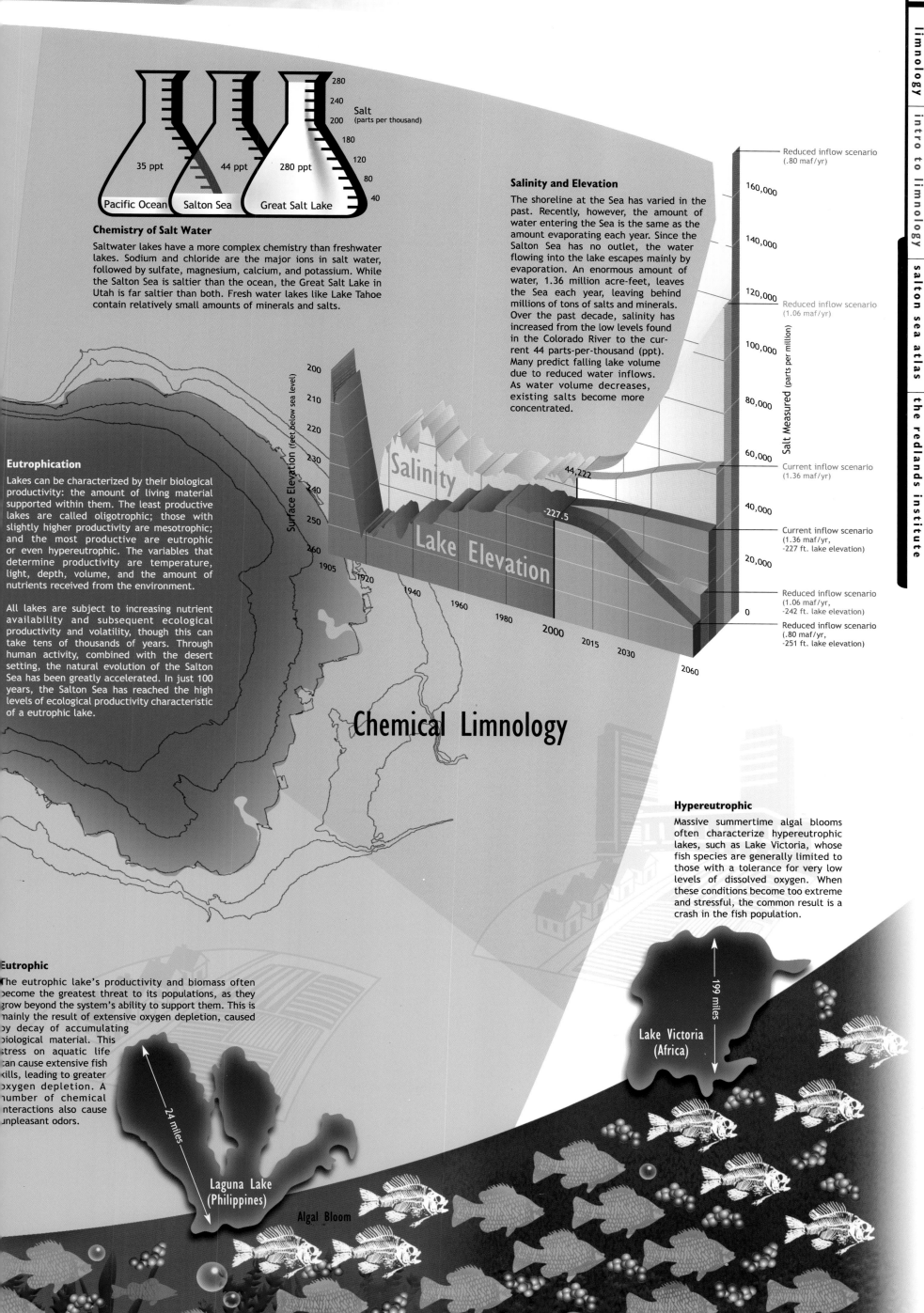

Chemistry of Salt Water

Saltwater lakes have a more complex chemistry than freshwater lakes. Sodium and chloride are the major ions in salt water, followed by sulfate, magnesium, calcium, and potassium. While the Salton Sea is saltier than the ocean, the Great Salt Lake in Utah is far saltier than both. Fresh water lakes like Lake Tahoe contain relatively small amounts of minerals and salts.

Salt (parts per thousand)

280 240 200 180 120 80 40

35 ppt — Pacific Ocean
44 ppt — Salton Sea
280 ppt — Great Salt Lake

Salinity and Elevation

The shoreline at the Sea has varied in the past. Recently, however, the amount of water entering the Sea is the same as the amount evaporating each year. Since the Salton Sea has no outlet, the water flowing into the lake escapes mainly by evaporation. An enormous amount of water, 1.36 million acre-feet, leaves the Sea each year, leaving behind millions of tons of salts and minerals. Over the past decade, salinity has increased from the low levels found in the Colorado River to the current 44 parts-per-thousand (ppt). Many predict falling lake volume due to reduced water inflows. As water volume decreases, existing salts become more concentrated.

Reduced inflow scenario (.80 maf/yr) — 160,000
140,000
Reduced inflow scenario (1.06 maf/yr) — 120,000
100,000
80,000
60,000
Current inflow scenario (1.36 maf/yr) — 44,222
40,000
Current inflow scenario (1.36 maf/yr, -227 ft. lake elevation) — -227.5
20,000
Reduced inflow scenario (1.06 maf/yr, -242 ft. lake elevation)
0 — Reduced inflow scenario (.80 maf/yr, -251 ft. lake elevation)

Salt Measured (parts per million)

Surface Elevation (feet below sea level)

200 210 220 230 240 250 260

Salinity

Lake Elevation

1905 1920 1940 1960 1980 2000 2015 2030 2060

Eutrophication

Lakes can be characterized by their biological productivity: the amount of living material supported within them. The least productive lakes are called oligotrophic; those with slightly higher productivity are mesotrophic; and the most productive are eutrophic or even hypereutrophic. The variables that determine productivity are temperature, light, depth, volume, and the amount of nutrients received from the environment.

All lakes are subject to increasing nutrient availability and subsequent ecological productivity and volatility, though this can take tens of thousands of years. Through human activity, combined with the desert setting, the natural evolution of the Salton Sea has been greatly accelerated. In just 100 years, the Salton Sea has reached the high levels of ecological productivity characteristic of a eutrophic lake.

Chemical Limnology

Hypereutrophic

Massive summertime algal blooms often characterize hypereutrophic lakes, such as Lake Victoria, whose fish species are generally limited to those with a tolerance for very low levels of dissolved oxygen. When these conditions become too extreme and stressful, the common result is a crash in the fish population.

Eutrophic

The eutrophic lake's productivity and biomass often become the greatest threat to its populations, as they grow beyond the system's ability to support them. This is mainly the result of extensive oxygen depletion, caused by decay of accumulating biological material. This stress on aquatic life can cause extensive fish kills, leading to greater oxygen depletion. A number of chemical interactions also cause unpleasant odors.

199 miles

Lake Victoria (Africa)

24 miles

Laguna Lake (Philippines)

Algal Bloom

Spring and Summer Circulation & Stratification

Figures 1 & 2
Northern Basin: Stratification persists throughout the spring and summer months. Currents are erratic. Surface and bottom waters may flow in opposing or similar directions, often influenced by currents from the southern basin.

Southern Basin: Water is well mixed, with infrequent periods of stratification. Water generally moves in a counterclockwise gyre. Due to mixing by wind, the upper and lower water layers move in the same direction.

figure 1

Northern Basin   Southern Basin

figure 2

Physical dimensions and climactic setting affect the waters of the Sea. The extreme climate acts on the Sea's large surface area; because of the shallow depth, external forces cause rapid changes in the Sea. A small rise at the bottom of the Sea, a natural berm, makes the Sea shallower in the middle, dividing the lake into two basins, north and south.

Fresh water entering a body of salt water will float over the more dense, saline water in a wedge. In the Salton Sea, fresh water mixes rapidly, with a small wedge at the mouths of the New, Alamo, and Whitewater Rivers.

Though the lake is shallow, at times the water forms distinct layers top to bottom. This layering, or stratification, is generally caused by differences in temperature or salinity. Cooler and more saline water is denser, so it sinks, while warmer and fresher water floats at the surface.

From midwinter to early fall, when the air temperature warms, the lake becomes more stratified. From early fall through midwinter, cooler water temperatures create less stratification.

Wind in the valley blows predominantly from the northwest to the southeast, stronger in the spring and weaker in the summer. As the wind pushes water, it makes the surface at the southeastern end slightly higher.

Stratification

Water in most lakes changes with depth—cooler, saltier, and less oxygenated water exists at the bottom. Environments at each level of stratification differ. At the surface, increased temperatures and evaporation lead to upwelling and mixing. Wind also drives change, mixing oxygen-poor bottom water with oxygen-rich surface water. Currents stir up sediments, releasing them back into the water.

wind

evaporation

warmer
less dense
fresher

cooler
more dense
salter

Process of Stratification

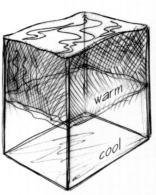

Temperature
Temperature differences cause water to stratify in distinct layers. Warmer water floats on denser, cooler water. Infrequent mixing can lead to wider temperature differences between surface water and deeper water.

warm

cool

less dense

dense

figure 3   Northern Basin   Southern Basin

figure 4

Fall and Winter Circulation & Stratification

Figures 3 & 4

Northern Basin: Strongest in fall, increased winds lead to increased mixing. Currents from the south have greater influence on the northern basin in fall and winter, driving circulation in a clockwise gyre. Currents are more consistent.

Southern Basin: Currents and stratification in the southern basin are consistent throughout the year. A counterclockwise gyre and well-mixed waters are typical.

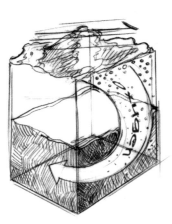

Dissolved Oxygen

Waves at the surface mix air with water. Along with oxygen-producing plants, surface waters contain more oxygen. In addition to chemical processes, the breakdown of organic material reduces oxygen at the bottom of the lake. Mixing blends oxygen-poor waters with surface water, reducing the concentration of oxygen in the lake.

Sediment Uptake

Mixing brings sediment from the lake bottom (and the metals and nutrients it contains) back into the water. Chemical and biological changes can result from the new availability of this material. Sediment also clouds the water, limiting sun penetration and algae growth.

Results

Turnover

Salinity

Salt water is denser than fresh water. In water bodies where fresh water meets saltier water (such as an estuary), fresh water floats on top. The rivers that feed the Salton Sea contain far less salt than the lake itself, creating a shallow plume of fresh water at the surface near the river deltas.

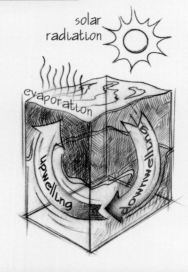

Convection

Most lakes mix their deeper, cooler water twice a year during spring warming and autumn cooling. The Salton Sea, however, mixes more frequently. The possibility of stratification increases during the summer due to higher solar energy and extreme day and night temperature differences. Where deeper water and surface water temperature differences persist, vertical mixing does not occur.

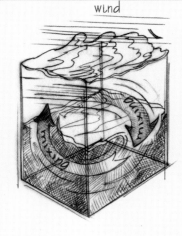

Wind

Wind creates higher velocity surface currents. Frequent windstorms in autumn months can mix waters throughout the lake, often ending long periods of stratification.

The unique geographic setting and adjacent human activity influence complex physical, chemical, and biological processes. At the formation of the current Sea, the waters were relatively fresh. Today, various salts comprise more than 99 percent of the dissolved chemicals. Over the past century, accumulation of salts, minerals, and nutrients from inflow has led to a changing environment. While a thriving ecology, this change causes environmental stress—taxing the ability of some species to adjust.

As salinity has increased, overall oxygen solubility has decreased. Areas already limited in oxygen, such as bottom waters, can become completely anoxic (oxygen free) more frequently and over longer time periods, leading to environmental stress in fish populations.

Lack of oxygen has additional impacts. In anoxic conditions, the breakdown of organic material produces sulfides. Because they are insoluble in water, these new compounds become trapped in sediment, reducing the amount of heavy metals in the water. This improves one aspect of water quality by balancing the constant inflow of heavy metals.

Over the past 30 years the amount of phosphorus entering the Sea has doubled—but phosphorus levels in Salton Sea water have remained stable. Phosphorus and nitrogen from agricultural runoff stimulate and fuel algae growth. In spite of more phosphorus entering the system, the biology of the Sea continues to grow to accommodate it. Phosphorus might also be incorporated in sediment and eliminated from the water through certain chemical reactions with fish tissue and bones.

Historically, alarming health warnings have led to public misconception of the Sea's condition. Today, pollutants, such as heavy metals and pesticides in the sea, are not considered significant health threats to humans and wildlife.

Chemical Constituents of the Salton Sea

Myths and Realities

Perception of Salton Sea water quality has long been shrouded in mystery—or myth. Pesticides and heavy metals are often perceived as significant threats to human and wildlife health at the Sea—a widespread misconception. Research indicates that pesticide and heavy metal levels in sediment and water are below toxic thresholds. Salts and other major ions comprise the vast majority of dissolved chemicals in the Sea.

Heavy metals 0.079%

Nutrients 0.011%

Pesticides 0.002%

Salt & Major Ions 99.097%

Why Does the Salton Sea Stink?

A combination of factors leads to an ever-changing riot of smells at the Salton Sea. Changing physical, biological, and chemical processes produce a variety of odors: from the familiar rotten-egg stench of hydrogen sulfide (produced by bacteria when oxygen is low), to the crisp sea-salt smell of the saline waters. Other influences around the Sea include: agriculture, geothermal power plants, vibrant wetland habitats, and decaying fish. Processes internal to the Sea, as well as external influences (such as wind, heat, sunlight, and the quality of inflow), vary throughout the year, yielding the dynamic and unique smell characteristic of the Sea.

Cl^-

Water (H_2O)

Na^+

Sodium Chloride (NaCl)

The Chemistry of Water

Many chemicals dissolve in water—primarily due to their molecular structure. Water molecules consist of a central oxygen atom bonded to two hydrogen atoms. Oxygen is more electronegative than hydrogen. The different charge of oxygen and hydrogen results in unequal sharing of electrons, with hydrogen being partially positive and oxygen being partially negative.

Many compounds, such as sodium chloride (NaCl), are soluble in water because their ions are attracted to one of the poles of the water molecule. When sodium ions (Na+) and chloride ions (Cl-) disperse in water, water molecules surround sodium ions with their negative ends (oxygen atoms) toward the ion. Positive ends (hydrogen atoms) surround the negative chloride ions. Other chemical compounds retain their chemical structure in water and will evaporate or precipitate and settle on the bottom.

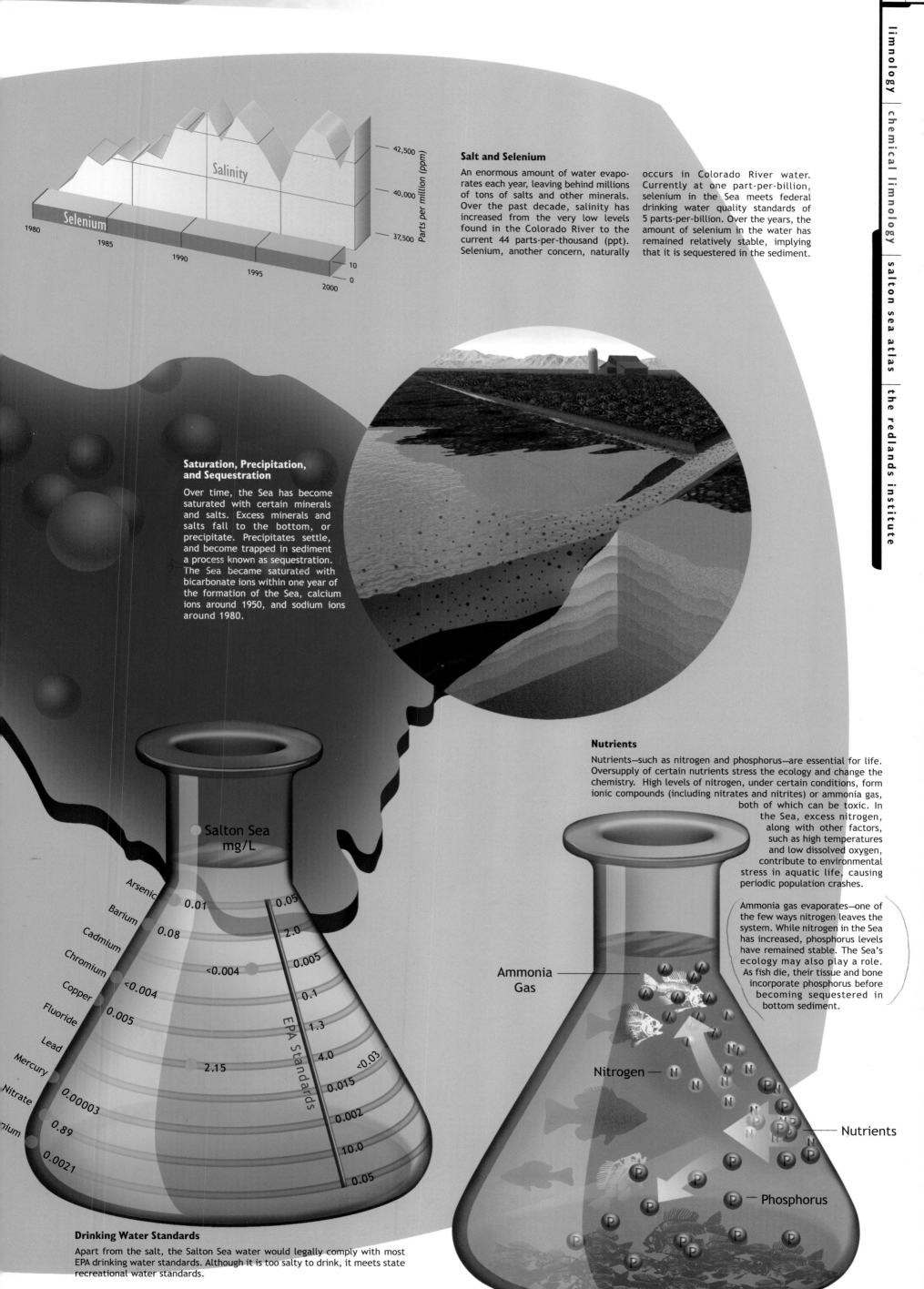

Salt and Selenium

An enormous amount of water evaporates each year, leaving behind millions of tons of salts and other minerals. Over the past decade, salinity has increased from the very low levels found in the Colorado River to the current 44 parts-per-thousand (ppt). Selenium, another concern, naturally occurs in Colorado River water. Currently at one part-per-billion, selenium in the Sea meets federal drinking water quality standards of 5 parts-per-billion. Over the years, the amount of selenium in the water has remained relatively stable, implying that it is sequestered in the sediment.

Saturation, Precipitation, and Sequestration

Over time, the Sea has become saturated with certain minerals and salts. Excess minerals and salts fall to the bottom, or precipitate. Precipitates settle, and become trapped in sediment a process known as sequestration. The Sea became saturated with bicarbonate ions within one year of the formation of the Sea, calcium ions around 1950, and sodium ions around 1980.

Nutrients

Nutrients—such as nitrogen and phosphorus—are essential for life. Oversupply of certain nutrients stress the ecology and change the chemistry. High levels of nitrogen, under certain conditions, form ionic compounds (including nitrates and nitrites) or ammonia gas, both of which can be toxic. In the Sea, excess nitrogen, along with other factors, such as high temperatures and low dissolved oxygen, contribute to environmental stress in aquatic life, causing periodic population crashes.

Ammonia gas evaporates—one of the few ways nitrogen leaves the system. While nitrogen in the Sea has increased, phosphorus levels have remained stable. The Sea's ecology may also play a role. As fish die, their tissue and bone incorporate phosphorus before becoming sequestered in bottom sediment.

Ammonia Gas

Nitrogen — N

Nutrients

Phosphorus

Salton Sea mg/L / EPA Standards

	Salton Sea mg/L	EPA Standards
Arsenic	0.01	0.05
Barium	0.08	2.0
Cadmium		0.005
Chromium	<0.004	0.1
Copper	<0.004	1.3
Fluoride	0.005	4.0
Lead		0.015
Mercury	2.15	<0.03
Nitrate	0.00003	0.002
	0.89	10.0
	0.0021	0.05

Drinking Water Standards

Apart from the salt, the Salton Sea water would legally comply with most EPA drinking water standards. Although it is too salty to drink, it meets state recreational water standards.

Salinity / Selenium chart

Parts per million (ppm)

42,500
40,000
37,500

1980 1985 1990 1995 2000

Salinity

Selenium

10
0

The Salton Sea has become increasingly rich with life. As water from agricultural fields continues to drain into it, the water evaporates —leaving the nutrients and salts behind. Rising nutrient levels lead to increased biological productivity—a process called eutrophication. While highly productive, eutrophic lakes often exhibit rapid and extreme environmental changes. The cumulative impact of these changes can stress wildlife, leading to disease and even death.

Biological productivity in a lake begins with primary producers. Composed of photosynthetic algae and phyto (plant) plankton, primary producers thrive on sunlight and nutrients. Small planktonic animals, such as brine shrimp (*Artemia satina*) and barnacle larvae (*Balanus amphitrite saltonensis*), eat the primary producers —and are in turn eaten by pileworms (*Neanthes succinea*). Plankton and pileworms are the basic food source for a thriving fish population.

As primary producers thrive, they provide energy for larger organisms. When plants and animals die, decomposers (bacteria) break them down, cycling nutrients back into the system. High nutrient levels, increased growth, and subsequent decomposition make the Salton Sea highly productive.

But increased growth can cause environmental instability, as populations exceed capacity. Nourished by the nutrient-rich broth, populations of algae and plankton explode in summer months, covering the Sea with carpets of algal blooms. Bacteria that break down these vast algae masses use up oxygen in the process. As water temperatures increase, dissolved oxygen declines even further, causing stress for aquatic organisms.

A changing environment brought on by a harsh geographic setting, physical, chemical, and biological processes causes stress on wildlife. Human influences at the Salton Sea, including increased nutrient input, have greatly accelerated natural processes. Rapid change causes environmental stress, and is the root of most visible health consequences at the Sea, including catastrophic fish die-offs and disease in birds.

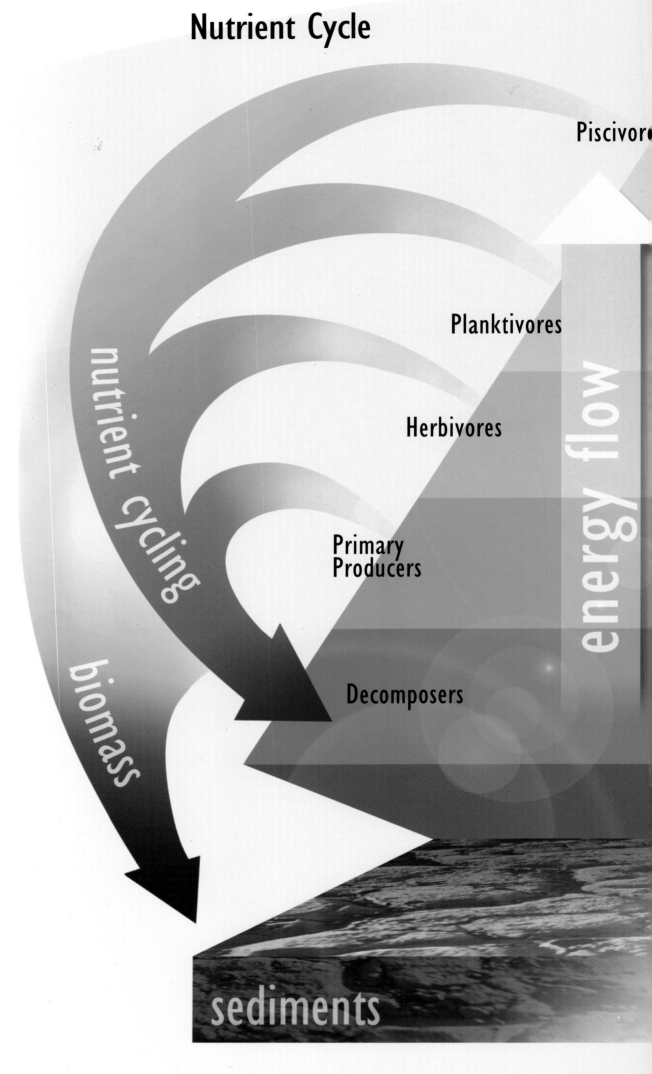

Nutrient Cycle

Piscivore

Planktivores

Herbivores

Primary Producers

Decomposers

nutrient cycling

biomass

energy flow

sediments

Bioaccumulation

Through bioaccumulation, contaminants, such as selenium, become more and more concentrated in organisms. Selenium in fish tissue has been a principal human health concern at the Salton Sea. Naturally occurring in Salton Sea water, selenium can be concentrated to toxic levels by bioaccumulation.

Plankton contain small amounts of selenium in their cells, absorbed from the selenium in the Sea. As other organisms eat

plankton, and fish eat these organisms, and so forth, the selenium level in cells increases. Thus pileworms have a higher concentration of selenium than plankton, and fish have a higher concentration still. Birds, and even humans, are feeding on progressively higher levels of selenium.

Like many things, a little may be healthy, but too much can be toxic. Humans, just like creatures in the Sea, only require so much. Some fish contain selenium levels high enough to cause human health concerns— higher than harmless amounts found naturally in the water.

Selenium

The Resilient Tilapia

Tilapia are a type of cichlid, a fresh-water fish native to Lake Tanganyika in East Africa. Introduced in the 1940s as a method of controlling vegetation in irrigation drains in Imperial Valley, tilapia are now the dominant fish species in the Salton Sea. The three tilapia species include *Oreochromis mossambicus, O. urolepis hornorum,* and *Tilapia zillii.* An estimated 90 million tilapia live in the Salton Sea.

Known for thriving in a wide range of potentially hostile environments, tilapia can survive with limited maintenance. Today, tilapia are a major source of protein in the developing world, particularly in tropical and subtropical areas.

Tilapia in the Salton Sea are not your ordinary tilapia. Although there are over 1,500 varieties of tilapia (and other cichlids), no others breed in salt water. Some live in salty lakes, but they all migrate up river to fresher water to lay their eggs. Salton Sea tilapia will nest in the bottom of the sea where oxygen is low and salinity is high.

Because these particular tilapia seem so adaptable, it is uncertain what environmental conditions they can tolerate. This makes setting and managing salinity levels in the Sea a challenge.

nitrogen and phosphorus

sunlight

outside nutrients

Tea-Colored Water

The water in the Salton Sea is not quite blue. Depending principally on how much suspended sediments and algae are in the water, the lake will be bluish-green, green, or even brown. Highly variable water color is typical of eutrophic lakes.

Wildlife Tolerances and Disease

Organisms can survive in different conditions. Each species has its own tolerance level. Disease can affect one species but not others; a certain amount of a pollutant can impair one organism while killing another. Sometimes environmental conditions will stress one part of a species life-cycle, but not the entire species population. For example, some levels of salinity will limit fish breeding, while even higher levels would kill a fish outright.

At the Salton Sea, environmental change is so rapid species are stressed by multiple environmental conditions simultaneously. These numerous stresses can lead to impaired health, and even disease. Since the formation of the current Sea, disease in bird populations has increased in variety, frequency, and scale. As recently as 1996, for example, 15,000 white pelicans (approximately 15–20 percent of the western population) died from type C avian botulism; more than 1,000 endangered brown pelicans died as well.

F ew other places on the planet support as diverse a bird population as the Salton Sea. Among the most vital bird habitats globally, the Sea is visited by more species of birds than any other location in the United States. A complex and varied ecology supports this avian mecca. From the lowliest microbe to the introduced fish species, the Sea's biological diversity and health is key for many western migratory birds.

Different bird species require different habitats — and their habitat needs vary according to their life stage and time of year. Over the past 200 years, the size, range, and diversity of wetland habitats in North America has drastically declined. As a result, the Sea and its environs not only provide critical types of year-round habitats for many different bird species, but it is increasingly one of the few places in the region to offer such resources.

ecology

Barnacles

The Salton Sea is one of few inland lakes in the world that hosts a thriving barnacle population. The free-floating barnacle larvae attach themselves to rocks, dock piers, fish, or even each other. The barnacle shell develops around the animal, which lives the rest of its life attached backwards to its substrate. Barnacles are filter feeders, combing plankton from the water with their feathery legs. Because of this feeding habit, researchers thought the barnacles would be good indicators of pollutants in the Sea. To their surprise, examination of the barnacle shells did not reveal any elevated levels of pesticides or other chemicals. Perplexed at the lack of pollutants found in the barnacle shells, the researchers guessed that perhaps the pollutants were being sequestered in sediments or in the Sea water in some way that prevented the uptake of these elements by the barnacles. They did not realize that the Salton Sea is not highly polluted—it is simply too rich with nutrients.

Nutrients

energy flow

Phytoplankton

Zooplankton

Barnacle larvae
Balanus amphitrite saltonensis

nutrient cloud

Nutrient-rich inflows

Adult barnacle colony
Balanus amphitrite saltonensis

A Keystone Species: Pileworms

Like a house of cards, a keystone species is one that, if removed from the ecosystem, would result in the collapse of many other species. The lowly pileworm is the keystone species in the Salton Sea ecosystem. Pileworms provide the critical link between the organic detritus that settles on the sea floor and the higher organisms, such as fish and birds. Pileworms comprise the primary food for croaker and juvenile corvina, which are in turn consumed by fish-eating birds, such as pelicans and cormorants. If the Sea loses its pileworms due to increasing salinity or deoxygenation, then these other dependent species will also be threatened or even lost.

Pileworms
Neanthes succinea

The Salton Sea is teeming with life, and microscopic plants and animals form the base of this highly productive ecosystem. Called plankton, these minuscule floating organisms are not only plentiful in the Sea, but are surprisingly diverse as well. Researchers at San Diego State University have identified more than 400 species of microorganisms in the Salton Sea, several of them new to science.

Readily available nutrients, largely from nitrogen and phosphorus-rich inflows, along with sunlight, power a complex web of life. The nutrient-rich water and propitious sunlight sustain microscopic plants (phytoplankton, such as the tire-shaped *Cyclotellus*), which use photosynthesis to produce energy that becomes the base of the aquatic food chain.

These primary producers are eaten by other zooplankton, such as tiny brine shrimp (*Artemia satina*) or barnacle larvae (*Balanus amphitrite saltonensis*), and in turn are eaten by larger invertebrates, such as adult barnacles and pileworms (*Neanthes succinea*). There are only 14 species of macroinvertebrates (visible animals without backbones) documented in

Tolerances

Biologists do not know exactly how much salt these creatures can tolerate. Laboratory investigations may give
some indications of the limits of salinity, temperature, and
other variables affecting the Sea's invertebrates, but they
cannot replicate the actual conditions of the open sea.
Furthermore, the fauna of the Salton Sea has adapted to
these changing conditions over past generations, in isola-
tion from other populations of the same species elsewhere.
Therefore, many of the Sea's creatures show greater tolerance for salinity than other populations, surviving in the
Sea beyond the lethal limits of others of its kind. Ongoing
research is attempting to determine tolerances of key
species, such as the Salton Sea pileworms.

Algal bloom

the Sea. The Salton Sea barnacle was probably introduced via hulls of
military seaplanes, vessels, or buoys during military exercises in 1944.
Isolated from its more widespread oceanic parent population, the Salton
Sea variety of the species has since then evolved to become a uniquely
identifiable subspecies. So widespread is the Salton Sea barnacle, its
shells make up the bulk of Salton Sea beach "sand."

Pileworms, introduced from San Diego's Mission Bay around 1930, are
the dominant macroinvertebrate on the Sea bottom, providing the key
food source for many fish and birds. Pileworms break down organic
material in the bottom sediment. As prey for many fish and birds, pileworms are a vital link between detritus accumulating on bottom sediments and species at higher levels in the food chain. Pileworms comprise the major portion of the diet of adult croaker (*Bairdiella icistia*) and
juvenile orangemouth corvina (*Cynoscion xanthulus*).

For many species of migratory birds, the high biological productivity of
the Salton Sea—particularly of pileworms—is critical for the survival of
many populations, such as the million-plus eared grebes (*Podiceps nigricollis*) that winter at the Sea.

Fish health

Fish tolerances for salinity, temperature, and oxygen depletion vary greatly. The fish species living in the Sea are all adapted to high salinity, but no one knows to what degree these particular populations have adapted to saline conditions in the Sea, or what the limits of salt tolerance may be for any particular species.

Salt is not a significant factor in the fish kills occurring at the Sea today—which result from other environmental stresses. Episodes of summer and fall fish die-offs correspond to high water temperatures and low, dissolved oxygen content, exacerbated by the hypereutrophic conditions of the Sea. Winter fish kills of tilapia may be the result of low water temperatures. Parasites on fish gills may impair ability to absorb already low, dissolved oxygen levels.

The Prolific Tilapia

Tilapia, native to Africa, are widespread in the tropics and subtropics around the world. One of the most widespread tilapia species, the Mozambique tilapia (*Oreochromis mossambicus*), is presently found in coastal regions of Southern and Central California, as well as the Salton Sea and adjacent drains. Two other tilapia species found in the Sea include *O. urolepis hornorum*, and *Tilapia zillii*. Today, tilapia represent the dominant fish species in the Sea by number—estimated at about 90 million. They range in size up to four pounds and reproduce at a stunning rate. They thrive in warm water, but cannot survive in water less than 55°F—a contributing factor in occasional winter fish kills.

The Salton Sea tilapia have adapted to the saline water. No other population of tilapia are known to breed in salt water. Salton Sea tilapia forage, nest, and breed at the bottom of the Sea—where oxygen is low and salinity is high.

Croaker

Croaker (*Bairdiella icistia*) represent the second most abundant fish species in the Salton Sea, and are native to the Gulf of California. Croaker are generally small, rarely reaching over one pound (0.6 kg), and are unimportant as game fish in the Salton Sea. It has been suggested as a significant forage fish for the corvinas. The Salton Sea population is descended from only 67 fish introduced in 1950-51.

Orangemouth Corvina

The orangemouth corvina (*Cynoscion xanthulus*) are native to the Gulf of California and represent the most important game fish in the Salton Sea. Corvina were first stocked in the 1950s, followed by other introductions through 1956. Approximately 250 specimens were introduced during that period. A 1970 California Fish and Game report estimated the corvina population in the Sea at one to three million fish. Adult corvina are predators and inhabit principally the open water areas of the Sea. Anglers in the nearshore also readily catch the fish. The maximum reported size is 32 pounds and over 30 inches in length.

Sargo
Anisotremus davidsonii

Croaker
Bairdiella icistia

Tilapia
Oreochromis mossambicus

Diverse aquatic habitats at the Salton Sea support a thriving fish population. Carp (*Cyprinus carpio*), catfish (*Clarias batrachus*), and mosquitofish (*Gambusia affinis*) use freshwater areas of the New and Alamo Rivers. Brackish waters near river deltas provide essential habitats for spawning fish. Shoreline areas and subsurface springs are important habitats for spawning tilapia and desert pupfish (*Cyprinodon macularius*). Deltas and near shore waters generally have higher dissolved oxygen content, and fish seem to crowd these areas during summer months when oxygen levels decline elsewhere. The open waters provide habitat for adult tilapia, croaker (*Bairdiella icistia*), sargo (*Anisotremus davidsonii*),

and orangemouth corvina (*Cynoscion xanthulus*). Corvina are the "sharks of the Sea"—top-level predators cruising for smaller fish prey.

During periods of inundation, ancient Lake Cahuilla supported large populations of Colorado River fish species, such as the bony-tail (*Gila elegans*), razorback sucker (*Xyrauchen texanus*), and desert pupfish—the only native species surviving in the Salton Sea today. During the Sea's creation in 1905-7, the Colorado River reintroduced freshwater fish to the Sea. With increasing salinity, these populations declined rapidly by 1929. The main fish species at the time were Colorado River trout (*Salmo pleuriticus*),

Sargo

Sargo (*Anisotremus davidsonii*) range from central to southern Baja California and into the northern Gulf of California. Sargo in the Salton Sea are descended from just 65 fish introduced from the Gulf of California in 1951. Recently, fishermen have reported catching sargo with deformed bodies or incomplete gill flaps— a possible sign of genetic inbreeding resulting from the small size of the initial founder stock. Sargo are larger than croaker (reaching 2 kg) and it is assumed that this fish is an important prey for the corvinas. Sargo are also a popular recreational fish.

Pupfish—Desert Survivors

After Lake Cahuilla receded, about 300 hundred years ago, the desert pupfish (*Cyprinodon macularius*) retreated to springs, seeps, and slow-moving waters along the lower Colorado River and in the Salton Basin. Pupfish thrived along streams, such as Fish Creek in Anza-Borrego State Park, occasionally getting washed downstream during floods. Upon reinundation of Lake Cahuilla, or with the present filling of the Salton Sea, the pupfish redispersed through the lake, and up the desert washes of San Felipe and Salt Creek. Today the pupfish occur in shoreline pools around the near-shore environment and in the agricultural drains, as well as their ancestral refugia.

Desert pupfish have adapted to the scarce waters of harsh desert environments. They can withstand high and varying temperatures, low oxygen levels, and salinity levels ranging from freshwater to nearly twice that of sea-water. The desert pupfish was listed as an endangered species in 1980 (state) and 1986 (federal) because of predation by introduced species and impacts to its ancestral habitat in Fish Creek.

Desert Pupfish
Cyprinodon macularius

Orangemouth corvina
Cynoscion xanthulus

The Tilapia
The three tilapia species in the Salton Sea include *Oreochromis mossambicus*, *O. urolepis hornorum*, and *Tilapia zillii*. An estimated 90 million tilapia live in the Salton Sea.

mosquitofish (*Gambusia affinis*), and humpback suckers (*Xyrauchen cypho*). In the early 1950s, the California Department of Fish and Game (CDFG) stocked 20 marine species in the Sea—mostly from the San Felipe area of the Gulf of California—to create a sport fishery. Of these, only orange-mouth corvina, croaker, and sargo are currently abundant.

In the mid-1960s, tilapia (*Oreochromis mossambicus*), an exotic species originating from Africa, was introduced to the Sea from an aquarist fish farm and irrigation ditches. By the early 1980s, tilapia was the dominant fish species and the most important prey for the increasing numbers of pis-civorous birds; tilapia is now a popular fish for recreational fishing. Nurtured by the abundant invertebrates, the Sea's fishery is among the most productive in the world. At its peak during the 1970s, more than 9,267 corvina were caught with a catch rate of 1.88 fish per angler hour—one of the best catch rates ever recorded in the state. Even now in its hypereutrophic condition, fishermen frequently catch their limit of corvina, with many specimens coming in over 20 pounds, and a day with over 100 tilapia is not unusual.

Desert

The desert uplands around the Salton Sea provide year-round habitats for many species of birds adapted to the extremes of heat and drought. Gambel's quail (*Callipepla gambelii*) scurry for shade under mesquite trees, while the large-billed race of savannah sparrow (*Passerculus sandwichensis*) is found only in saltbush scrub around the Sea itself. A declining species elsewhere in California, burrowing owls (*Athene cunicularia*) take refuge in their cool underground burrows during the heat of the day.

Burrowing owl
Athene cunicularia

Gambel's quail
Callipepla gambelii

Savannah sparrow
Passerculus sandwichensis

Palm Oasis

Providing shade and scarce water, the palm oases are essential habitat for many birds. Hooded orioles (*Icterus cucullatus*) use strings of the leaves for nest material, while many others make their homes in the thick skirts of thatch that adorn the stately palms. A Salton Sea specialty is the Abert's towhee (*Pipilo aberti*), found only in the Salton Basin, along the Lower Colorado River, and southern Arizona.

Hooded oriole
Icterus cucullatus

Abert's towhee
Pipilo aberti

Open Sea

The open water is used by tens of millions of waterbirds each year, including millions of eared grebes. Hoards of pelicans, cormorants, ducks, gulls, and terns make ready use of the abundant water and its resources. The diverse habitats surrounding the Sea, in combination with the productive and bountiful open waters make the Salton Sea a unique resource for a large number of bird species.

Caspian tern
Sterna caspia

Eared grebe
winter plumage

Eared grebe
Podiceps nigricollis

Great egrets
Ardea alba

Cattle egret
Bubulcus ibis

Snags

Rising water levels in the 1950s and 1960s drowned many mesquites, salt cedars, and cottonwoods that grew near the shoreline, especially around river mouths. Drowned trees persist as snags used by numerous breeding double-crested cormorants (*Phalacrocorax auritus*), herons, and egrets. The largest cattle egret colony in recent years numbered over 30,000 nests. Other species regularly form colonies of 100-300 nests.

Great blue heron
Ardea herodias

Birdlife is rich at the Salton Sea, perhaps as rich as it is anywhere. The region hosts over 400 species of birds. A fourth of these species breed at the Sea, some of which breed nowhere else in North America. Not only is there a large diversity of species, some species at the Sea number in the millions. The sheer diversity and number of bird species at the Sea is extraordinary.

From the everglades of Florida to the Mai Po marshes of Hong Kong to the Pantanal of Brazil, there are few places on the globe that support as many birds as the Salton Sea. Whether millions of migrating eared grebes (*Podiceps nigricollis*), hundreds of thousands of wintering gulls, or tens of thousands of breeding egrets, herons, and cormorants, the spectacle of birds dotting the water and sky can be breathtaking.

It is the diverse habitats at the Salton Sea region that support this wealth of birds. Breeding subtropical seabirds use barnacle covered spits in the Sea; breeding herons, egrets, and ibis drape snags jutting from the Sea and freshwater lakes; breeding shorebirds dot the shoreline and bordering impoundments; and breeding landbirds are found throughout the riparian areas along

Agricultural Fields

Unfarmed fields provide habitats for numerous wintering birds, from northern harriers (*Circus cyaneus*) and short-eared owls (*Asio flammeus*) to western meadowlarks (*Stumella neglecta*) and various sparrows, especially savannahs (*Passerculus sandwhichensis*). Burning harvested fields is common; such burns provide critical habitats for wintering mountain plovers (*Charadrius montanus*) and frequently support large numbers of wintering horned larks (*Eremophila alpestris*) and American pipits (*Anthus rubescens*). Flooded fields often support a wealth of waterbirds, including tens of thousands of wintering ring-billed gulls (*Larus delawarensis*), thousands of year-round cattle egrets (*Bubulcus ibis*) and white-faced ibis (*Plegadis chihi*), and hundreds of migratory shorebirds. As many as 30,000 snow geese (*Chen caerulescens*) winter at the Salton Sea, foraging in flooded fields and roosting at the Sea.

Snow goose
Chen caerulescens

Northern pintail
Anas acuta

Magnificent frigatebird
Fregata magnificens

Brown pelican
Pelecanus occidentalis

Wood stork
Mycteria americana

Fresh Water Habitats

Fresh water marsh provides habitat to migratory and resident bird species alike. The Sea is the year-round home to the largest breeding population of the Yuma clapper-rail (*Rallus longirostris*), endemic to the American Southwest. Wood storks (*Mycteria americana*) and yellow-headed blackbird (*Xanthocephalus xanthocephalus*) are also found at the Sea throughout the year. The migratory gull-billed tern (*Sterna nilotica*) requires open freshwater marsh and agricultural fields for foraging on terrestrial and aquatic invertebrates and small fish.

Yellow-headed blackbird
Xanthocephalus xanthocephalus

Clapper-rail
Rallus longirostris

Double-crested cormorant
Phalacrocorax auritus

White pelicans
Pelecanus erythrorhynchos

Island

Mullet Island, a volcanic formation at the south end of the Sea near the Alamo River Delta, provides birds a safe haven from terrestrial predators, such as coyote (*Canis latrans*). Tens of thousands of white and brown pelicans, as well as double-crested cormorants, nest on Mullet Island and forage open water throughout the Sea.

Smaller islands are found throughout the near-shore areas. The gull-billed tern (*Sterna nilotica*) and black skimmer (*Rynchops niger*) (both California Species of Concern), the Forster's tern (*Sterna forsteri*) and the Caspian tern (*Sterna caspia*) all nest on islands with a sandy substrate at the north and south ends of the Salton Sea. The numbers of gull-billed terns using the Salton Sea can exceed 600, and comprise approximately one-third of known nesting for the western population of this species.

Brown pelican
Pelecanus occidentalis

Black skimmer
Rynchops niger

Shoreline

The shoreline varies from mudflats to barnacle beaches. Breakwaters, jetties, marinas, pilings, and embankments provide roosts and forage sites for pelicans, shorebirds, gulls, and terns, and some provide nest sites for tern colonies. Shallow impoundments of fresh or brackish water that border the Sea provide abundant foraging habitat for shorebirds. Foraging herons and ibis use similar ponds with deeper water and a marshy fringe.

Black-necked stilt
Himantopus mexicanus

American avocet
Recurvirostra americana

Long-billed curlew
Numenius americanus

Gull-billed tern
Sterna nilotica

Killdeer
Charadrius vociferus

rivers and lakes and the suburban habitats associated with ubiquitous humans. While many of the same species frequent the Colorado River region, the Sea offers habitats to hundreds of other species. Notable absentees from the Colorado River region are the cattle egret, which nests in the Basin in the tens of thousands, and the white-faced ibis. Other breeding herons and egrets are the least bittern (*Ixobrychus exilis*), great blue heron (*Ardea herodias*) and green herons (*Butorides virescens*), great egrets (*Ardea alba*) and snowy egrets (*Egretta thula*), and black-crowned night-heron (*Nycticorax nycticorax*). The Salton Sea is the principal breeding locale in the interior Southwest for the double-crested cormorant (*Phalacrocorax*

auritus). Loss of migratory birds from disease at the Salton Sea has become a problem of increased importance since the 1990s. This phenomenon is not unique to the Salton Sea, nor is disease outbreak at the Sea a new occurrence. Increase in wildlife disease both nationally and internationally has mirrored the major increases in environmental change. Large-scale bird die-offs at the Salton Sea have occurred since at least 1917, but during recent years the frequency of disease outbreaks and types of diseases have increased. As the changes in aquatic and terrestrial environments at the Sea and elsewhere continue, so will wildlife disease. The complexity of this situation poses a major challenge for today's decision makers.

Wetland Loss

Wetlands have historically been regarded as wastelands —sources of mosquitoes, flies, unpleasant odors, and disease. People thought of wetlands as places to avoid or even eliminate. Largely because of this view, more than half of America's wetlands have been destroyed, drained and converted to farmlands, filled for housing or industrial developments, or as dumps for industrial and municipal waste.

California leads the nation in wetland habitat loss. Of California's estimated five million acres of wetlands, circa 1800, only 450,000 acres were still present in 2000 — a net loss of 91 percent.

In centuries past, during dry periods of the Salton Basin, migratory birds were not so dependent on the Salton Sea because there were plenty of additional wetland habitats along the California Coast and Central Valley. Now, the Salton Sea has become a last oasis for many species—if they cannot stop, rest, and fatten up at the Sea, they may perish during their return migration.

91%

2000

9%

Greater flamingo
Phoenicopterus ruber

Yellow-footed gull
Larus livens

Blue-footed booby
Sula nebouxii

The Salton Sea is an essential stopover for many species during migration. As many as 3.5 million eared grebes (*Podiceps nigricollis*), 90 percent of the continental population, spend their winters there, fattening up on pileworms and invertebrates before their perilous journey back across the desert to the Great Salt Lake and beyond for nesting. More than 30,000 white pelicans (*Pelecanus erythrorhynchos*), 80 percent of the western continental population, winter on the open Sea, feasting on the abundant fishery. Hundreds of thousands of shorebirds of 44 different species pass through the Salton Basin during their migrations on the Pacific Flyway, and

25,000 snow geese (*Chen caerulescens*) and Ross' geese (*Chen rossii*) enjoy the balmy winter temperatures at the Sea.

Many of the migratory birds follow the coast, north and south, along the Pacific Flyway. East Coast species tend to follow the Atlantic Flyway, and other birds migrate from the Gulf of Mexico to Canada and back along the Mississippi River or Central Flyway. An analysis of bird banding data showed the expected concentration of data points through the Central Valley of California and up along the Pacific Coast.

Seasonal Flyways

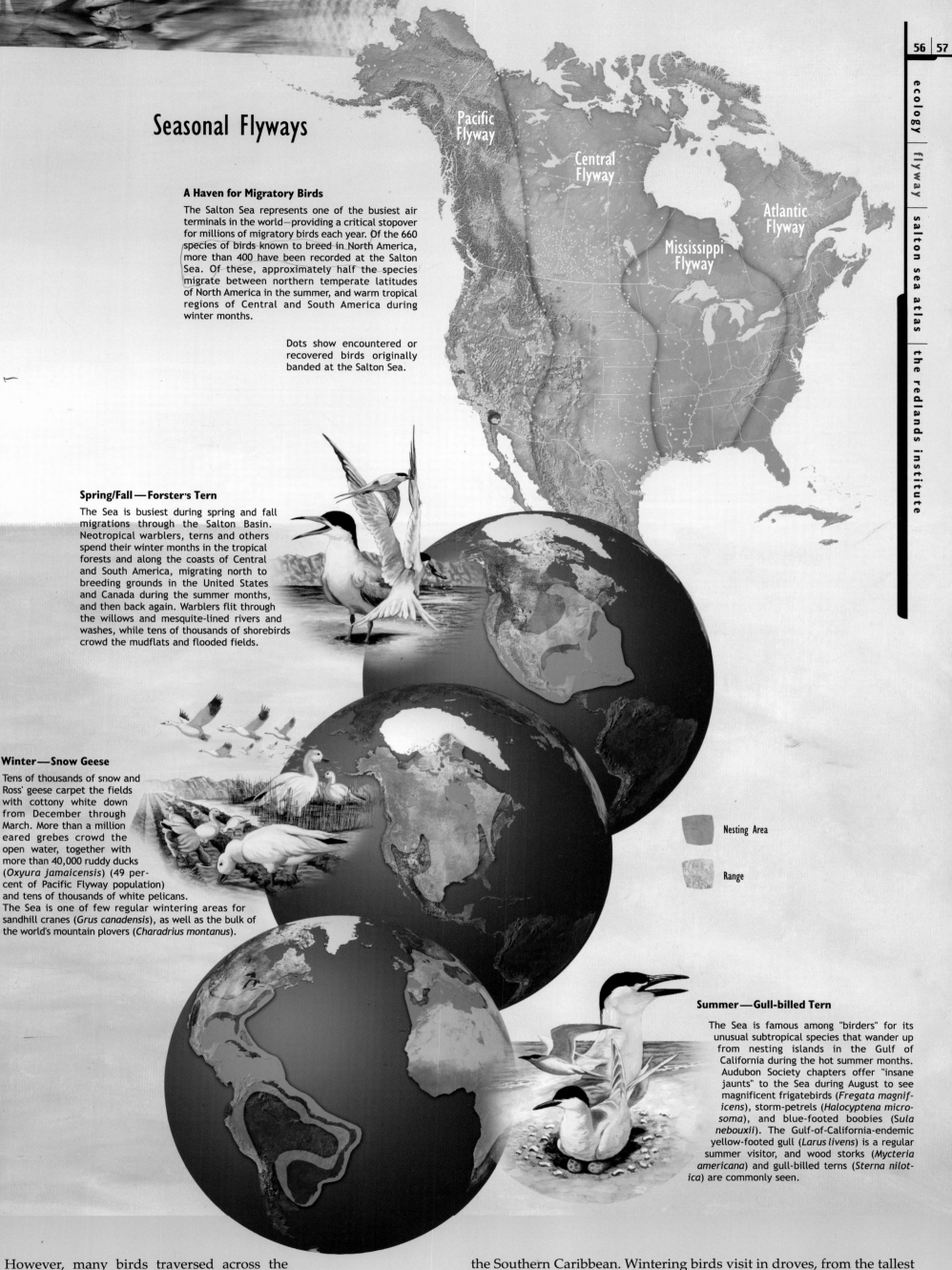

Pacific Flyway

Central Flyway

Atlantic Flyway

Mississippi Flyway

A Haven for Migratory Birds

The Salton Sea represents one of the busiest air terminals in the world—providing a critical stopover for millions of migratory birds each year. Of the 660 species of birds known to breed in North America, more than 400 have been recorded at the Salton Sea. Of these, approximately half the species migrate between northern temperate latitudes of North America in the summer, and warm tropical regions of Central and South America during winter months.

Dots show encountered or recovered birds originally banded at the Salton Sea.

Spring/Fall—Forster's Tern

The Sea is busiest during spring and fall migrations through the Salton Basin. Neotropical warblers, terns and others spend their winter months in the tropical forests and along the coasts of Central and South America, migrating north to breeding grounds in the United States and Canada during the summer months, and then back again. Warblers flit through the willows and mesquite-lined rivers and washes, while tens of thousands of shorebirds crowd the mudflats and flooded fields.

Winter—Snow Geese

Tens of thousands of snow and Ross' geese carpet the fields with cottony white down from December through March. More than a million eared grebes crowd the open water, together with more than 40,000 ruddy ducks (*Oxyura jamaicensis*) (49 percent of Pacific Flyway population) and tens of thousands of white pelicans. The Sea is one of few regular wintering areas for sandhill cranes (*Grus canadensis*), as well as the bulk of the world's mountain plovers (*Charadrius montanus*).

Nesting Area

Range

Summer—Gull-billed Tern

The Sea is famous among "birders" for its unusual subtropical species that wander up from nesting islands in the Gulf of California during the hot summer months. Audubon Society chapters offer "insane jaunts" to the Sea during August to see magnificent frigatebirds (*Fregata magnificens*), storm-petrels (*Halocyptena microsoma*), and blue-footed boobies (*Sula nebouxii*). The Gulf-of-California-endemic yellow-footed gull (*Larus livens*) is a regular summer visitor, and wood storks (*Mycteria americana*) and gull-billed terns (*Sterna nilotica*) are commonly seen.

However, many birds traversed across the Mojave Desert and Great Basin to the Great Salt Lake, and then to breeding grounds in the prairie pothole country of south central Canada and the north central plains of the United States. From there, they might fly back to the Salton Sea or, more likely, to the Gulf of Mexico. There are a surprising number of bird band recoveries along the Arctic North Slope, extending out along the Aleutian Islands to Kamchatka and northern Siberia. Three wayward birds were recovered in Hawaii, probably dead-end migrations of lost fall migrants from the Aleutians; while a fair number of bands were returned from Central America, and a few from

the Southern Caribbean. Wintering birds visit in droves, from the tallest crane to the smallest sparrow, and a host of migratory waterbirds, shorebirds, and landbirds would have a desperate journey through the bleak desert were it not for the Salton Sea.

Besides providing a haven for waterbirds in an intensely arid region, the Sea also provides a modicum of relief for the loss of wetlands in California, which is estimated at over 90 percent during the past century.

The Salton Sea is at a crossroads. We are faced with immediate decisions—eclipsed in scale only by their ecological consequences. The Sea itself has seen—and revisited—perpetual changes at the hand of the fickle flows of a raging Colorado River. Today, even with the highly controlled flows of the Colorado, environmental change at the Sea is ever present. These changes—at the root of highly visible, wildlife health problems—are only warnings of far more drastic consequences to come.

As water chemistry and biological systems continue to change, the ecosystem faces radical alteration. Among the immediate concerns, rising salinity, if continued unchecked, will ultimately make the Sea unable to support existing fish species. Without a plentiful food supply at the Salton Sea, no amount of wetland habitat will sustain the Sea's current role as a vital stopover for migratory birds in North America.

As the already-scarce water supplies of the American Southwest are strained to meet the needs of a burgeoning population, we face increasingly difficult decisions on managing our declining wetland habitats and the valuable water that sustains them. In the context of massive habitat loss elsewhere, and the continued escalation in demand for water resources, the future of the Salton Sea is of vital importance for both wildlife and growing human populations.

future
of the
salton
sea

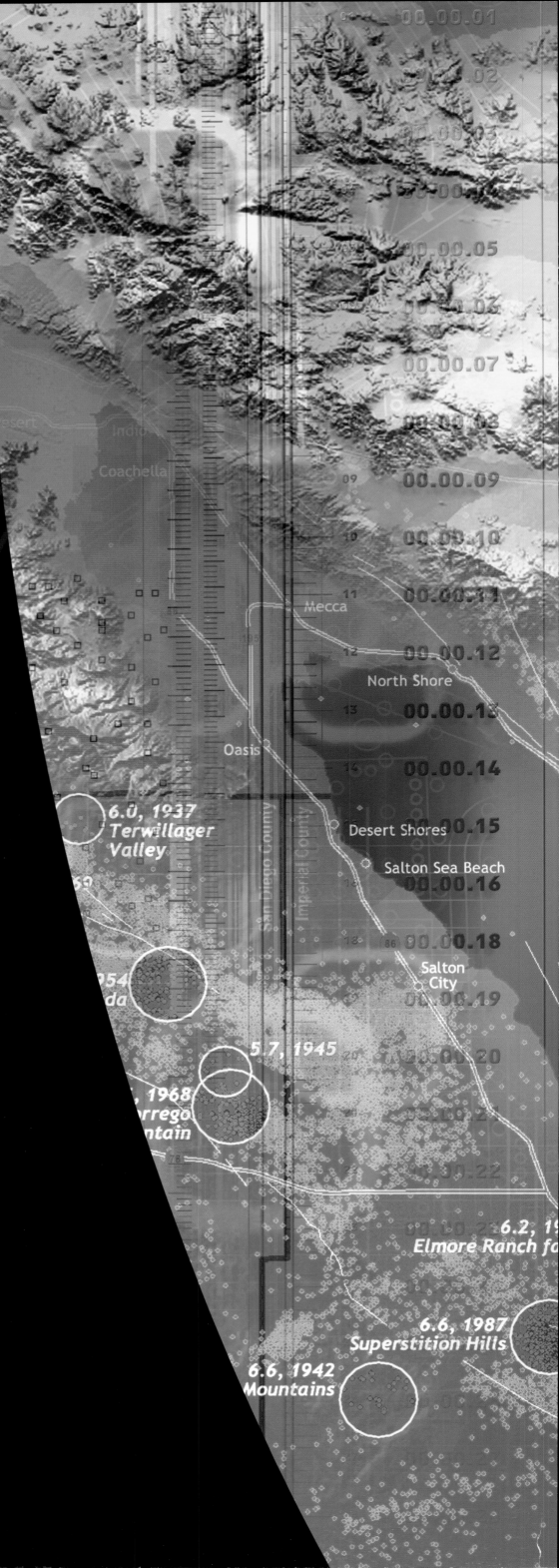

W̲e are living in the midst of a data flood. The computer revolution has made data capture an exponentially faster and more comprehensive process. These digital representations of reality flow from many disciplines, sciences, and areas of interest: geology, economics, biology, real estate, forestry, agriculture—all adding another facet to a bigger picture.

Though diverse in content, geographic location is the common denominator enabling widely disparate data sources to be joined. Tools for leveraging geographic information, GIS, integrate a broad range of data and improve communication and understanding of complex interrelated concepts and information.

The Salton Sea is a striking example of this data convergence—government agencies, scientists, and private companies generate data from multiple sources in a variety of formats for diverse needs. The resulting multi-layered maps reveal important concepts at a glance, with details and complex relationships emerging with each subsequent examination.

maps

Bombay
Beach

1942

Niland

5.7, 1981
Westmorland

Calipatria

5.5, 1950

5.5, 1979

Westmorland

Brawley

5.8, 1951

5.5, 1953

Southern California

15	Interstate highway
60	State highway
2	Mexico highway
	Major road
	Railway
	Urban area
	County line
	Federal recreation land
	State recreation land
	Major river
	Major canal
	Perennial lake
	Dry lake

Albers equal area conic projection,
standard parallels at 33°15' and 34°00'.

5   0   5   10   15   20   25 Miles

116°0'W · 115°30'W · 115°0'W · 114°30'W

Twentynine Palms

Bristol Lake

Cadiz Lake

Danby Lake

Dale Lake

OREGON
IDAHO
MONTANA
SOUTH DAKOTA
WYOMING
NEBRASKA
NEVADA
UTAH
COLORADO
KANSAS
OKLAHOMA
CALIFORNIA
ARIZONA
NEW MEXICO
Pacific Ocean
MEXICO
TEXAS
Area enlarged below

34°0'N

San Bernardino County
Riverside County

Joshua Tree National Park

177

Palen Lake

Hayfield Lake

Ford Dry Lake

10

Blythe

Coachella Canal

Sea Level

CALIFORNIA
ARIZONA

North Shore

33°30'N

Salton Sea State Recreation Area

Riverside County
Imperial County

Palo Verde

Desert Shores

Salton Sea Beach

Cibola National Wildlife Refuge

111

Bombay Beach

Imperial Wildlife Area Wister Unit

Salton Sea

Salton City

Niland

Salton Sea Test Base

Sonny Bono Salton Sea National Wildlife Refuge

Imperial Wildlife Area Hazard Unit

Sonny Bono Salton Sea National Wildlife Refuge

78

San Felipe Creek

Sea Level

Sonny Bono Salton Sea National Wildlife Refuge

Calipatria

Imperial Wildlife Area Ramer Unit

Imperial National Wildlife Refuge

111

115

Picacho State Recreation Area

La Paz Co.
Yuma Co.

Westmorland
-163 ft.

33°0'N

Brawley

New River

Alamo River

Sea Level

Coachella Canal

Martinez Lake

86

111

115

Colorado River

Seeley

Holtville

Gila River

El Centro

8

New River

Yuma

Ocotillo

Sea Level

All American Canal

Imperial County

Rio Colorado

Calexico International Airport

Calexico

Mexicali

Yuma International Airport

8

CALIFORNIA - UNITED STATES
BAJA CALIFORNIA - MEXICO

Rodolfo Sanchez Taboada Airport

32°30'N

2

5

San Luis

Yuma County ARIZONA - UNITED STATES
SONORA - MEXICO

Laguna Salada

116°0'W · 115°30'W · 115°0'W · 114°30'W

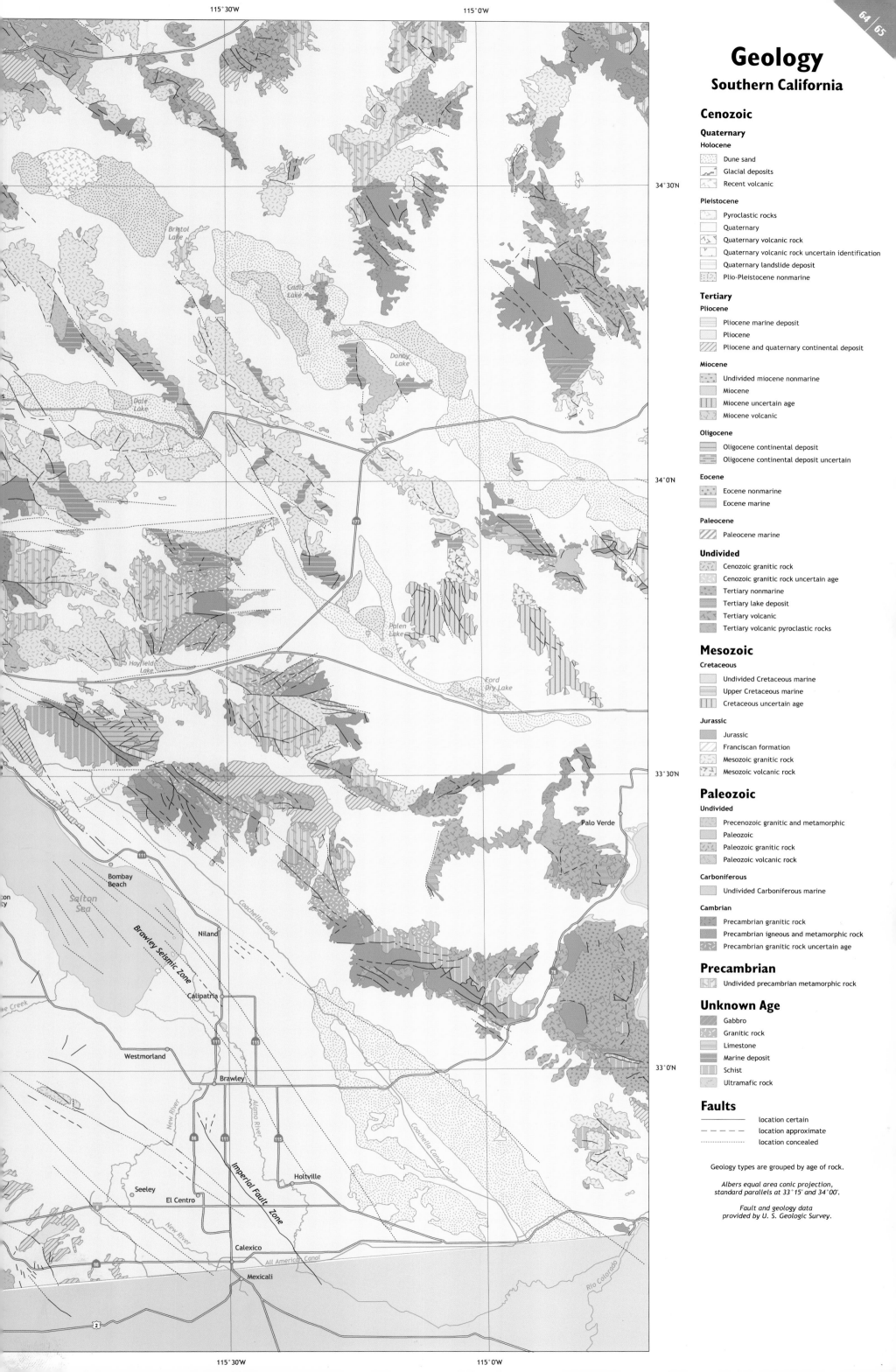

Geology
Southern California

Cenozoic

Quaternary

Holocene

- Dune sand
- Glacial deposits
- Recent volcanic

Pleistocene

- Pyroclastic rocks
- Quaternary
- Quaternary volcanic rock
- Quaternary volcanic rock uncertain identification
- Quaternary landslide deposit
- Plio-Pleistocene nonmarine

Tertiary

Pliocene

- Pliocene marine deposit
- Pliocene
- Pliocene and quaternary continental deposit

Miocene

- Undivided miocene nonmarine
- Miocene
- Miocene uncertain age
- Miocene volcanic

Oligocene

- Oligocene continental deposit
- Oligocene continental deposit uncertain

Eocene

- Eocene nonmarine
- Eocene marine

Paleocene

- Paleocene marine

Undivided

- Cenozoic granitic rock
- Cenozoic granitic rock uncertain age
- Tertiary nonmarine
- Tertiary lake deposit
- Tertiary volcanic
- Tertiary volcanic pyroclastic rocks

Mesozoic

Cretaceous

- Undivided Cretaceous marine
- Upper Cretaceous marine
- Cretaceous uncertain age

Jurassic

- Jurassic
- Franciscan formation
- Mesozoic granitic rock
- Mesozoic volcanic rock

Paleozoic

Undivided

- Precenozoic granitic and metamorphic
- Paleozoic
- Paleozoic granitic rock
- Paleozoic volcanic rock

Carboniferous

- Undivided Carboniferous marine

Cambrian

- Precambrian granitic rock
- Precambrian igneous and metamorphic rock
- Precambrian granitic rock uncertain age

Precambrian

- Undivided precambrian metamorphic rock

Unknown Age

- Gabbro
- Granitic rock
- Limestone
- Marine deposit
- Schist
- Ultramafic rock

Faults

- —————— location certain
- – – – – – location approximate
- ·············· location concealed

Geology types are grouped by age of rock.

*Albers equal area conic projection,
standard parallels at 33°15' and 34°00'.*

*Fault and geology data
provided by U. S. Geologic Survey.*

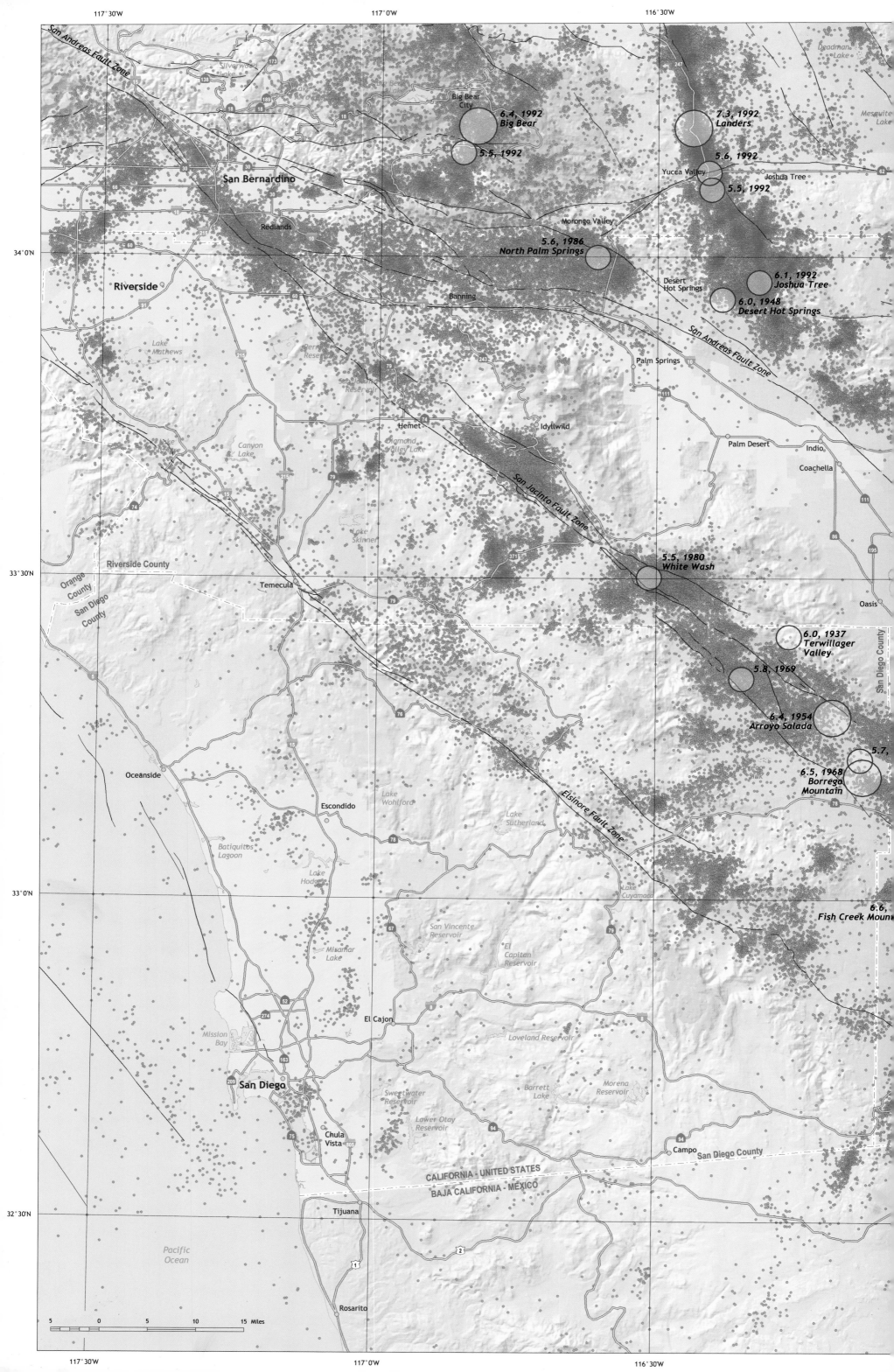

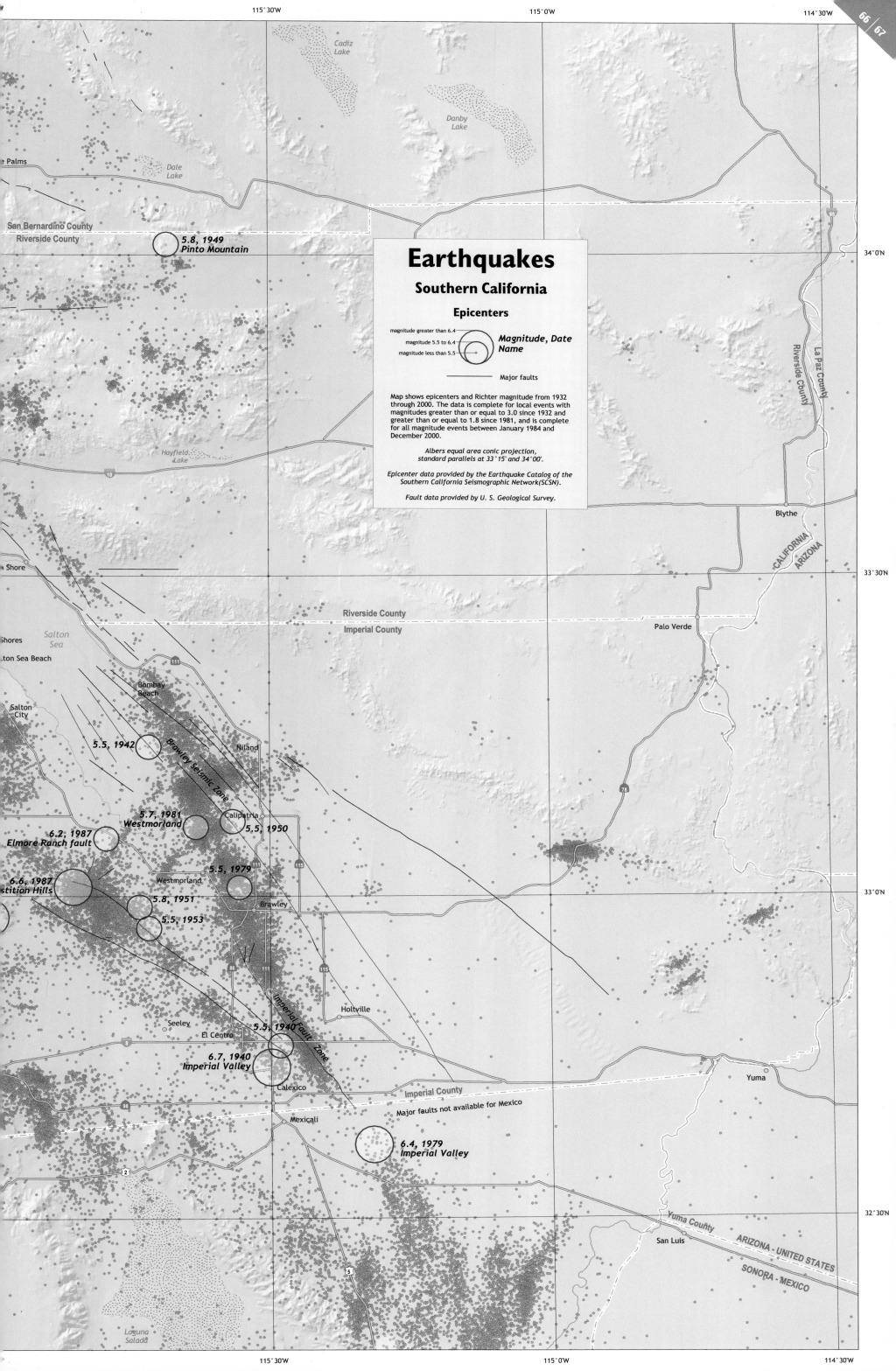

Earthquakes
Southern California
Epicenters

magnitude greater than 6.4
magnitude 5.5 to 6.4
magnitude less than 5.5

*Magnitude, Date
Name*

Major faults

Map shows epicenters and Richter magnitude from 1932
through 2000. The data is complete for local events with
magnitudes greater than or equal to 3.0 since 1932 and
greater than or equal to 1.8 since 1981, and is complete
for all magnitude events between January 1984 and
December 2000.

Albers equal area conic projection,
standard parallels at 33°15' and 34°00'.

Epicenter data provided by the Earthquake Catalog of the
Southern California Seismographic Network(SCSN).

Fault data provided by U. S. Geological Survey.

*5.8, 1949
Pinto Mountain*

5.5, 1942

Brawley Seismic Zone

*5.7, 1981
Westmorland*

5.5, 1950

*6.2, 1987
Elmore Ranch fault*

5.5, 1979

*6.6, 1987
stition Hills*

5.8, 1951

5.5, 1953

5.5, 1940

*6.7, 1940
Imperial Valley*

Imperial Fault Zone

Major faults not available for Mexico

*6.4, 1979
Imperial Valley*

San Bernardino County
Riverside County

Riverside County
Imperial County

Imperial County

CALIFORNIA
ARIZONA

La Paz County

Riverside County

Yuma County

ARIZONA - UNITED STATES

SONORA - MEXICO

Cadiz
Lake

Danby
Lake

Dale
Lake

Hayfield
Lake

Salton
Sea

Bombay
Beach

Niland

Calipatria

Westmorland

Brawley

Holtville

Seeley

El Centro

Calexico

Mexicali

Salton
City

Blythe

Palo Verde

Yuma

San Luis

Laguna
Salada

e Palms

Shore

Shores

ton Sea Beach

34°0'N

33°30'N

33°0'N

32°30'N

115°30'W

115°0'W

114°30'W

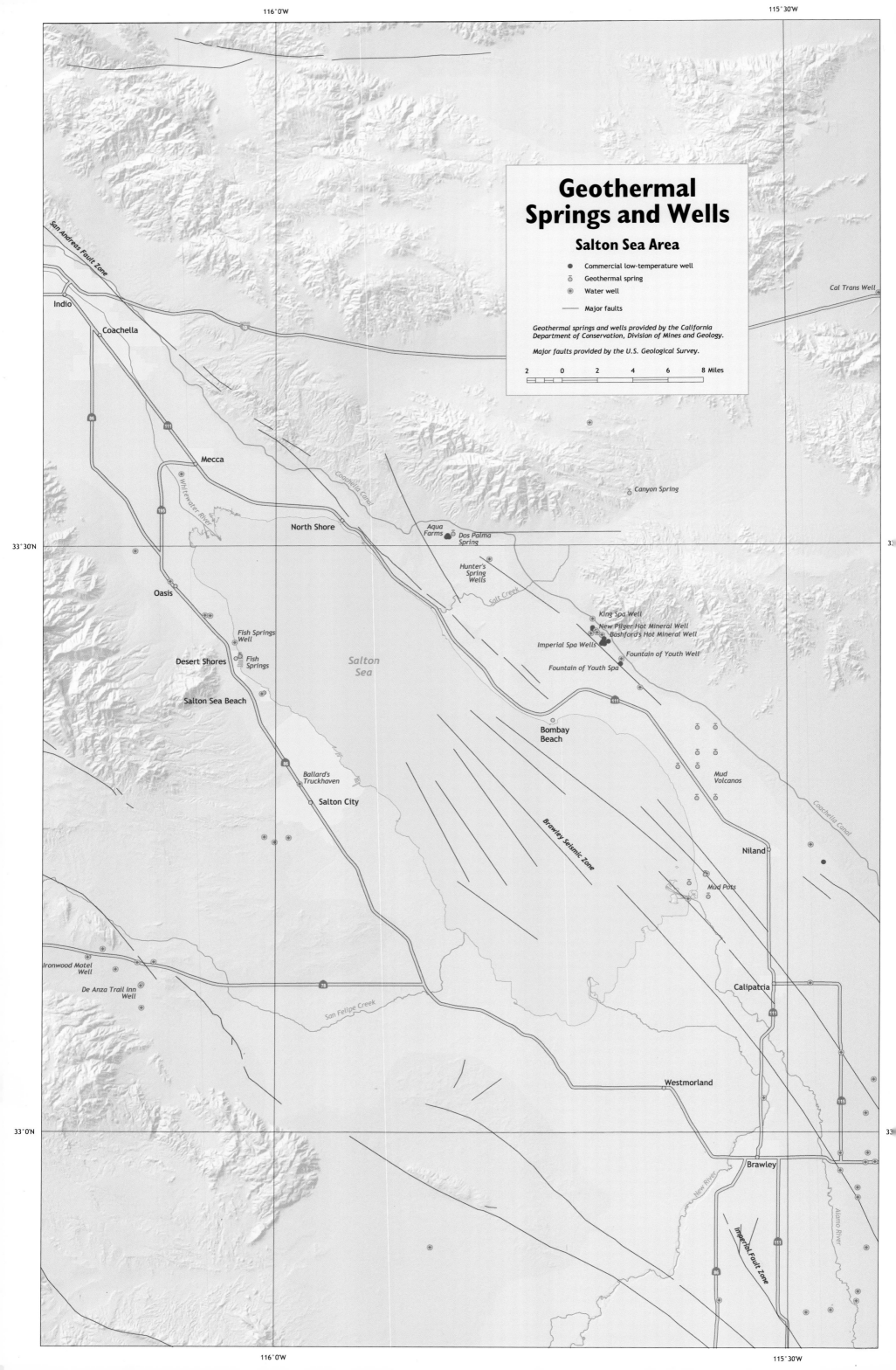

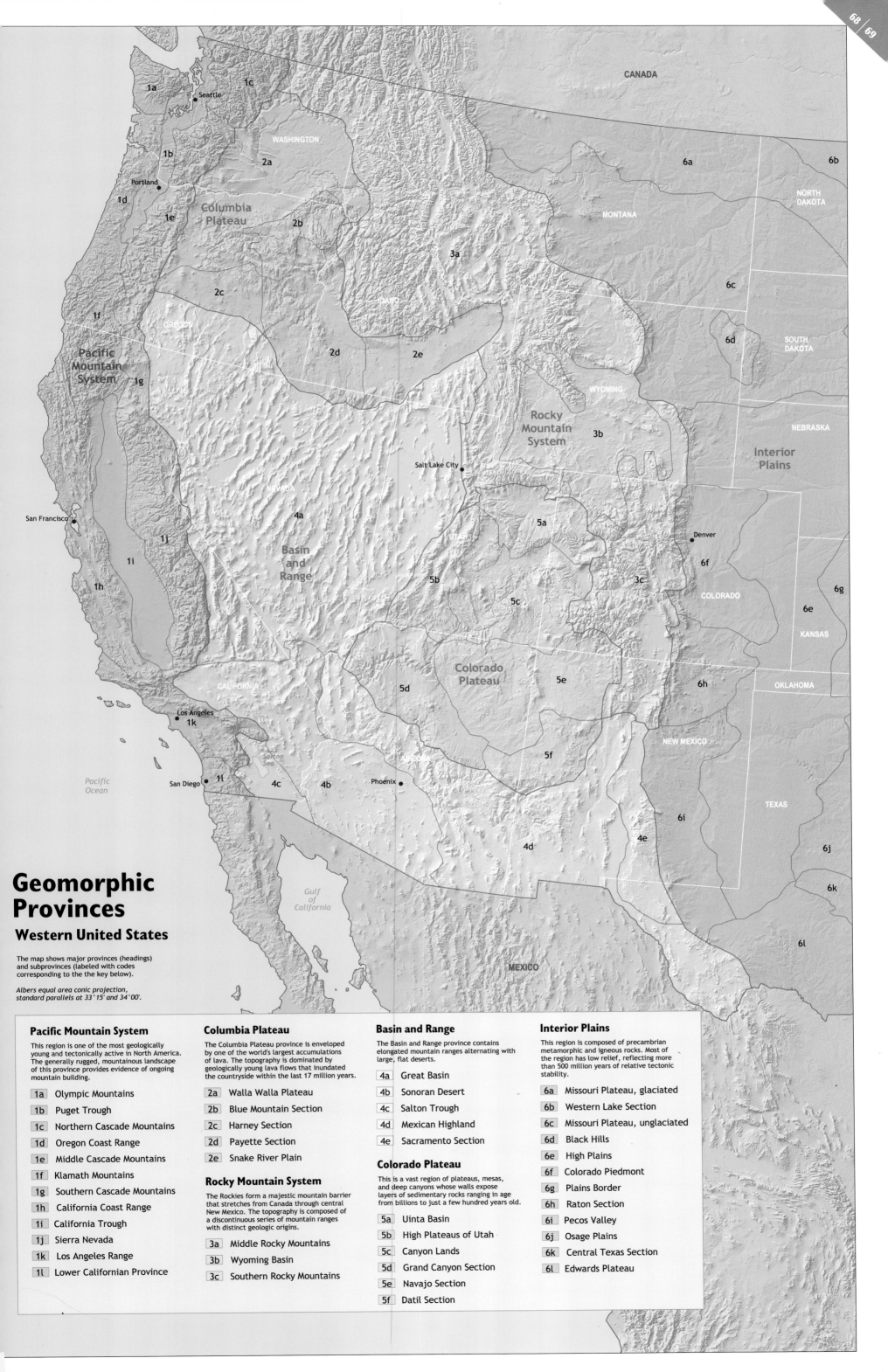

Geomorphic Provinces

Western United States

The map shows major provinces (headings)
and subprovinces (labeled with codes
corresponding to the the key below).

*Albers equal area conic projection,
standard parallels at 33°15' and 34°00'.*

Pacific Mountain System

This region is one of the most geologically
young and tectonically active in North America.
The generally rugged, mountainous landscape
of this province provides evidence of ongoing
mountain building.

1a	Olympic Mountains
1b	Puget Trough
1c	Northern Cascade Mountains
1d	Oregon Coast Range
1e	Middle Cascade Mountains
1f	Klamath Mountains
1g	Southern Cascade Mountains
1h	California Coast Range
1i	California Trough
1j	Sierra Nevada
1k	Los Angeles Range
1l	Lower Californian Province

Columbia Plateau

The Columbia Plateau province is enveloped
by one of the world's largest accumulations
of lava. The topography is dominated by
geologically young lava flows that inundated
the countryside within the last 17 million years.

2a	Walla Walla Plateau
2b	Blue Mountain Section
2c	Harney Section
2d	Payette Section
2e	Snake River Plain

Rocky Mountain System

The Rockies form a majestic mountain barrier
that stretches from Canada through central
New Mexico. The topography is composed of
a discontinuous series of mountain ranges
with distinct geologic origins.

3a	Middle Rocky Mountains
3b	Wyoming Basin
3c	Southern Rocky Mountains

Basin and Range

The Basin and Range province contains
elongated mountain ranges alternating with
large, flat deserts.

4a	Great Basin
4b	Sonoran Desert
4c	Salton Trough
4d	Mexican Highland
4e	Sacramento Section

Colorado Plateau

This is a vast region of plateaus, mesas,
and deep canyons whose walls expose
layers of sedimentary rocks ranging in age
from billions to just a few hundred years old.

5a	Uinta Basin
5b	High Plateaus of Utah
5c	Canyon Lands
5d	Grand Canyon Section
5e	Navajo Section
5f	Datil Section

Interior Plains

This region is composed of precambrian
metamorphic and igneous rocks. Most of
the region has low relief, reflecting more
than 500 million years of relative tectonic
stability.

6a	Missouri Plateau, glaciated
6b	Western Lake Section
6c	Missouri Plateau, unglaciated
6d	Black Hills
6e	High Plains
6f	Colorado Piedmont
6g	Plains Border
6h	Raton Section
6i	Pecos Valley
6j	Osage Plains
6k	Central Texas Section
6l	Edwards Plateau

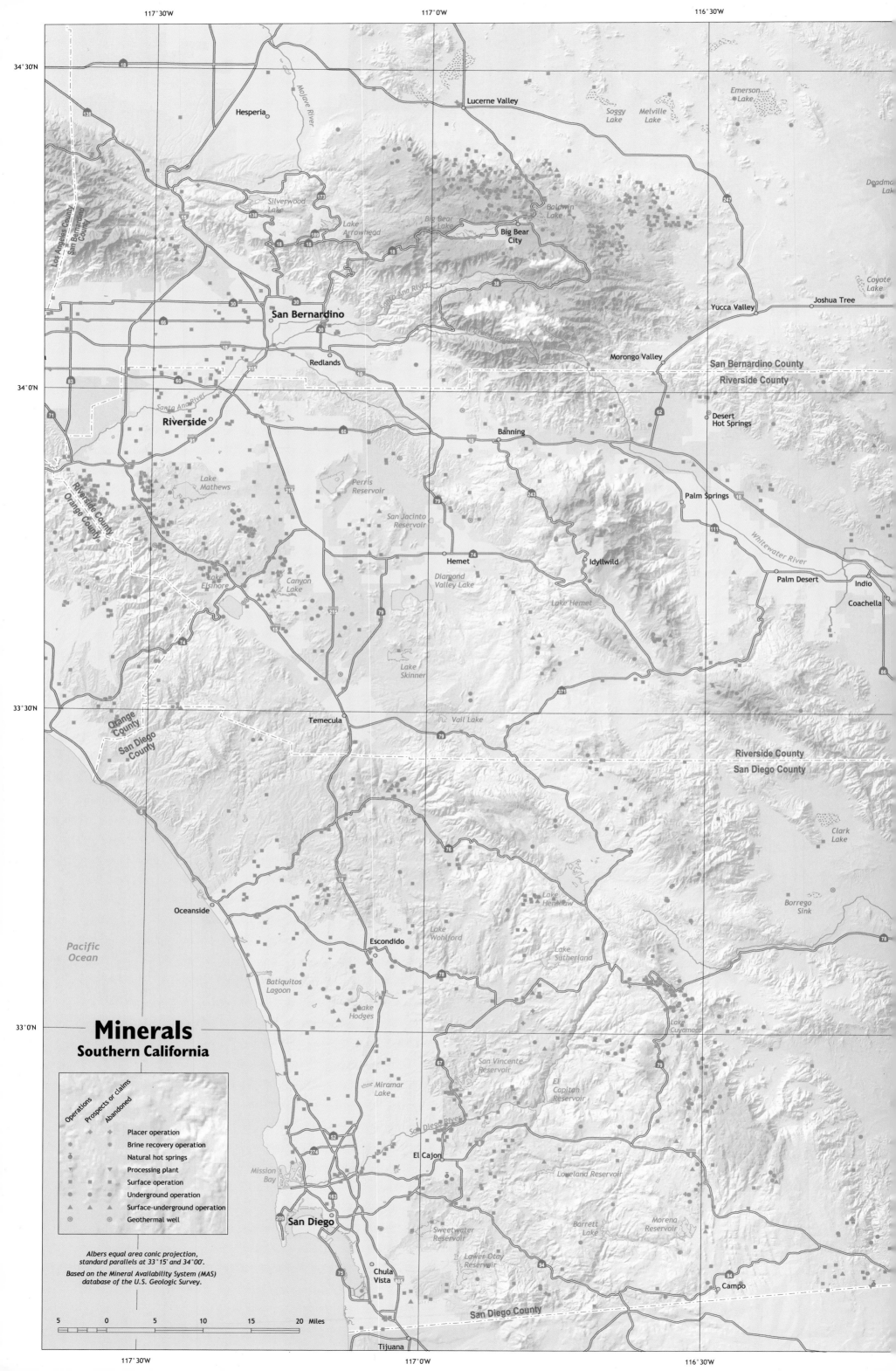

Minerals
Southern California

	Operations	Prospects or claims	Abandoned	
	+	+	+	Placer operation
	●	●	●	Brine recovery operation
	○	○	○	Natural hot springs
	▽	▽	▽	Processing plant
	■	■	■	Surface operation
	●	●	●	Underground operation
	▲	▲	▲	Surface-underground operation
	⊙	⊙	⊙	Geothermal well

Albers equal area conic projection,
standard parallels at 33°15' and 34°00'.

Based on the Mineral Availability System (MAS)
database of the U.S. Geologic Survey.

5 0 5 10 15 20 Miles

116°0'W 115°30'W 115°0'W

34°30'N

34°0'N

33°30'N

33°0'N

Bristol
Lake

Cadiz
Lake

Danby
Lake

Dale
Lake

Twentynine Palms

62

177

Palen
Lake

Hayfield
Lake

Ford
Dry Lake

10

Mecca

North Shore

Blythe

Riverside County

Imperial County

Palo Verde

Desert Shores

Salton Sea Beach

Bombay
Beach

86

Salton
City

Salton
Sea

111

Coachella Canal

Salt Creek

Niland

78

Calipatria

San Felipe Creek

111 115

Coachella Canal

Westmorland

Brawley

New River

Alamo River

86 111 115

CALIFORNIA
ARIZONA

Holtville

Seeley

El Centro

8

Ocotillo

Calexico

New River

Imperial County

Yuma

98

CALIFORNIA - UNITED STATES

BAJA CALIFORNIA - MEXICO

Mexicali

All American Canal

Rio Colorado

Colorado River

2

116°0'W 115°30'W 115°0'W

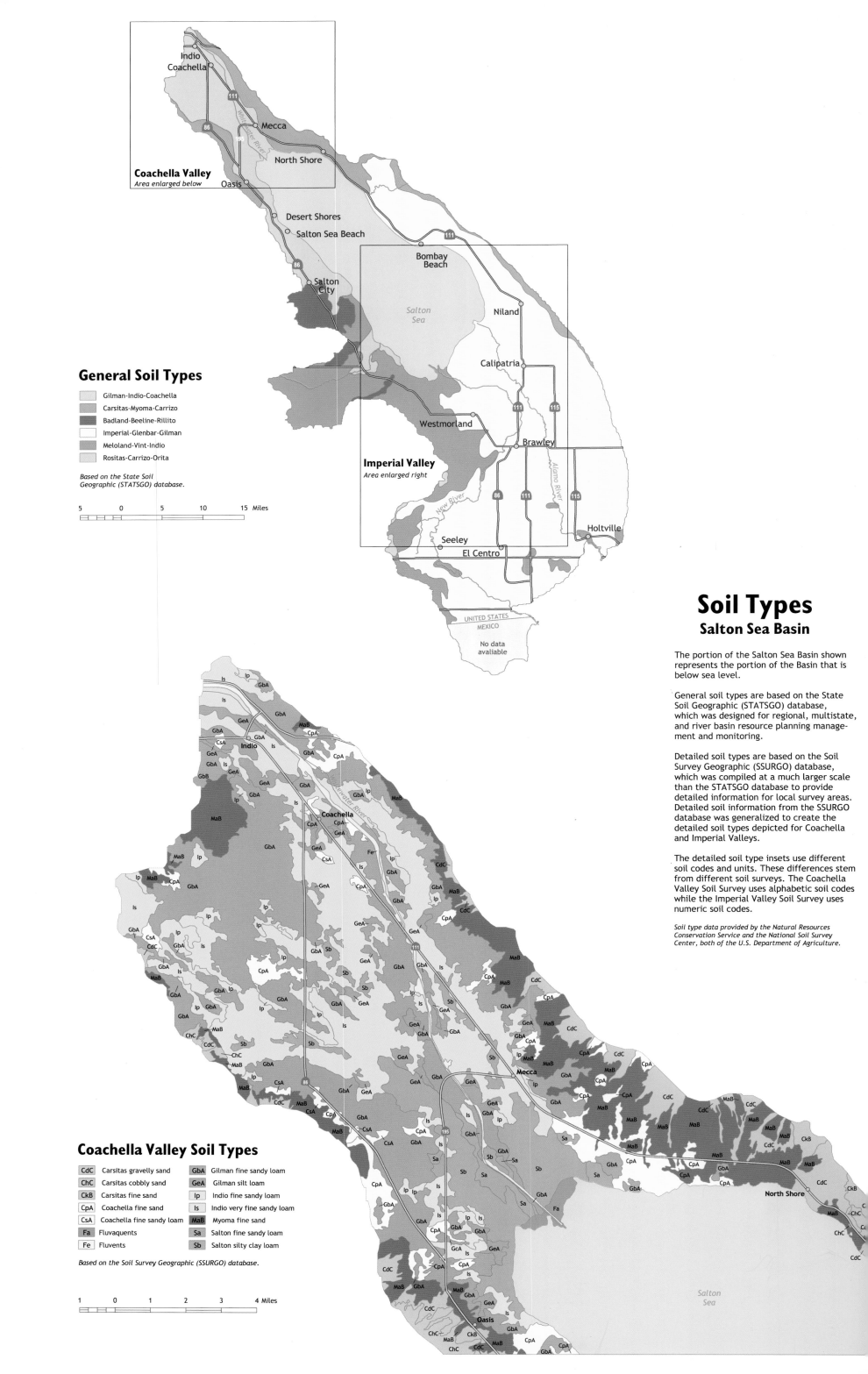

Soil Types
Salton Sea Basin

General Soil Types

- Gilman-Indio-Coachella
- Carsitas-Myoma-Carrizo
- Badland-Beeline-Rillito
- Imperial-Glenbar-Gilman
- Meloland-Vint-Indio
- Rositas-Carrizo-Orita

Based on the State Soil Geographic (STATSGO) database.

5   0   5   10   15 Miles

Coachella Valley
Area enlarged below

Imperial Valley
Area enlarged right

The portion of the Salton Sea Basin shown represents the portion of the Basin that is below sea level.

General soil types are based on the State Soil Geographic (STATSGO) database, which was designed for regional, multistate, and river basin resource planning management and monitoring.

Detailed soil types are based on the Soil Survey Geographic (SSURGO) database, which was compiled at a much larger scale than the STATSGO database to provide detailed information for local survey areas. Detailed soil information from the SSURGO database was generalized to create the detailed soil types depicted for Coachella and Imperial Valleys.

The detailed soil type insets use different soil codes and units. These differences stem from different soil surveys. The Coachella Valley Soil Survey uses alphabetic soil codes while the Imperial Valley Soil Survey uses numeric soil codes.

Soil type data provided by the Natural Resources Conservation Service and the National Soil Survey Center, both of the U.S. Department of Agriculture.

Coachella Valley Soil Types

Code	Description	Code	Description
CdC	Carsitas gravelly sand	GbA	Gilman fine sandy loam
ChC	Carsitas cobbly sand	GeA	Gilman silt loam
CkB	Carsitas fine sand	Ip	Indio fine sandy loam
CpA	Coachella fine sand	Is	Indio very fine sandy loam
CsA	Coachella fine sandy loam	MaB	Myoma fine sand
Fa	Fluvaquents	Sa	Salton fine sandy loam
Fe	Fluvents	Sb	Salton silty clay loam

Based on the Soil Survey Geographic (SSURGO) database.

1   0   1   2   3   4 Miles

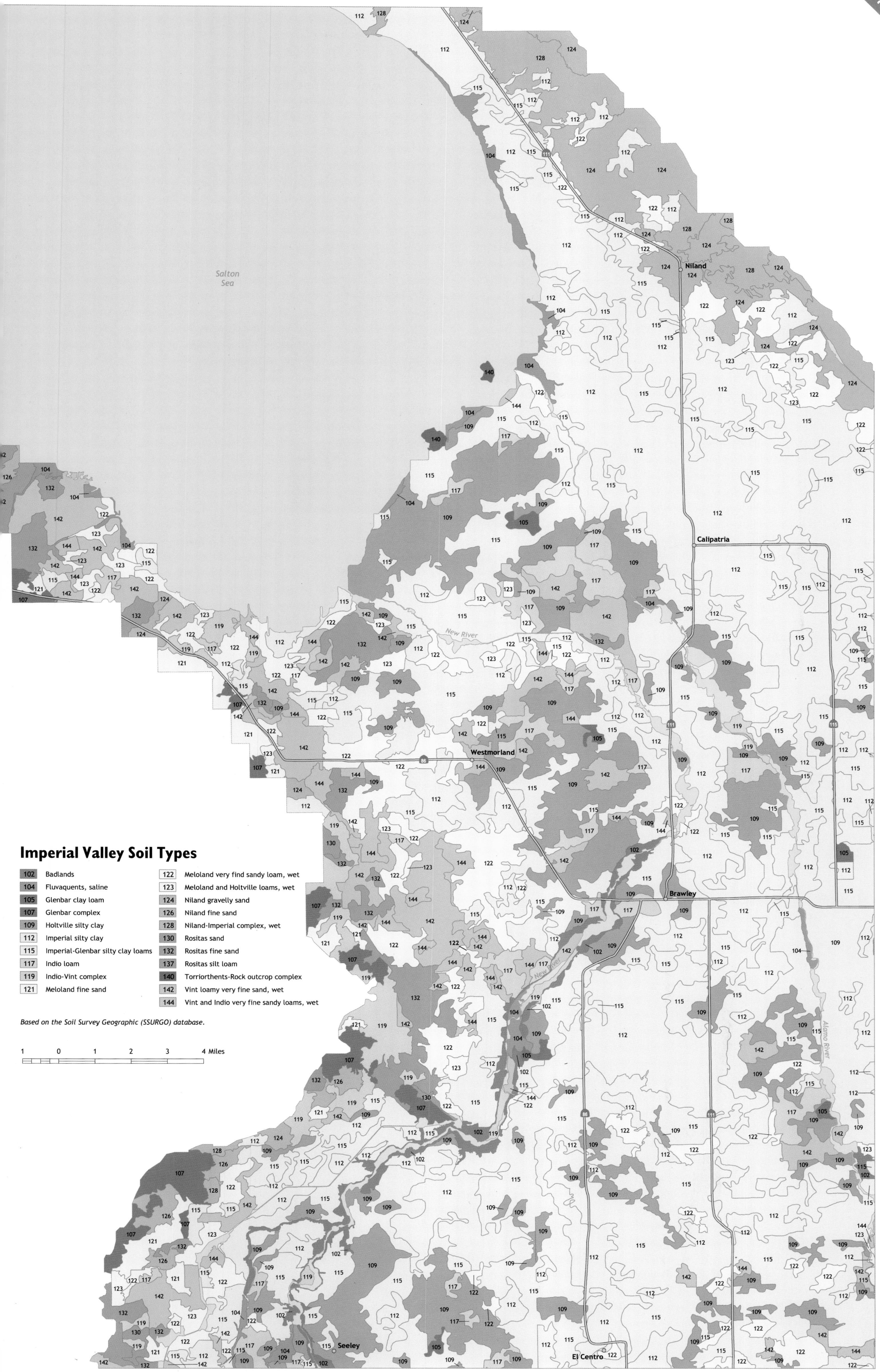

Imperial Valley Soil Types
102 Badlands
104 Fluvaquents, saline
105 Glenbar clay loam
107 Glenbar complex
109 Holtville silty clay
112 Imperial silty clay
115 Imperial-Glenbar silty clay loams
117 Indio loam
119 Indio-Vint complex
121 Meloland fine sand
122 Meloland very find sandy loam, wet
123 Meloland and Holtville loams, wet
124 Niland gravelly sand
126 Niland fine sand
128 Niland-Imperial complex, wet
130 Rositas sand
132 Rositas fine sand
137 Rositas silt loam
140 Torriorthents-Rock outcrop complex
142 Vint loamy very fine sand, wet
144 Vint and Indio very fine sandy loams, wet
Based on the Soil Survey Geographic (SSURGO) database.
1 0 1 2 3 4 Miles
Salton Sea
Niland
Calipatria
Westmorland
Brawley
El Centro
Seeley
New River
Alamo River
111
115
86

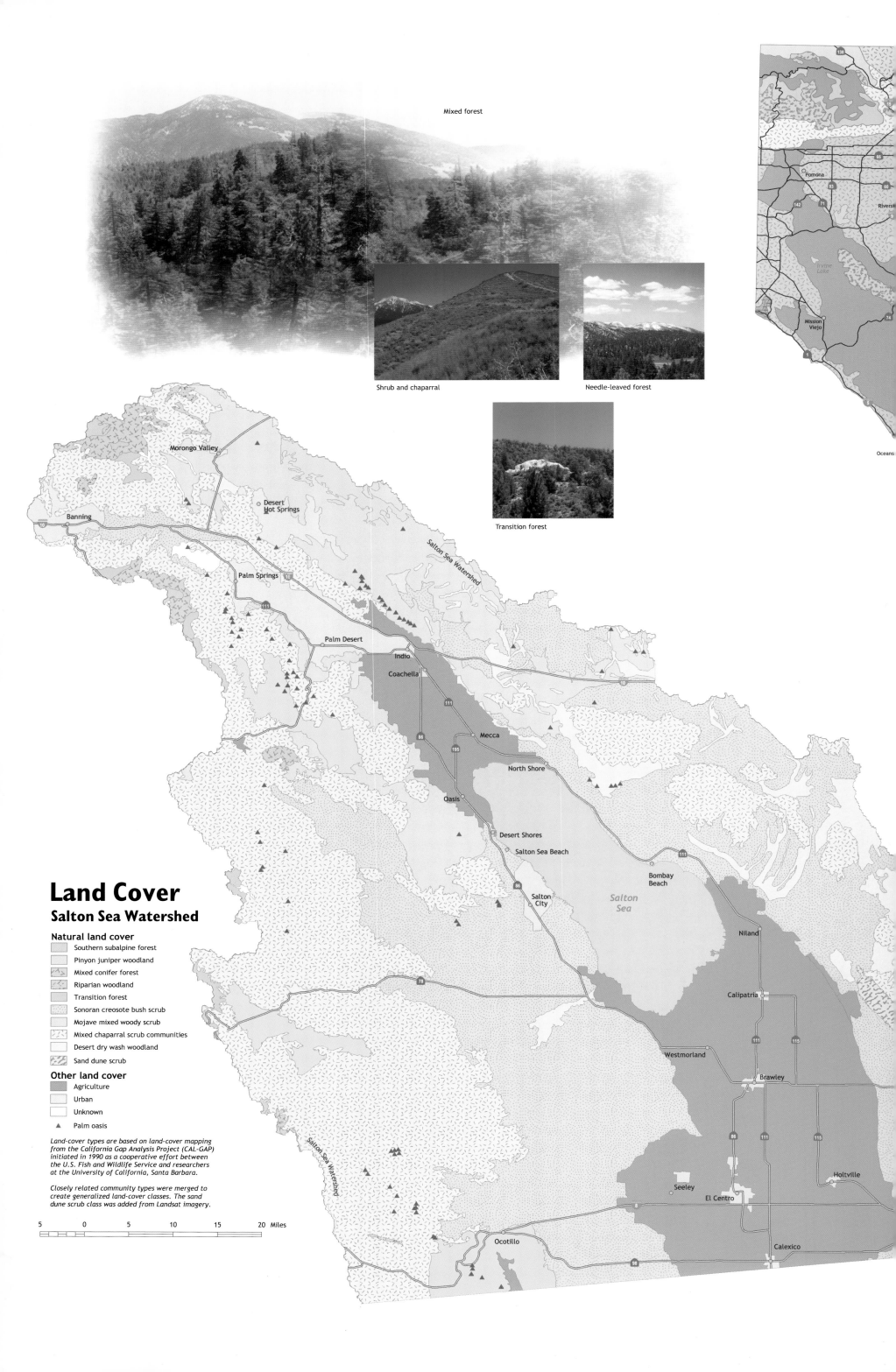

Mixed forest

Shrub and chaparral

Needle-leaved forest

Transition forest

Morongo Valley

Banning

Desert
Hot Springs

Palm Springs

Palm Desert

Indio

Coachella

Mecca

North Shore

Oasis

Desert Shores

Salton Sea Beach

Bombay
Beach

Salton
Sea

Salton
City

Niland

Calipatria

Westmorland

Brawley

Seeley

El Centro

Holtville

Ocotillo

Calexico

Pomona

Riverside

Mission
Viejo

Oceans

Salton Sea Watershed

Salton Sea Watershed

Land Cover
Salton Sea Watershed

Natural land cover

Southern subalpine forest
Pinyon juniper woodland
Mixed conifer forest
Riparian woodland
Transition forest
Sonoran creosote bush scrub
Mojave mixed woody scrub
Mixed chaparral scrub communities
Desert dry wash woodland
Sand dune scrub

Other land cover

Agriculture
Urban
Unknown
▲ Palm oasis

*Land-cover types are based on land-cover mapping
from the California Gap Analysis Project (CAL-GAP)
initiated in 1990 as a cooperative effort between
the U.S. Fish and Wildlife Service and researchers
at the University of California, Santa Barbara.*

*Closely related community types were merged to
create generalized land-cover classes. The sand
dune scrub class was added from Landsat imagery.*

5   0   5   10   15   20 Miles

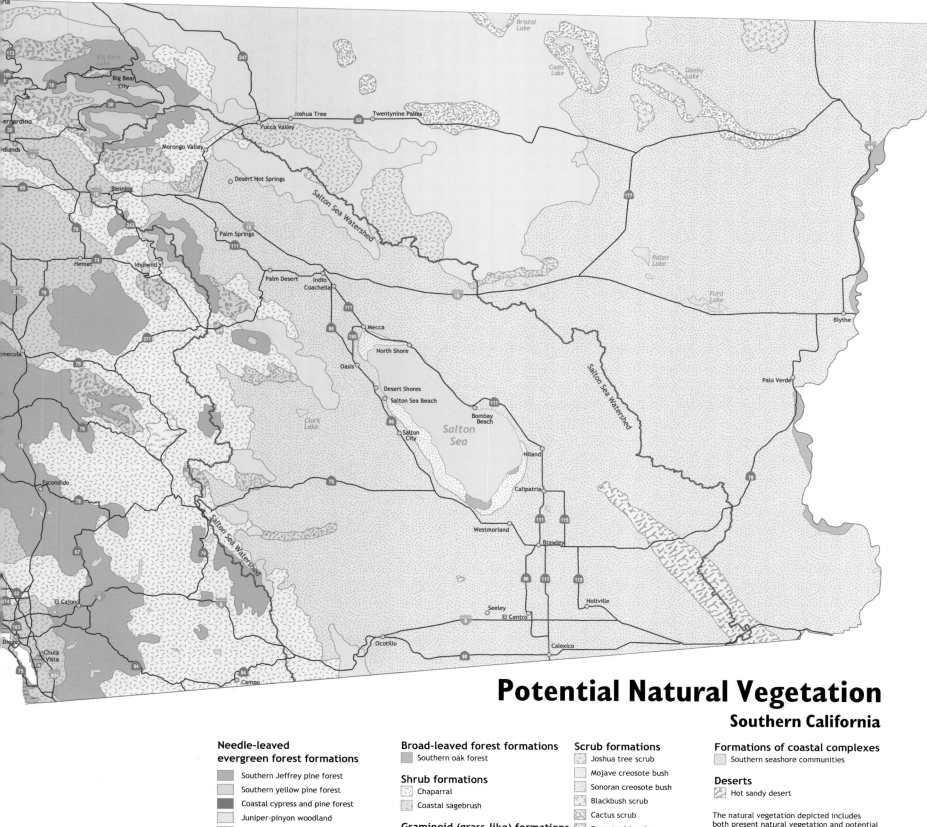

Potential Natural Vegetation
Southern California

Needle-leaved evergreen forest formations
- Southern Jeffrey pine forest
- Southern yellow pine forest
- Coastal cypress and pine forest
- Juniper-pinyon woodland
- Southern montane-subalpine forest

Mixed broad-leaved and needle-leaved forest formations
- Mixed hardwood forest

Broad-leaved forest formations
- Southern oak forest

Shrub formations
- Chaparral
- Coastal sagebrush

Graminoid (grass-like) formations
- California prairie
- Coastal saltmarsh

Scrub formations
- Joshua tree scrub
- Mojave creosote bush
- Sonoran creosote bush
- Blackbush scrub
- Cactus scrub
- Desert saltbrush
- Salton Sea saltbrush
- Alkali scrub-woodland

Formations of coastal complexes
- Southern seashore communities

Deserts
- Hot sandy desert

The natural vegetation depicted includes both present natural vegetation and potential natural vegetation. Potential natural vegetation is the natural vegetation that would likely return if man-altered areas were abandoned.

After "The Map of the Natural Vegetation of California" A. W. Küchler, 1977.

10   0   10   20   30   40   Miles

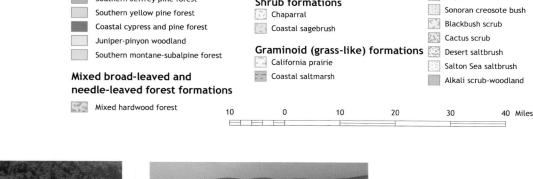

Broad-leaved forest

Desert

Scrub

Palm oasis

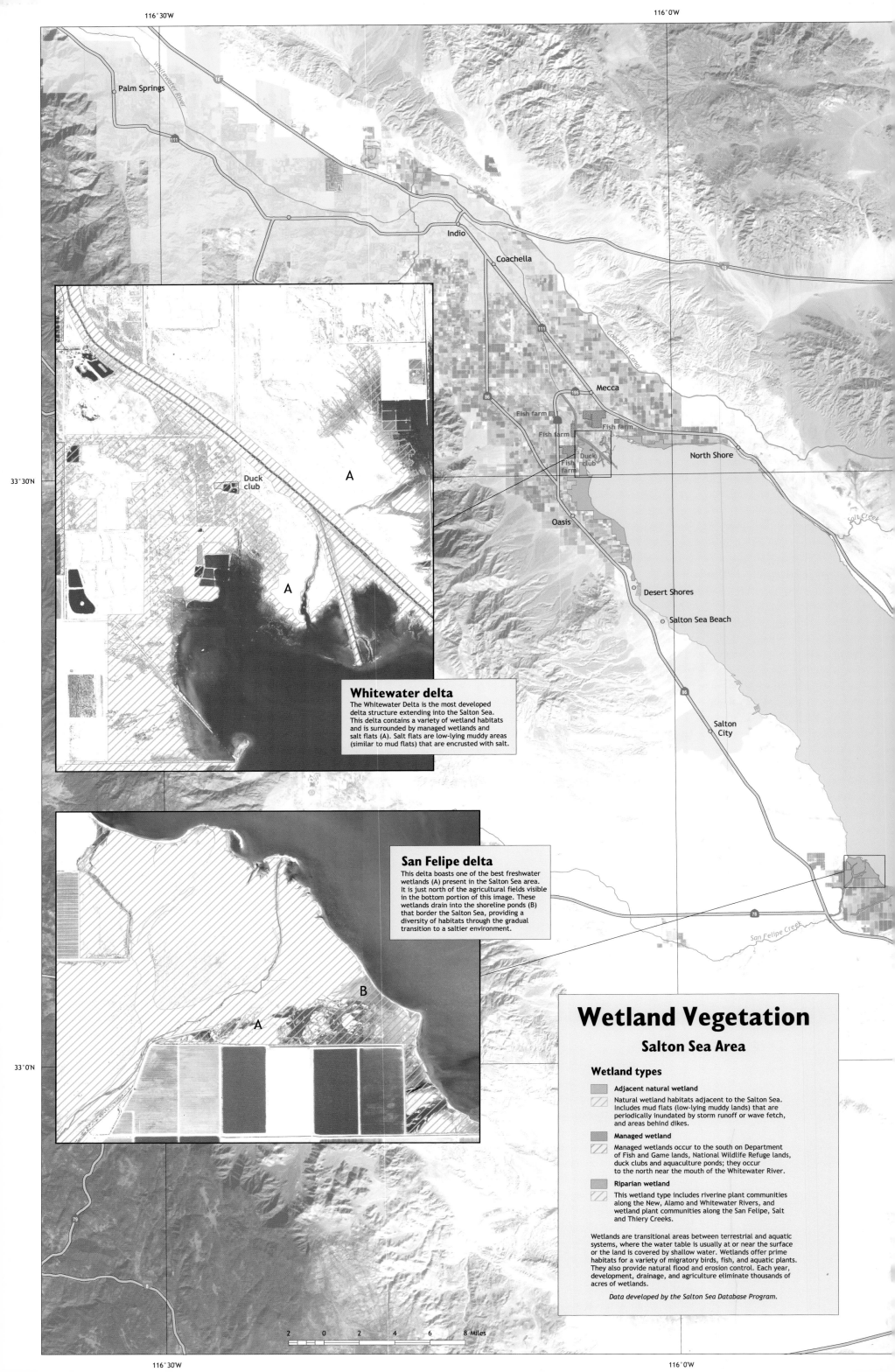

116°30'W

116°0'W

Palm Springs

Indio

Coachella

Mecca

Fish farm

Fish farm

Fish farm

Fish farm

Duck club

North Shore

Oasis

Duck club

A

A

33°30'N

Desert Shores

Salton Sea Beach

Salton City

Whitewater delta

The Whitewater Delta is the most developed delta structure extending into the Salton Sea. This delta contains a variety of wetland habitats and is surrounded by managed wetlands and salt flats (A). Salt flats are low-lying muddy areas (similar to mud flats) that are encrusted with salt.

San Felipe delta

This delta boasts one of the best freshwater wetlands (A) present in the Salton Sea area. It is just north of the agricultural fields visible in the bottom portion of this image. These wetlands drain into the shoreline ponds (B) that border the Salton Sea, providing a diversity of habitats through the gradual transition to a saltier environment.

B

A

San Felipe Creek

Wetland Vegetation

Salton Sea Area

Wetland types

Adjacent natural wetland

Natural wetland habitats adjacent to the Salton Sea. Includes mud flats (low-lying muddy lands) that are periodically inundated by storm runoff or wave fetch, and areas behind dikes.

Managed wetland

Managed wetlands occur to the south on Department of Fish and Game lands, National Wildlife Refuge lands, duck clubs and aquaculture ponds; they occur to the north near the mouth of the Whitewater River.

Riparian wetland

This wetland type includes riverine plant communities along the New, Alamo and Whitewater Rivers, and wetland plant communities along the San Felipe, Salt and Thiery Creeks.

Wetlands are transitional areas between terrestrial and aquatic systems, where the water table is usually at or near the surface or the land is covered by shallow water. Wetlands offer prime habitats for a variety of migratory birds, fish, and aquatic plants. They also provide natural flood and erosion control. Each year, development, drainage, and agriculture eliminate thousands of acres of wetlands.

Data developed by the Salton Sea Database Program.

33°0'N

2   0   2   4   6   8 Miles

116°30'W

116°0'W

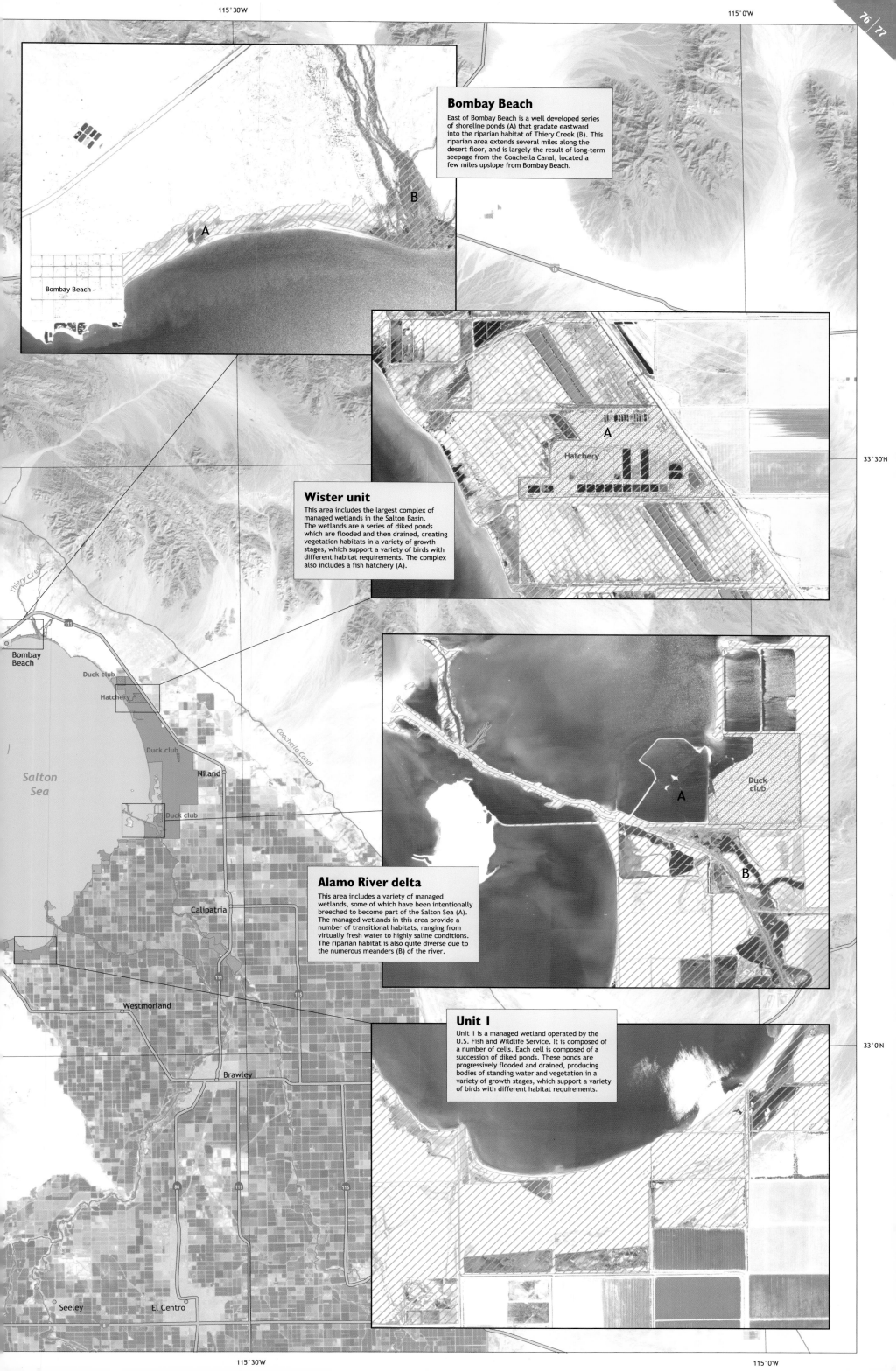

Bombay Beach

East of Bombay Beach is a well developed series of shoreline ponds (A) that gradate eastward into the riparian habitat of Thiery Creek (B). This riparian area extends several miles along the desert floor, and is largely the result of long-term seepage from the Coachella Canal, located a few miles upslope from Bombay Beach.

Wister unit

This area includes the largest complex of managed wetlands in the Salton Basin. The wetlands are a series of diked ponds which are flooded and then drained, creating vegetation habitats in a variety of growth stages, which support a variety of birds with different habitat requirements. The complex also includes a fish hatchery (A).

Alamo River delta

This area includes a variety of managed wetlands, some of which have been intentionally breeched to become part of the Salton Sea (A). The managed wetlands in this area provide a number of transitional habitats, ranging from virtually fresh water to highly saline conditions. The riparian habitat is also quite diverse due to the numerous meanders (B) of the river.

Unit 1

Unit 1 is a managed wetland operated by the U.S. Fish and Wildlife Service. It is composed of a number of cells. Each cell is composed of a succession of diked ponds. These ponds are progressively flooded and drained, producing bodies of standing water and vegetation in a variety of growth stages, which support a variety of birds with different habitat requirements.

115°30'W   115°0'W

33°30'N

33°0'N

Bombay Beach

Thiery Creek

Bombay Beach

Duck club

Hatchery

Duck club

Salton Sea

Niland

Coachella Canal

Duck club

Calipatria

Westmorland

Brawley

Seeley   El Centro

Hatchery

Duck club

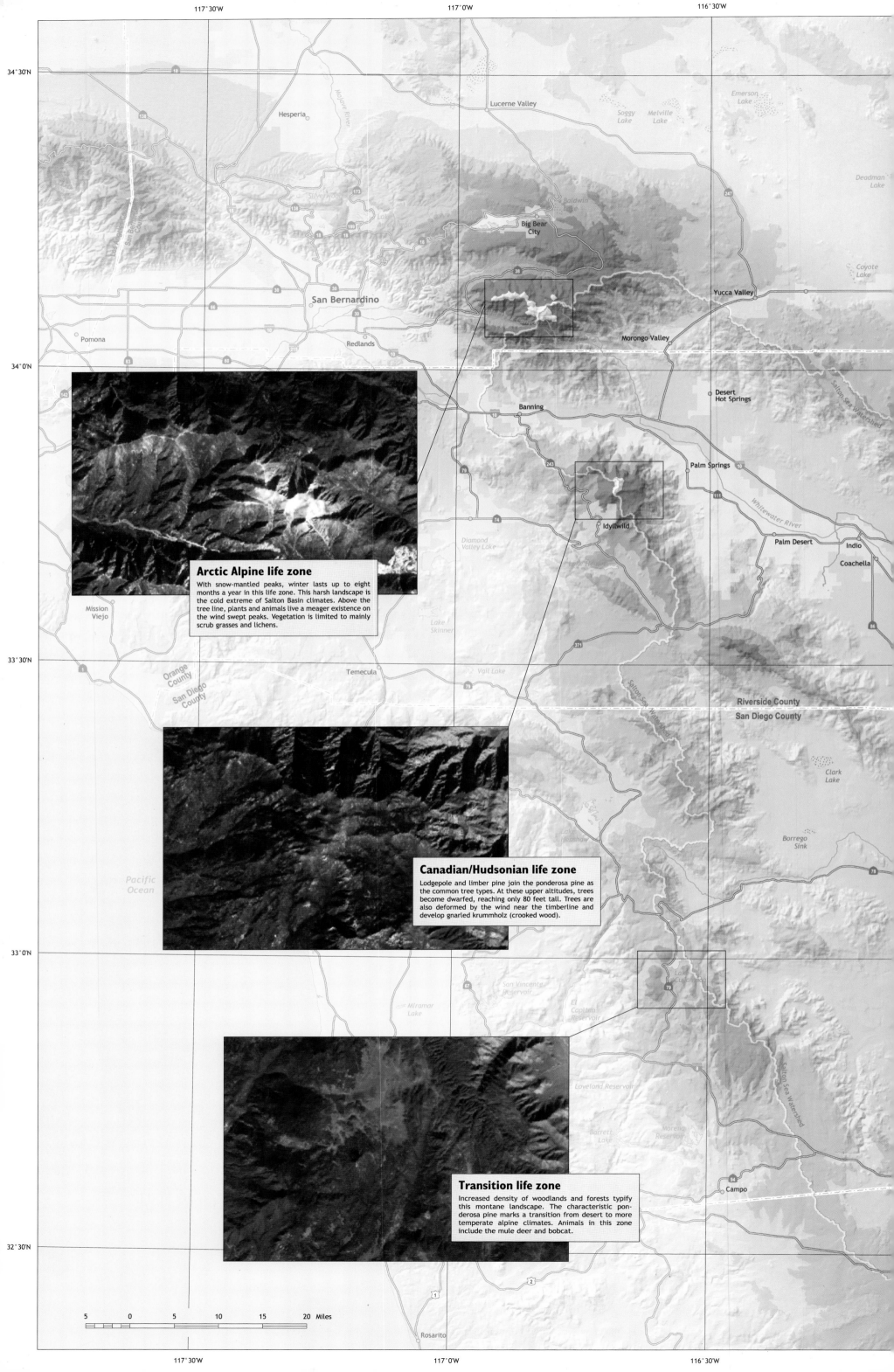

Arctic Alpine life zone

With snow-mantled peaks, winter lasts up to eight months a year in this life zone. This harsh landscape is the cold extreme of Salton Basin climates. Above the tree line, plants and animals live a meager existence on the wind swept peaks. Vegetation is limited to mainly scrub grasses and lichens.

Canadian/Hudsonian life zone

Lodgepole and limber pine join the ponderosa pine as the common tree types. At these upper altitudes, trees become dwarfed, reaching only 80 feet tall. Trees are also deformed by the wind near the timberline and develop gnarled krummholz (crooked wood).

Transition life zone

Increased density of woodlands and forests typify this montane landscape. The characteristic pon-derosa pine marks a transition from desert to more temperate alpine climates. Animals in this zone include the mule deer and bobcat.

5   0   5   10   15   20 Miles

Life Zones
Salton Sea Watershed Area

The Salton Basin comprises one of the most diverse collections of plants and animals in North America, principally due to its extreme topography and climates. From searing tropical-desert bajadas (shallow slopes at the base of rocky hills) to icy alpine summits, habitats change dramatically in very short distances. As elevation increases, the cooler temperatures support different species. These steep slopes support remarkably diverse plant and animal communities so distinct from one another they are termed "life zones."

Cooler climates lie at higher latitudes and elevations. In the Salton Basin, elevation has a large impact on climate. Climate ranges from subtropical desert in the valley, to arctic-alpine tundra at the top of the mountainous areas. From the lowest elevations in the Salton Basin to the highest peaks of the San Jacinto mountains, life zones range from Lower Sonoran to Canadian/Hudsonian in just several miles. This is the most abundant range of life zones to be located within such a short horizontal distance in North America.

Life zones as shown on background map

Arctic Alpine   Canadian/   Transition   Upper Sonoran   Lower Sonoran
                 Hudsonian

Inset images contain 2000 Landsat Thematic Mapper imagery for each life zone.

Albers equal area conic projection, standard parallels at 33°15′ and 34°00′.

Upper Sonoran life zone

Pine and oak woodlands, which include evergreen oaks, pinyon pine, and juniper are evidence of moister and cooler temperatures. Greater amounts of vegetation than the Lower Sonoran life zone support more numerous animal populations and larger predators, such as the gray fox.

Lower Sonoran life zone

With blistering heat and minimal precipitation, plants and animals adapt to hot days and cooler nights, in addition to surviving on scarce moisture and ground water. Succulents (cacti) store water in their prickly flesh. California fan palms cluster around oases, where ground water is close to the surface. The palo verde sends deep roots to tap distant ground water. Many animals seek shelter during the day, and forage in the cool night air.

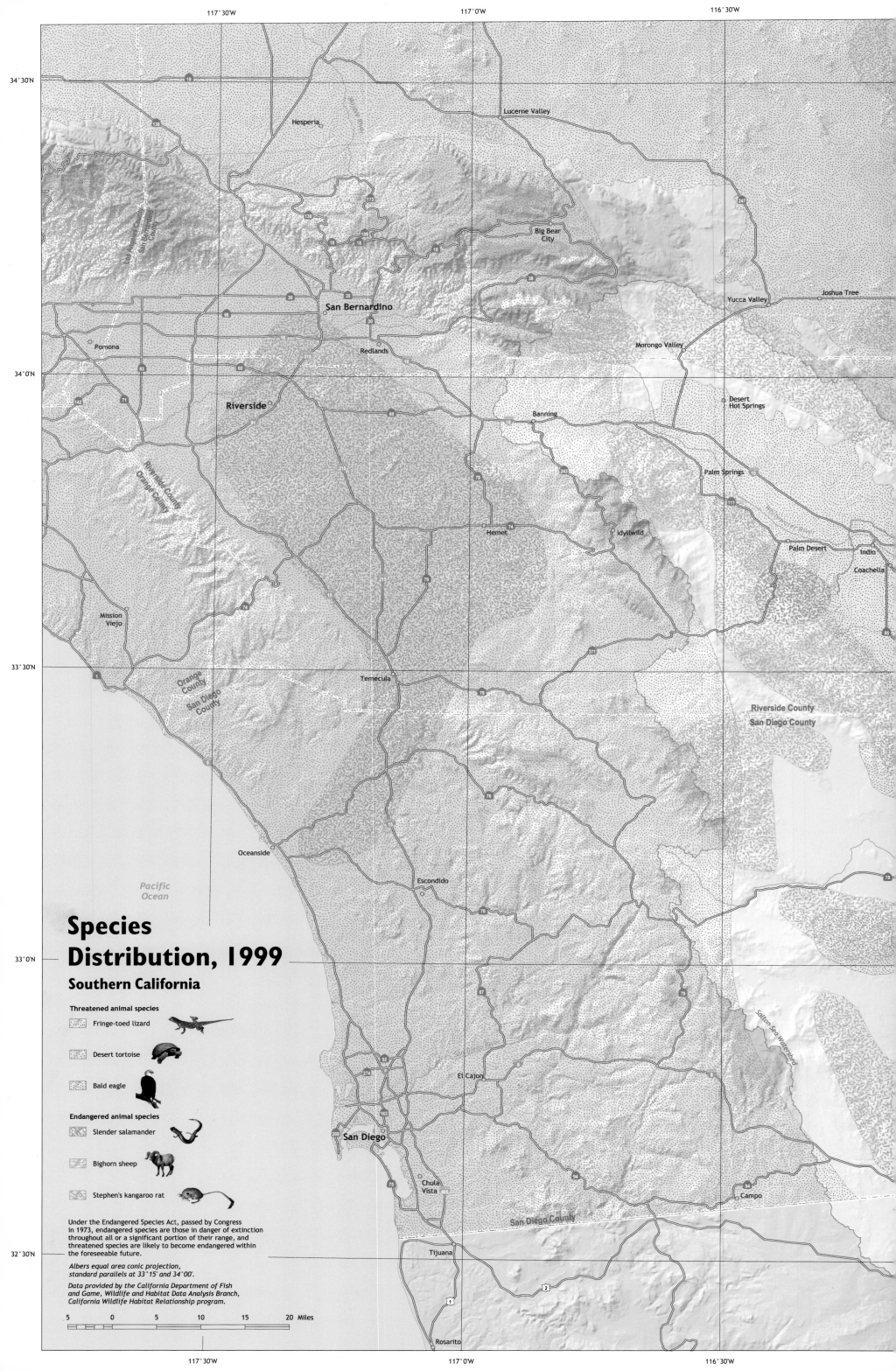

Species Distribution, 1999

Southern California

Threatened animal species

- Fringe-toed lizard
- Desert tortoise
- Bald eagle

Endangered animal species

- Slender salamander
- Bighorn sheep
- Stephen's kangaroo rat

Under the Endangered Species Act, passed by Congress in 1973, endangered species are those in danger of extinction throughout all or a significant portion of their range, and threatened species are likely to become endangered within the foreseeable future.

Albers equal area conic projection, standard parallels at 33°15' and 34°00'.

Data provided by the California Department of Fish and Game, Wildlife and Habitat Data Analysis Branch, California Wildlife Habitat Relationship program.

5 0 5 10 15 20 Miles

116°0'W   115°30'W   115°0'W   114°30'W

34°30'N

Twentynine Palms

San Bernardino County
Riverside County

34°0'N

Mecca

North Shore

Salton Sea Rater River

Riverside County
Imperial County

Blythe

CALIFORNIA
ARIZONA

Palo Verde

33°30'N

Desert Shores

Salton Sea Beach

Bombay
Beach

Salton
City

Salton
Sea

Niland

San Felipe Creek

Calipatria

La Paz Co.
Yuma Co.

Westmorland

33°0'N

Brawley

New River

Alamo River

Holtville

Seeley

El Centro

New River

Ocotillo

Calexico

Yuma

All American Canal

Imperial County

CALIFORNIA - UNITED STATES
BAJA CALIFORNIA - MEXICO

Mexicali

Rio Colorado

Gila River

Colorado River

32°30'N

San Luis

Yuma County ARIZONA - UNITED STATES
SONORA - MEXICO

116°0'W   115°30'W   115°0'W   114°30'W

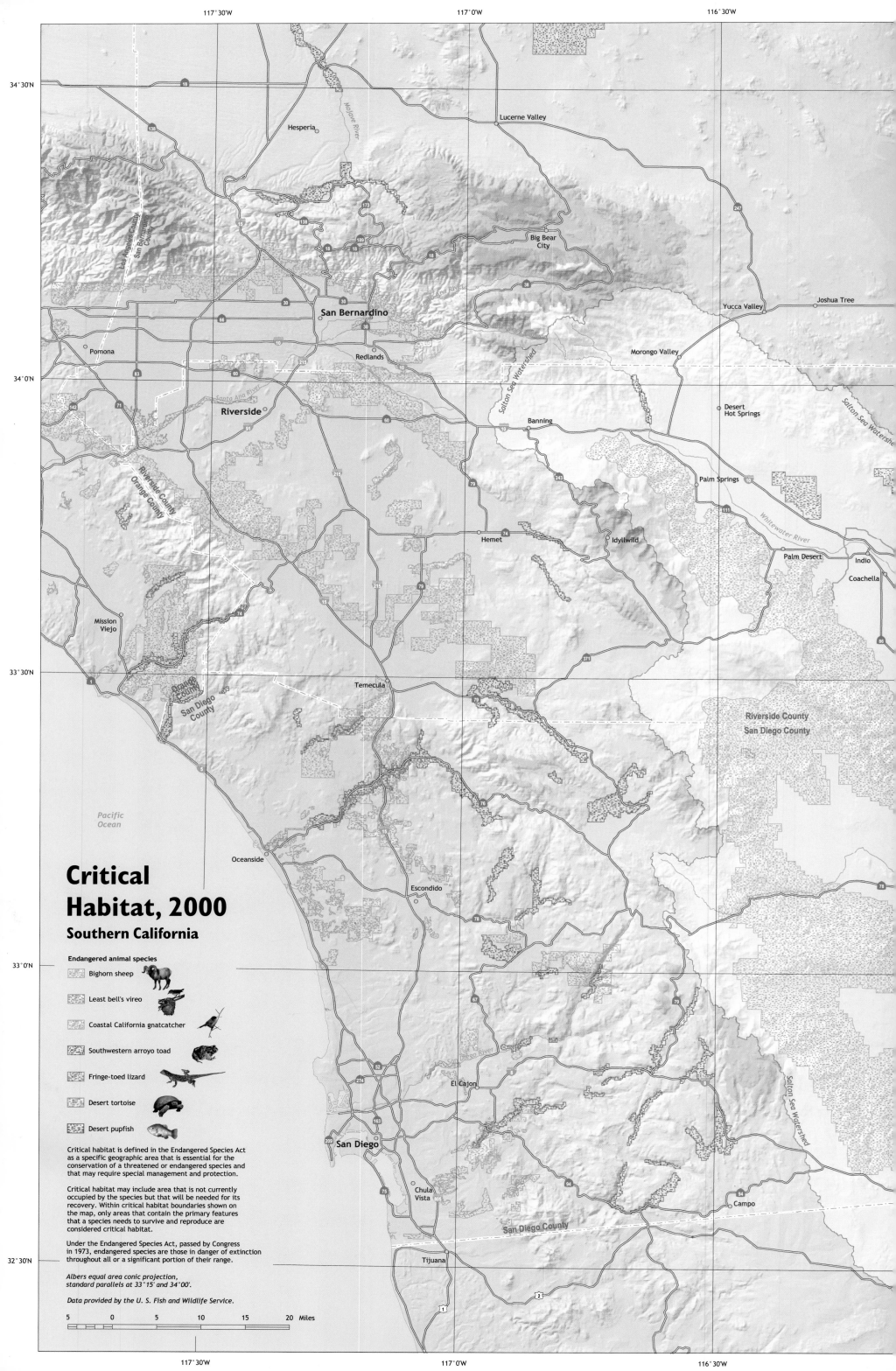

Critical Habitat, 2000

Southern California

Endangered animal species

- Bighorn sheep
- Least bell's vireo
- Coastal California gnatcatcher
- Southwestern arroyo toad
- Fringe-toed lizard
- Desert tortoise
- Desert pupfish

Critical habitat is defined in the Endangered Species Act as a specific geographic area that is essential for the conservation of a threatened or endangered species and that may require special management and protection.

Critical habitat may include area that is not currently occupied by the species but that will be needed for its recovery. Within critical habitat boundaries shown on the map, only areas that contain the primary features that a species needs to survive and reproduce are considered critical habitat.

Under the Endangered Species Act, passed by Congress in 1973, endangered species are those in danger of extinction throughout all or a significant portion of their range.

Albers equal area conic projection,
standard parallels at 33°15' and 34°00'.

Data provided by the U. S. Fish and Wildlife Service.

5   0   5   10   15   20 Miles

116°0'W   115°30'W   115°0'W   114°30'W

34°30'N

Twentynine Palms

62

San Bernardino County
Riverside County

34°0'N

177

95

cca   Coachella Canal

North Shore

Blythe

CALIFORNIA   ARIZONA

33°30'N

Desert Shores

Salton Sea Beach

111

Riverside County
Imperial County

Palo Verde

Colorado River

86

Bombay
Beach

Salton
Sea

Salt Creek

Salton
City

Niland

San Felipe Creek

Calipatria

La Paz Co.
Yuma Co.

111   115

33°0'N

Westmorland

New River

Brawley

Alamo River

Coachella Canal

86   111   115

Seeley

Holtville

El Centro

New River

Ocotillo

Calexico

Yuma

All American Canal   Imperial County

Rio Colorado

CALIFORNIA - UNITED STATES

98

Mexicali

BAJA CALIFORNIA - MEXICO

2

32°30'N

Yuma County   ARIZONA - UNITED STATES

San Luis

SONORA - MEXICO

5

116°0'W   115°30'W   115°0'W   114°30'W

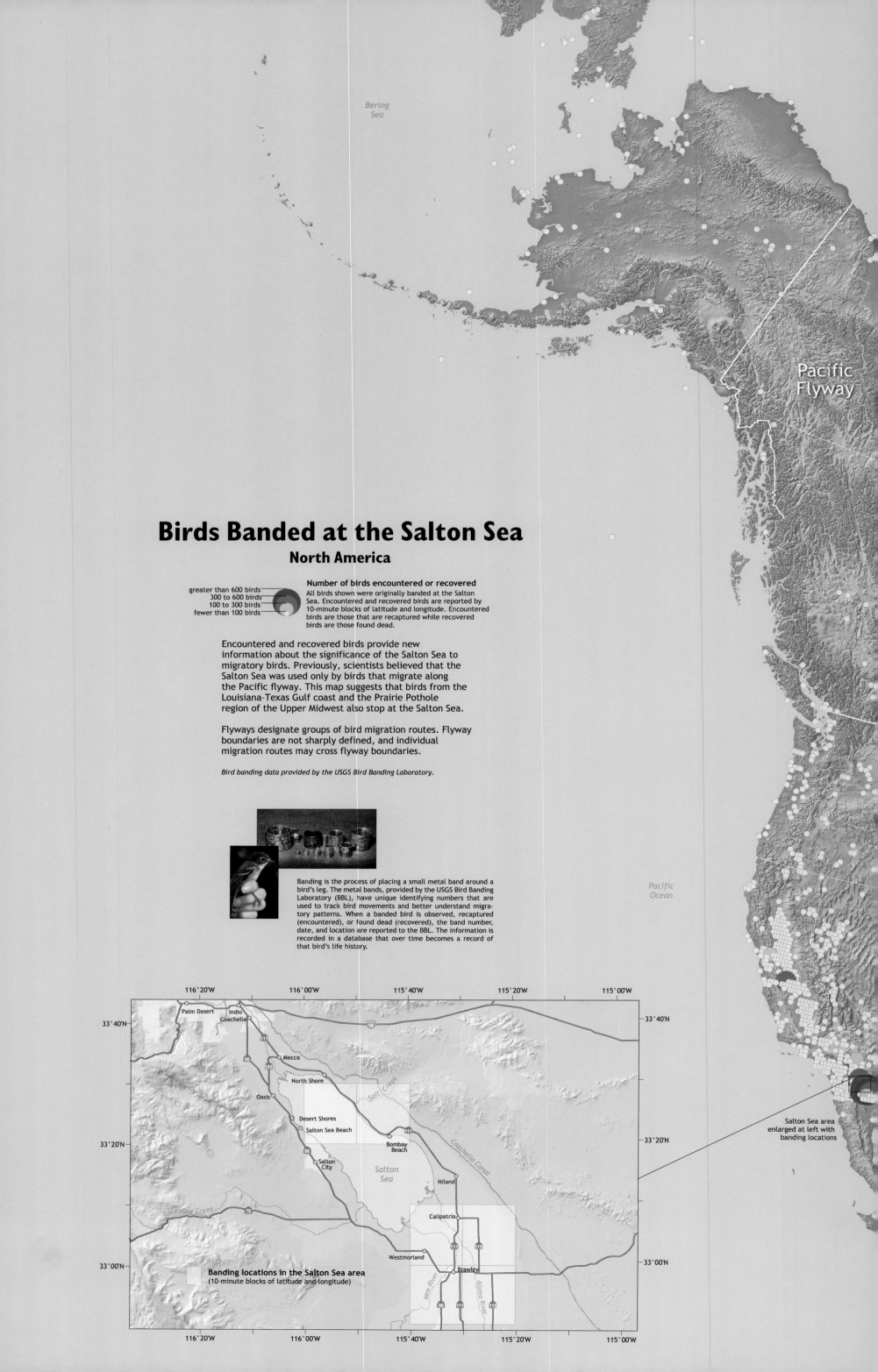

Birds Banded at the Salton Sea

North America

Number of birds encountered or recovered

greater than 600 birds
300 to 600 birds
100 to 300 birds
fewer than 100 birds

All birds shown were originally banded at the Salton Sea. Encountered and recovered birds are reported by 10-minute blocks of latitude and longitude. Encountered birds are those that are recaptured while recovered birds are those found dead.

Encountered and recovered birds provide new information about the significance of the Salton Sea to migratory birds. Previously, scientists believed that the Salton Sea was used only by birds that migrate along the Pacific flyway. This map suggests that birds from the Louisiana-Texas Gulf coast and the Prairie Pothole region of the Upper Midwest also stop at the Salton Sea.

Flyways designate groups of bird migration routes. Flyway boundaries are not sharply defined, and individual migration routes may cross flyway boundaries.

Bird banding data provided by the USGS Bird Banding Laboratory.

Banding is the process of placing a small metal band around a bird's leg. The metal bands, provided by the USGS Bird Banding Laboratory (BBL), have unique identifying numbers that are used to track bird movements and better understand migratory patterns. When a banded bird is observed, recaptured (encountered), or found dead (recovered), the band number, date, and location are reported to the BBL. The information is recorded in a database that over time becomes a record of that bird's life history.

Bering Sea

Pacific Flyway

Pacific Ocean

Salton Sea area enlarged at left with banding locations

Banding locations in the Salton Sea area
(10-minute blocks of latitude and longitude)

Palm Desert
Indio
Coachella
Mecca
North Shore
Oasis
Desert Shores
Salton Sea Beach
Bombay Beach
Salton City
Niland
Calipatria
Westmorland
Brawley

Salton Sea

Salt Creek
Coachella Canal
New River
Alamo River

GREENLAND

*Arctic
Ocean*

Central
Flyway

*Hudson
Bay*

Atlantic
Flyway

CANADA

Mississippi
Flyway

Prairie Pothole
Region

UNITED STATES

*Atlantic
Ocean*

MEXICO

Louisiana-Texas
Gulf Coast

*Gulf of
Mexico*

CUBA

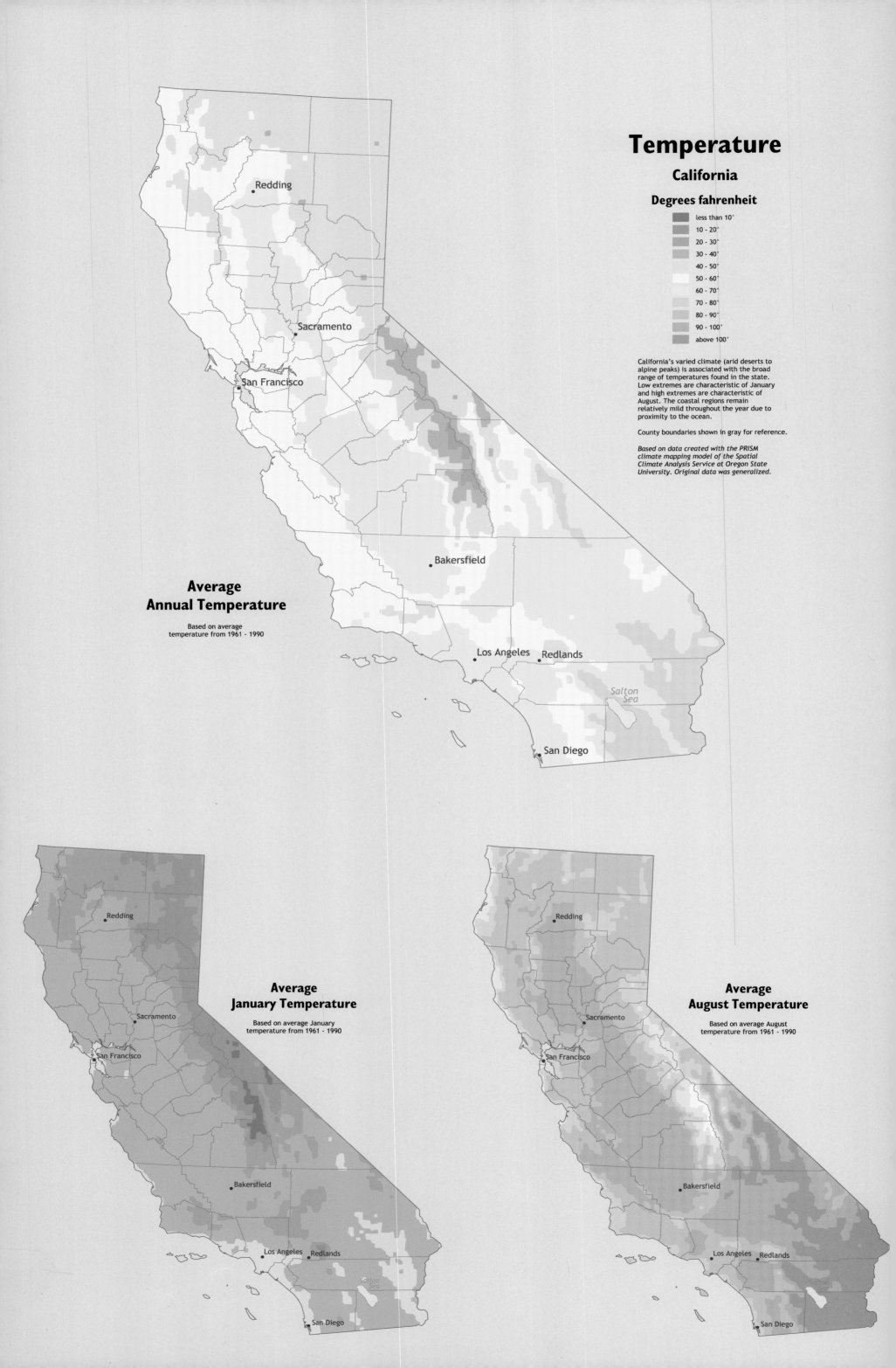

Temperature

California

Degrees fahrenheit

- less than 10°
- 10 - 20°
- 20 - 30°
- 30 - 40°
- 40 - 50°
- 50 - 60°
- 60 - 70°
- 70 - 80°
- 80 - 90°
- 90 - 100°
- above 100°

California's varied climate (arid deserts to alpine peaks) is associated with the broad range of temperatures found in the state. Low extremes are characteristic of January and high extremes are characteristic of August. The coastal regions remain relatively mild throughout the year due to proximity to the ocean.

County boundaries shown in gray for reference.

Based on data created with the PRISM climate mapping model of the Spatial Climate Analysis Service at Oregon State University. Original data was generalized.

Average Annual Temperature

Based on average
temperature from 1961 - 1990

Average January Temperature

Based on average January
temperature from 1961 - 1990

Average August Temperature

Based on average August
temperature from 1961 - 1990

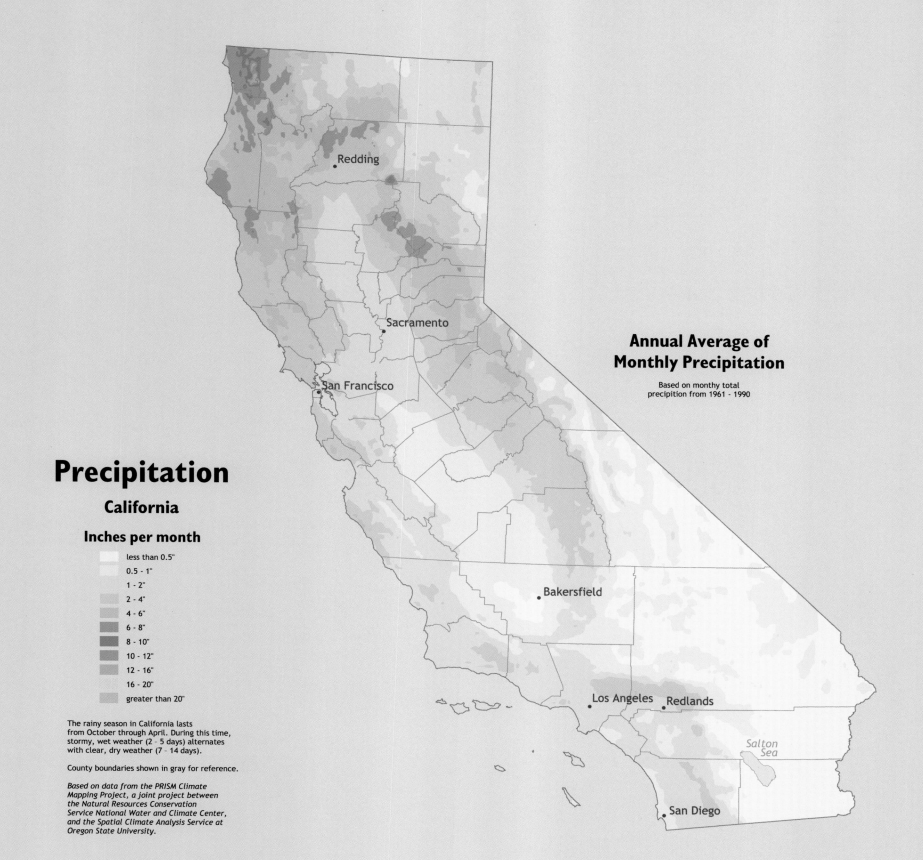

Annual Average of Monthly Precipitation

Based on monthy total
precipition from 1961 - 1990

Precipitation

California

Inches per month

- less than 0.5"
- 0.5 - 1"
- 1 - 2"
- 2 - 4"
- 4 - 6"
- 6 - 8"
- 8 - 10"
- 10 - 12"
- 12 - 16"
- 16 - 20"
- greater than 20"

The rainy season in California lasts
from October through April. During this time,
stormy, wet weather (2 – 5 days) alternates
with clear, dry weather (7 – 14 days).

County boundaries shown in gray for reference.

*Based on data from the PRISM Climate
Mapping Project, a joint project between
the Natural Resources Conservation
Service National Water and Climate Center,
and the Spatial Climate Analysis Service at
Oregon State University.*

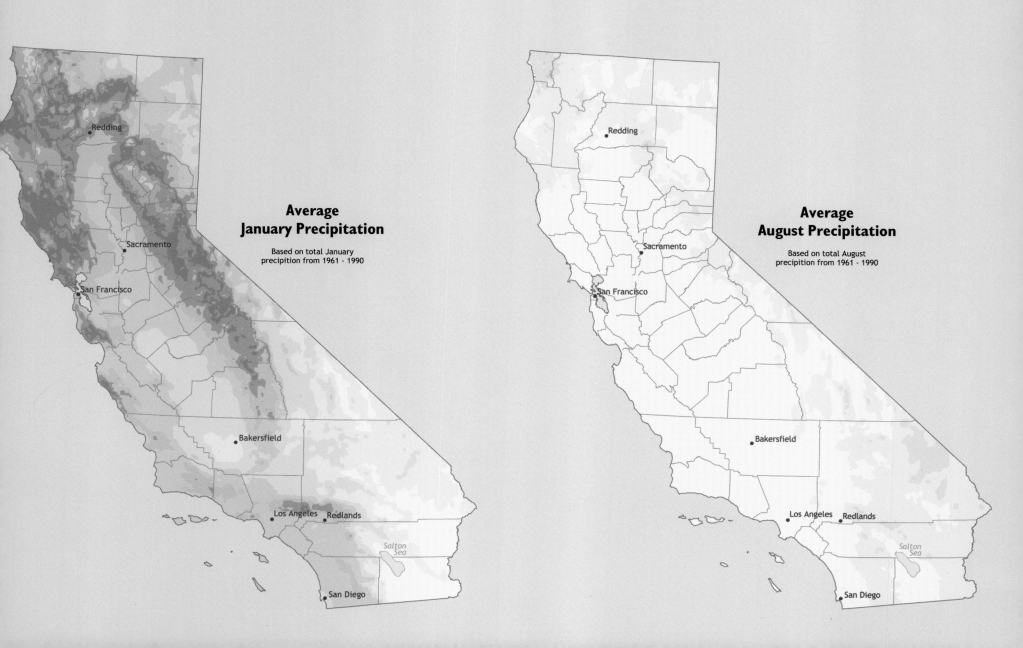

Average January Precipitation

Based on total January
precipition from 1961 - 1990

Average August Precipitation

Based on total August
precipition from 1961 - 1990

Wind-flow Patterns
California

Winter

Summer

Spring

Fall

For the majority of the year, the wind over the southern portion of California flows predominately from the ocean. It travels along the coastal plains, then up and over the mountain ranges. As it travels along the downslope of the mountains, it compresses, heats up and dries out, leading to temperature extremes and the dry desert climate of the Salton Basin.

Based on wind-flow patterns in "California: Patterns on the Land" (Durrenberger, 1965).

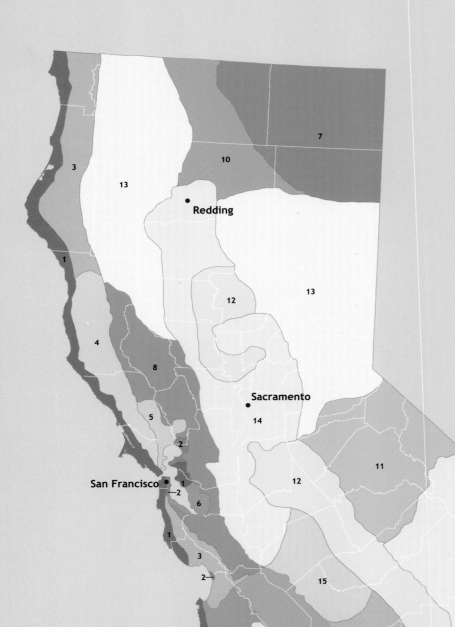

Reference evapotranspiration zones (as identified by CIMIS)

1	Coastal plains heavy fog zone
2	Coastal mixed fog area
3	Coastal valleys and plains and north coast mountains
4	South coast inland plains and mountains north of San Francisco
5	Northern inland valleys
6	Upland central coast and Los Angeles basin
7	Northeastern plains
8	Inland San Francisco Bay area
9	South coast marine to desert transition
10	North central plateau and central coast range
11	Central Sierra Nevada
12	East side Sacramento and San Joaquin Valley
13	Northern Sierra Nevada
14	Midcentral valley, southern Sierra Nevada, Tehachapi, and High Desert mountains
15	Northern and southern San Joaquin Valley
16	Westside San Joaquin Valley and mountains east and west of Imperial Valley
17	High Desert valleys
18	Imperial Valley, Death Valley, and Palo Verde

Monthly average evapotranspiration (inches per month)

Zone	Jan	Feb	Mar	Apr	May	Jun	Jul	Aug	Sep	Oct	Nov	Dec	To
1	0.93	1.40	2.48	3.30	4.03	4.50	4.65	4.03	3.30	2.48	1.20	0.62	33
2	1.24	1.68	3.10	3.90	4.65	5.10	4.96	4.65	3.90	2.79	1.90	1.24	39
3	1.86	2.24	3.72	4.80	5.27	5.70	5.58	5.27	4.20	3.41	2.40	1.86	46
4	1.86	2.24	3.41	4.50	5.27	5.70	5.89	5.58	4.50	3.41	2.40	1.86	46
5	0.93	1.68	2.79	4.20	5.58	6.30	6.51	5.89	4.50	3.10	1.50	0.93	43
6	1.86	2.24	3.41	4.80	5.58	6.30	6.51	6.20	4.80	3.72	2.40	1.86	49
7	0.62	1.40	2.48	3.90	5.27	6.30	7.44	6.51	4.80	2.79	1.20	0.62	43
8	1.24	1.68	3.41	4.80	6.20	6.90	7.44	6.51	5.10	3.41	1.80	0.93	49
9	2.17	2.80	4.03	5.10	5.89	6.60	7.44	6.82	5.70	4.03	2.70	1.86	55
10	0.93	1.68	3.10	4.50	5.89	7.20	8.06	7.13	5.10	3.10	1.50	0.93	49
11	1.55	2.24	3.10	4.50	5.89	7.20	8.06	7.44	5.70	3.72	2.10	1.55	53
12	1.24	1.96	3.41	5.10	6.82	7.80	8.06	7.13	5.40	3.72	1.80	0.93	53
13	1.24	1.96	3.10	4.80	6.51	7.80	8.99	7.75	5.70	3.72	1.80	0.93	54
14	1.55	2.24	3.72	5.10	6.82	7.80	8.68	7.75	5.70	4.03	2.10	1.55	57
15	1.24	2.24	3.72	5.70	7.44	8.10	8.68	7.75	5.70	4.03	2.10	1.24	57
16	1.55	2.52	4.03	5.70	7.75	8.70	9.30	8.37	6.30	4.34	2.40	1.55	62
17	1.86	2.80	4.65	6.00	8.06	9.00	9.92	8.68	6.60	4.34	2.70	1.86	66
18	2.48	3.36	5.27	6.90	8.68	9.60	9.61	8.68	6.90	4.96	3.00	2.17	71

Evapotranspiration
California

Evapotranspiration is a combination of water loss by evaporation and water transfer to the air through plant tissues.

The Salton Sea is located in evapotranspiration zone 18, which exibits the highest evapotranspiration in the state of California. High evaporation rates in the area contribute to a loss of 5.5 - 6.0 vertical feet of water each year from the Salton Sea.

County boundaries shown in white for reference.

Based on the map "Reference Evapotranspiration" from the California Irrigation Management Information System (CIMIS), 1999.

Ozone (O₃)

What is ozone?
Ozone is a major air pollutant that reacts with compounds in the atmosphere and the human body.

What can it do?
Ozone can cause lung and respiratory tract damage, and is corrosive to many materials. Plants and crops are adversely affected by the presence of ozone.

How is it measured?
Ozone is usually measured over 1-hour periods and reported as parts per million (ppm). The ppm values represent the number of ozone particles found in one million air particles. Daily reports of ozone usually cite the maximum 1-hour ppm value for that day.

What are the state and federal standards?
State and federal standards are based on a 1-hour sampling period. Ozone concentrations greater than the amounts below exceed the standards.

State: 0.09 ppm (in 1 hour)
Federal: 0.12 ppm (in 1 hour)

1990 Ozone
Annual average of the maximum 1-hour daily measurements (ppm)
- ◦ Within standards (less than 0.09)
- ◦ Exceeds state standards (0.09 - 0.12)
- ● Exceeds federal and state standards (greater than 0.12)

1999 Ozone
Annual average of the maximum 1-hour daily measurements (ppm)
- ◦ Within standards (less than 0.09)
- ◦ Exceeds state standards (0.09 - 0.12)
- ● Exceeds federal and state standards (greater than 0.12)

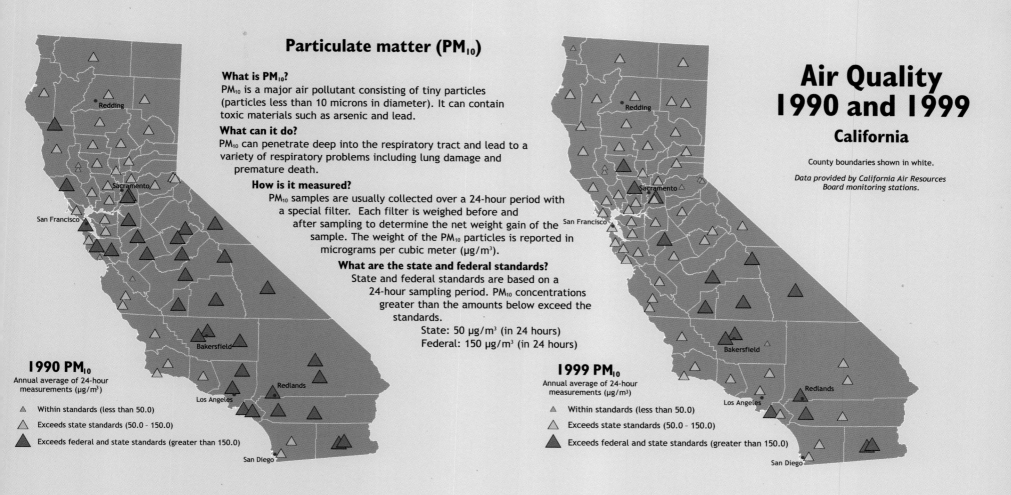

Particulate matter (PM₁₀)

What is PM₁₀?
PM₁₀ is a major air pollutant consisting of tiny particles (particles less than 10 microns in diameter). It can contain toxic materials such as arsenic and lead.

What can it do?
PM₁₀ can penetrate deep into the respiratory tract and lead to a variety of respiratory problems including lung damage and premature death.

How is it measured?
PM₁₀ samples are usually collected over a 24-hour period with a special filter. Each filter is weighed before and after sampling to determine the net weight gain of the sample. The weight of the PM₁₀ particles is reported in micrograms per cubic meter (µg/m³).

What are the state and federal standards?
State and federal standards are based on a 24-hour sampling period. PM₁₀ concentrations greater than the amounts below exceed the standards.

State: 50 µg/m³ (in 24 hours)
Federal: 150 µg/m³ (in 24 hours)

1990 PM₁₀
Annual average of 24-hour measurements (µg/m³)
- △ Within standards (less than 50.0)
- △ Exceeds state standards (50.0 - 150.0)
- ▲ Exceeds federal and state standards (greater than 150.0)

1999 PM₁₀
Annual average of 24-hour measurements (µg/m³)
- △ Within standards (less than 50.0)
- △ Exceeds state standards (50.0 - 150.0)
- ▲ Exceeds federal and state standards (greater than 150.0)

Air Quality 1990 and 1999
California

County boundaries shown in white.

Data provided by California Air Resources Board monitoring stations.

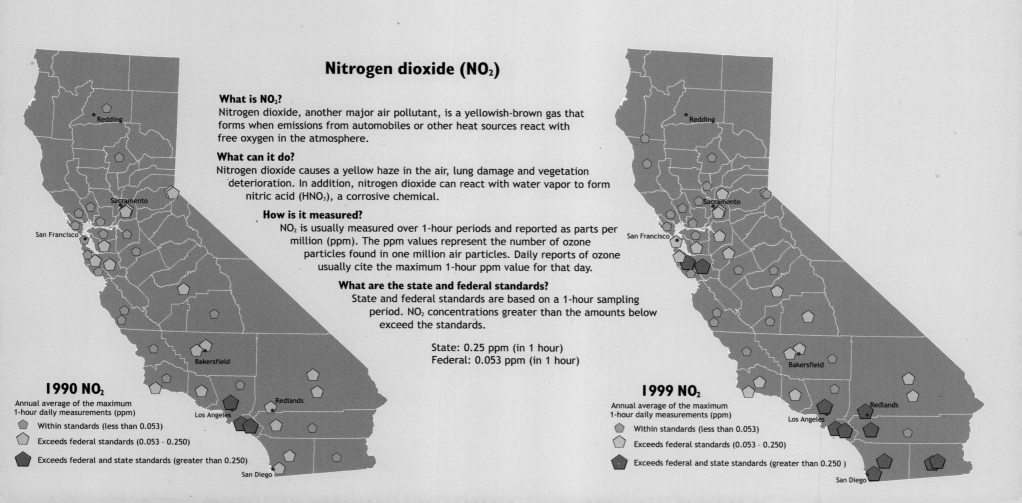

Nitrogen dioxide (NO₂)

What is NO₂?
Nitrogen dioxide, another major air pollutant, is a yellowish-brown gas that forms when emissions from automobiles or other heat sources react with free oxygen in the atmosphere.

What can it do?
Nitrogen dioxide causes a yellow haze in the air, lung damage and vegetation deterioration. In addition, nitrogen dioxide can react with water vapor to form nitric acid (HNO₃), a corrosive chemical.

How is it measured?
NO₂ is usually measured over 1-hour periods and reported as parts per million (ppm). The ppm values represent the number of ozone particles found in one million air particles. Daily reports of ozone usually cite the maximum 1-hour ppm value for that day.

What are the state and federal standards?
State and federal standards are based on a 1-hour sampling period. NO₂ concentrations greater than the amounts below exceed the standards.

State: 0.25 ppm (in 1 hour)
Federal: 0.053 ppm (in 1 hour)

1990 NO₂
Annual average of the maximum 1-hour daily measurements (ppm)
- ⬠ Within standards (less than 0.053)
- ⬠ Exceeds federal standards (0.053 - 0.250)
- ⬠ Exceeds federal and state standards (greater than 0.250)

1999 NO₂
Annual average of the maximum 1-hour daily measurements (ppm)
- ⬠ Within standards (less than 0.053)
- ⬠ Exceeds federal standards (0.053 - 0.250)
- ⬠ Exceeds federal and state standards (greater than 0.250)

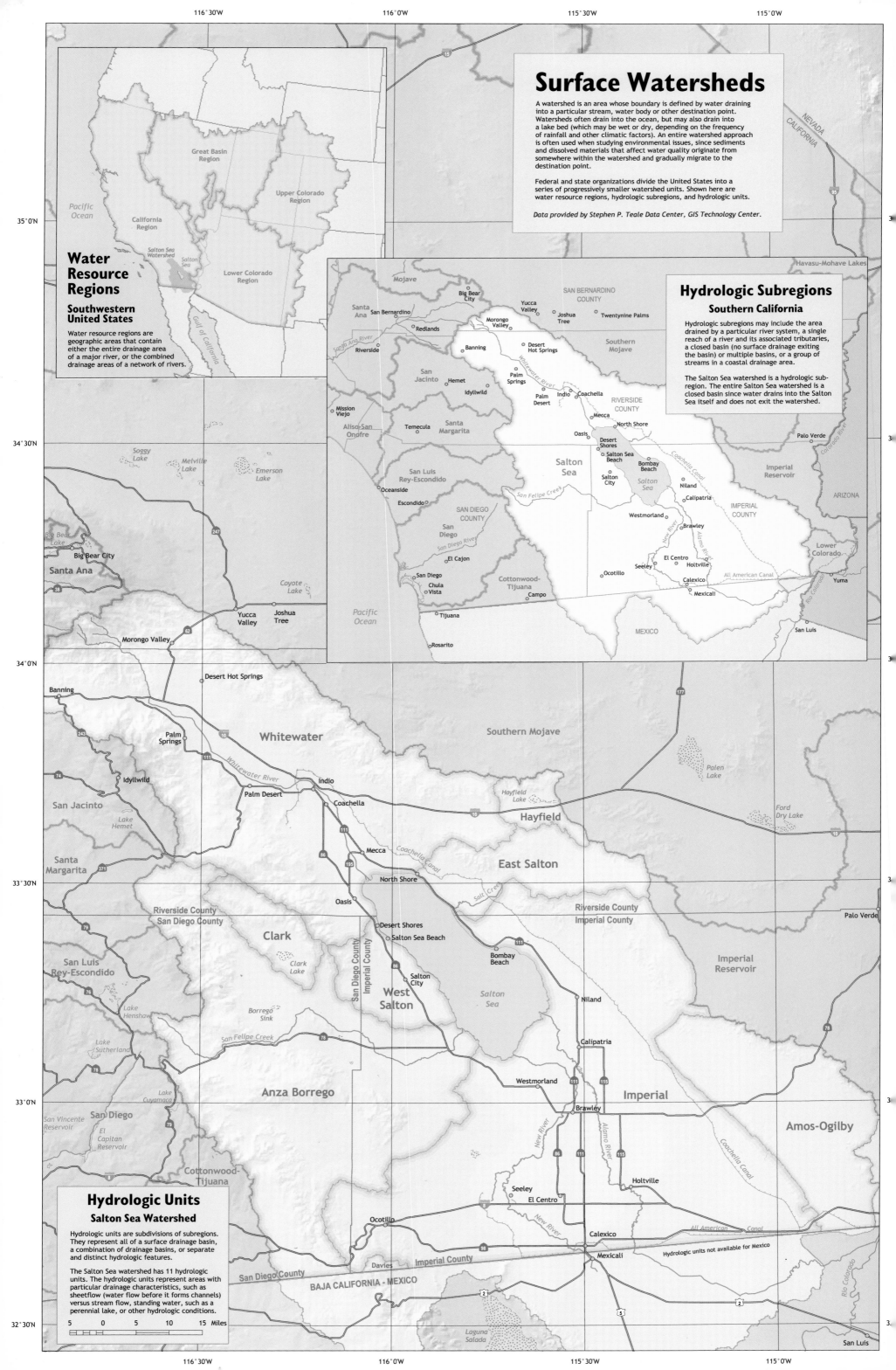

Surface Watersheds

A watershed is an area whose boundary is defined by water draining into a particular stream, water body or other destination point. Watersheds often drain into the ocean, but may also drain into a lake bed (which may be wet or dry, depending on the frequency of rainfall and other climatic factors). An entire watershed approach is often used when studying environmental issues, since sediments and dissolved materials that affect water quality originate from somewhere within the watershed and gradually migrate to the destination point.

Federal and state organizations divide the United States into a series of progressively smaller watershed units. Shown here are water resource regions, hydrologic subregions, and hydrologic units.

Data provided by Stephen P. Teale Data Center, GIS Technology Center.

Water Resource Regions
Southwestern United States

Water resource regions are geographic areas that contain either the entire drainage area of a major river, or the combined drainage areas of a network of rivers.

Hydrologic Subregions
Southern California

Hydrologic subregions may include the area drained by a particular river system, a single reach of a river and its associated tributaries, a closed basin (no surface drainage exiting the basin) or multiple basins, or a group of streams in a coastal drainage area.

The Salton Sea watershed is a hydrologic subregion. The entire Salton Sea watershed is a closed basin since water drains into the Salton Sea itself and does not exit the watershed.

Hydrologic Units
Salton Sea Watershed

Hydrologic units are subdivisions of subregions. They represent all of a surface drainage basin, a combination of drainage basins, or separate and distinct hydrologic features.

The Salton Sea watershed has 11 hydrologic units. The hydrologic units represent areas with particular drainage characteristics, such as sheetflow (water flow before it forms channels) versus stream flow, standing water, such as a perennial lake, or other hydrologic conditions.

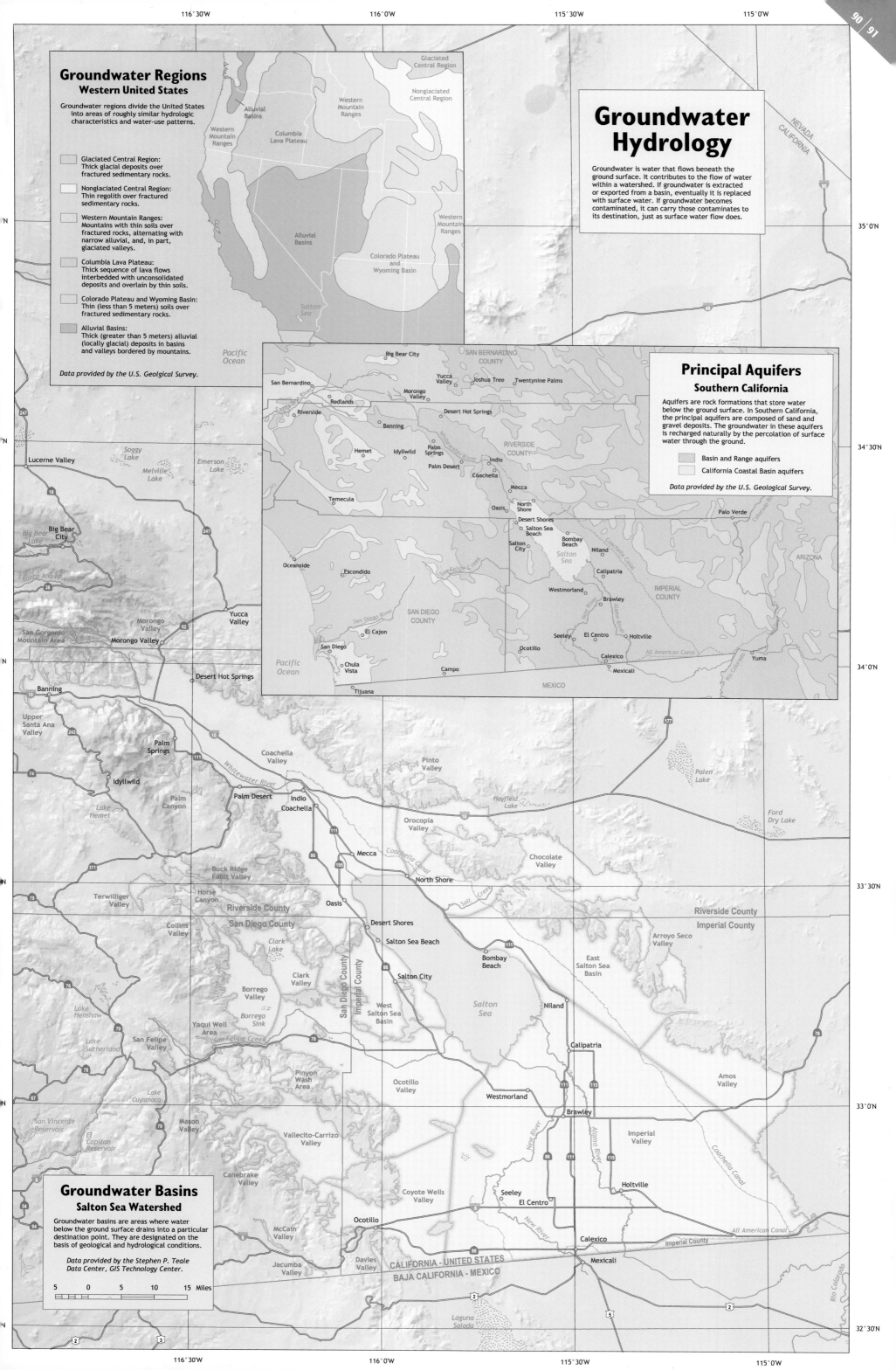

Groundwater Regions
Western United States

Groundwater regions divide the United States into areas of roughly similar hydrologic characteristics and water-use patterns.

- **Glaciated Central Region:** Thick glacial deposits over fractured sedimentary rocks.
- **Nonglaciated Central Region:** Thin regolith over fractured sedimentary rocks.
- **Western Mountain Ranges:** Mountains with thin soils over fractured rocks, alternating with narrow alluvial, and, in part, glaciated valleys.
- **Columbia Lava Plateau:** Thick sequence of lava flows interbedded with unconsolidated deposits and overlain by thin soils.
- **Colorado Plateau and Wyoming Basin:** Thin (less than 5 meters) soils over fractured sedimentary rocks.
- **Alluvial Basins:** Thick (greater than 5 meters) alluvial (locally glacial) deposits in basins and valleys bordered by mountains.

Data provided by the U.S. Geolgical Survey.

Groundwater Hydrology

Groundwater is water that flows beneath the ground surface. It contributes to the flow of water within a watershed. If groundwater is extracted or exported from a basin, eventually it is replaced with surface water. If groundwater becomes contaminated, it can carry those contaminates to its destination, just as surface water flow does.

Principal Aquifers
Southern California

Aquifers are rock formations that store water below the ground surface. In Southern California, the principal aquifers are composed of sand and gravel deposits. The groundwater in these aquifers is recharged naturally by the percolation of surface water through the ground.

- Basin and Range aquifers
- California Coastal Basin aquifers

Data provided by the U.S. Geological Survey.

Groundwater Basins
Salton Sea Watershed

Groundwater basins are areas where water below the ground surface drains into a particular destination point. They are designated on the basis of geological and hydrological conditions.

Data provided by the Stephen P. Teale Data Center, GIS Technology Center.

5 0 5 10 15 Miles

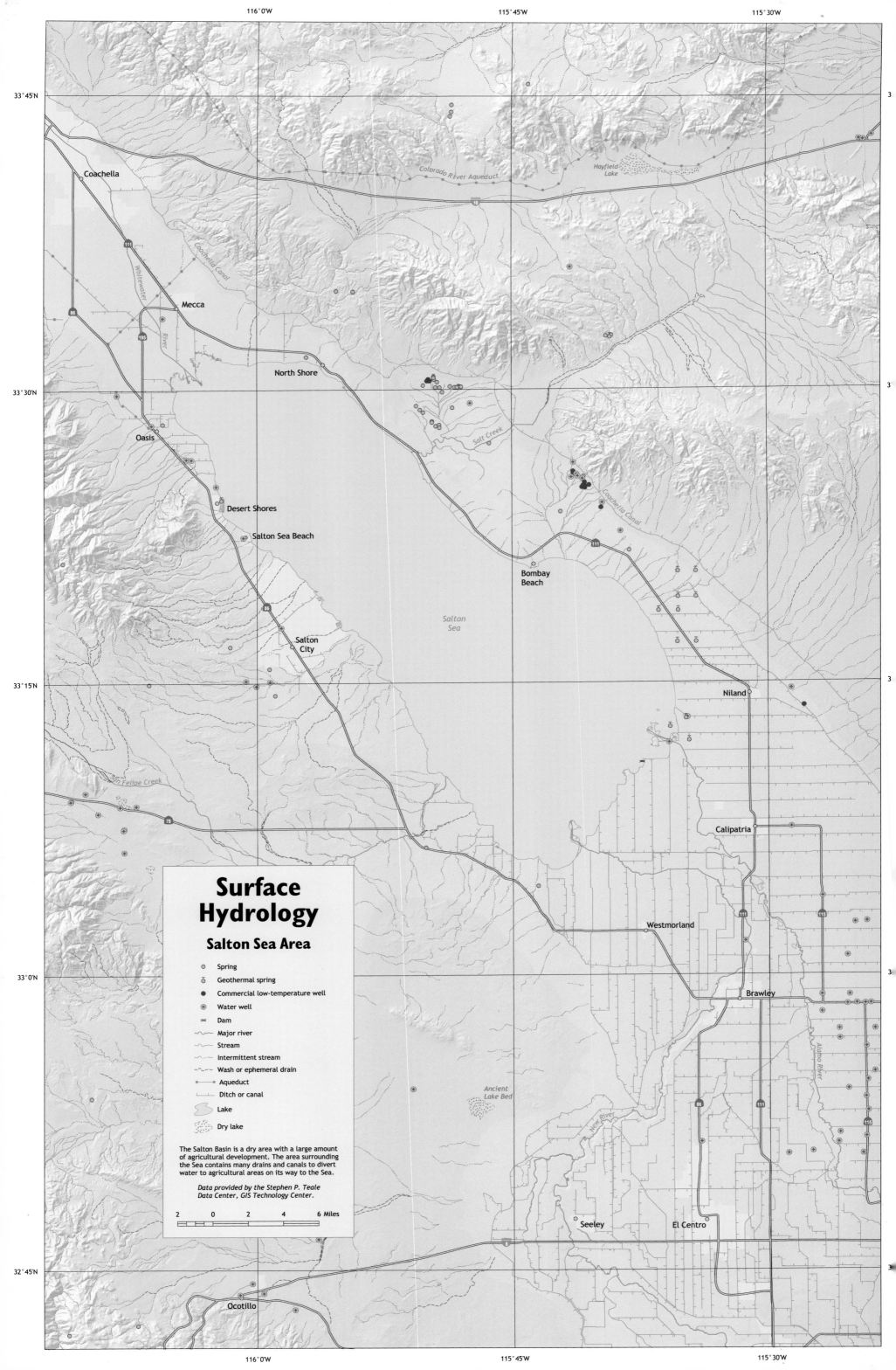

Surface Hydrology

Salton Sea Area

- ⊙ Spring
- ⊙ Geothermal spring
- ● Commercial low-temperature well
- ⊕ Water well
- ⊨ Dam
- ⌇ Major river
- ⌇ Stream
- ⌇ Intermittent stream
- ⌇ Wash or ephemeral drain
- •—•— Aqueduct
- ⊢⊢ Ditch or canal
- ◠ Lake
- ▒ Dry lake

The Salton Basin is a dry area with a large amount
of agricultural development. The area surrounding
the Sea contains many drains and canals to divert
water to agricultural areas on its way to the Sea.

*Data provided by the Stephen P. Teale
Data Center, GIS Technology Center.*

2   0   2   4   6 Miles

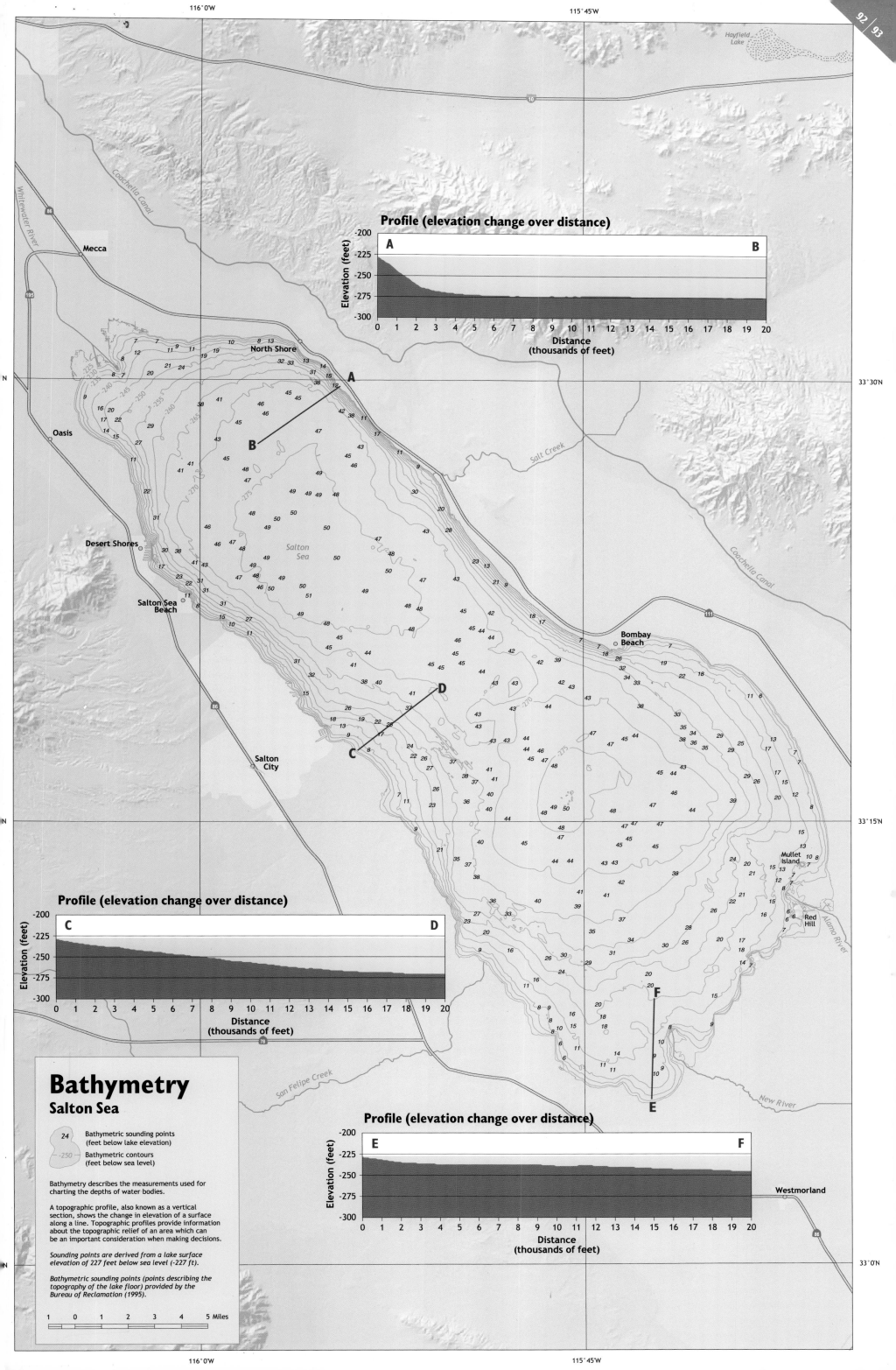

Profile (elevation change over distance)

Bathymetry
Salton Sea

24 — Bathymetric sounding points
(feet below lake elevation)

-250 — Bathymetric contours
(feet below sea level)

Bathymetry describes the measurements used for
charting the depths of water bodies.

A topographic profile, also known as a vertical
section, shows the change in elevation of a surface
along a line. Topographic profiles provide information
about the topographic relief of an area which can
be an important consideration when making decisions.

Sounding points are derived from a lake surface
elevation of 227 feet below sea level (-227 ft).

Bathymetric sounding points (points describing the
topography of the lake floor) provided by the
Bureau of Reclamation (1995).

Sediment Grainsize Distribution

Salton Sea

Sediments of the Salton Sea were analyzed for particle size. Sediments on the bottom of the Sea are comprised of silt, clay, and relatively fine-grained sands.

Clay grains are the smallest particles, with diameters less than 1/256 mm. Silt grains are larger than clay grains with diameters ranging from 1/256 mm to 1/16 mm. Sand grains are the largest. Sand grain diameters range from 1/16 mm to 2 mm.

Isobath interval is 5 feet. Negative values indicate feet below sea level.

Data provided by the Salton Sea Authority from a study conducted by LFR Levine-Fricke. Sample locations shown in blue (•).

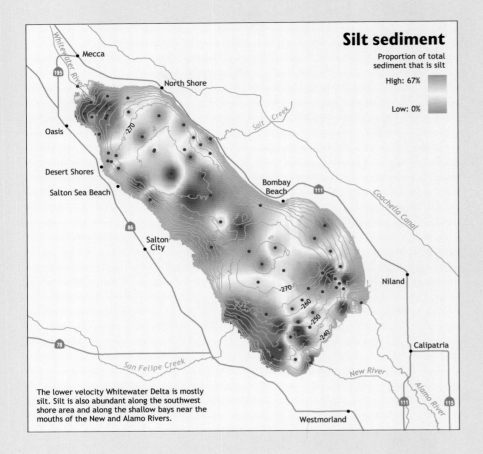

The lower velocity Whitewater Delta is mostly silt. Silt is also abundant along the southwest shore area and along the shallow bays near the mouths of the New and Alamo Rivers.

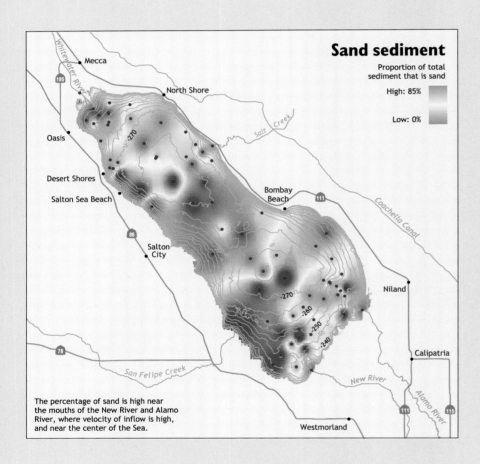

The percentage of sand is high near the mouths of the New River and Alamo River, where velocity of inflow is high, and near the center of the Sea.

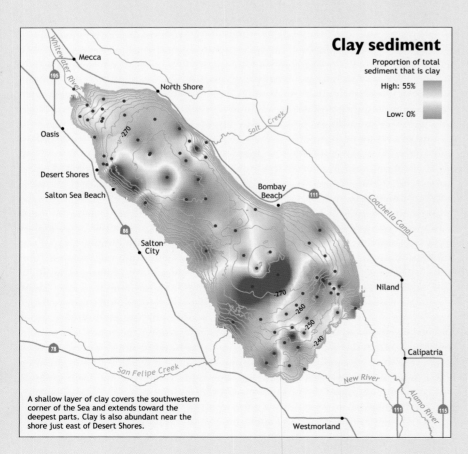

A shallow layer of clay covers the southwestern corner of the Sea and extends toward the deepest parts. Clay is also abundant near the shore just east of Desert Shores.

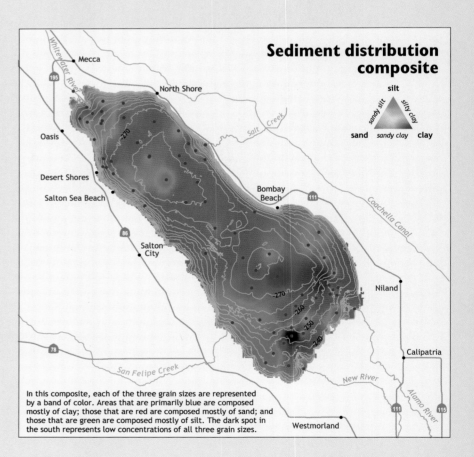

In this composite, each of the three grain sizes are represented by a band of color. Areas that are primarily blue are composed mostly of clay; those that are red are composed mostly of sand; and those that are green are composed mostly of silt. The dark spot in the south represents low concentrations of all three grain sizes.

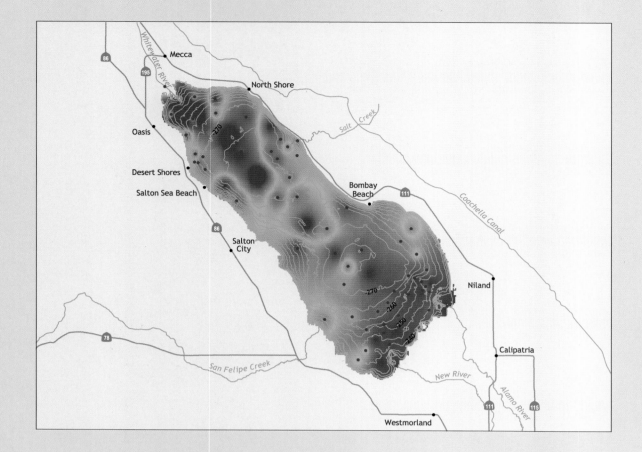

Organic Sediment Contaminants
Salton Sea

Sediments of the Salton Sea were tested for a number of organic contaminants. Elevated concentrations of organic substances were found primarily in the northern part of the Sea. However, only carbon disulfide, acetone, and 2-butanone were found in significant amounts.

Isobath interval is 5 feet. Negative values indicate feet below sea level.

Data provided by the Salton Sea Authority from a study conducted by LFR Levine·Fricke. Sample locations shown in blue (•).

5   0   5   10   15   20 Miles

Carbon disulfide
micrograms per kilogram (μg/kg), dry weight

High: 4.99 μg/kg

Low: 0.01 μg/kg

Carbon disulfide has the greatest concentrations near the mouth of the Whitewater River and in the northern portion of the Sea.

Acetone
micrograms per kilogram (μg/kg), dry weight

High: 1.53 μg/kg

Low: 0.02 μg/kg

Acetone is found in its highest concentrations throughout most of the northern portion of the Sea.

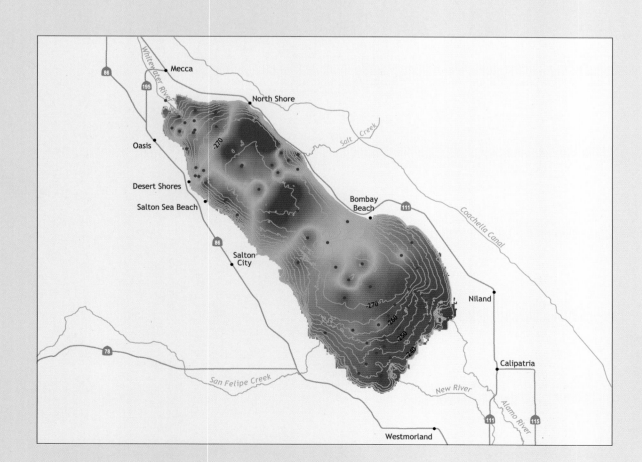

2-Butanone
micrograms per kilogram (μg/kg), dry weight

High: 0.54 μg/kg

Low: 0.01 μg/kg

The greatest concentrations of 2-butanone were found in the northern part of the Sea near North Shore, and in the deeper areas throughout the Sea.

Inorganic Sediment Contaminants

Salton Sea

Sediments of the Salton Sea were tested for a number of inorganic contaminants. The published NOAA standards "Biological Effects Range Low" (ERL) and "Biological Effects Range Medium" (ERM) are referenced as comparative values.

ERL and ERM concentration values are guidelines used to evaluate whether sediment chemical concentrations are within ranges that have been reported to be associated with biological effects. These guidelines were generated from a large national sediment database. ERM values are the concentrations at which 50 percent of the studies for a particular chemical showed biological effects resulting from those concentrations, and ERL values are the concentrations at which 10 percent of the studies showed biological effects resulting from those concentrations.

Selenium does not have an ERL or ERM standard published by NOAA. Instead guidelines for sediment suitable for wetlands creation from the California Regional Water Quality Control Board, San Francisco Region, were used to create surrogate ERL and ERM values.

Isobath interval is 5 feet. Negative values indicate feet below sea level.

Data provided by the Salton Sea Authority from a study conducted by LFR Levine·Fricke. Sample locations shown in blue (•).

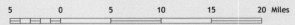

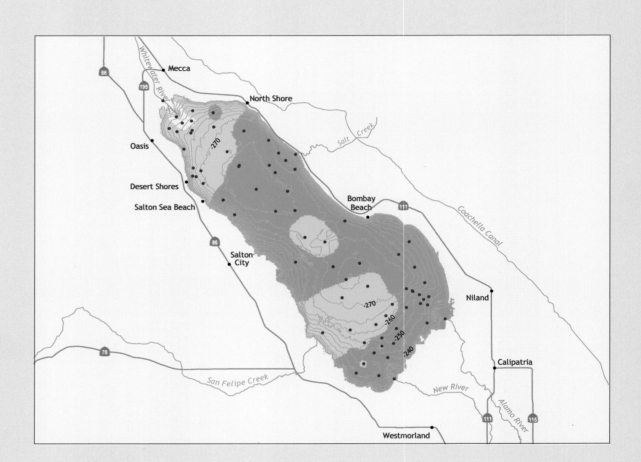

Copper

milligrams per kilogram (mg/kg), dry weight

34 mg/kg ——— ERL
15 mg/kg
0 mg/kg

The highest concentration of copper occurs near the mouth of the Whitewater River.

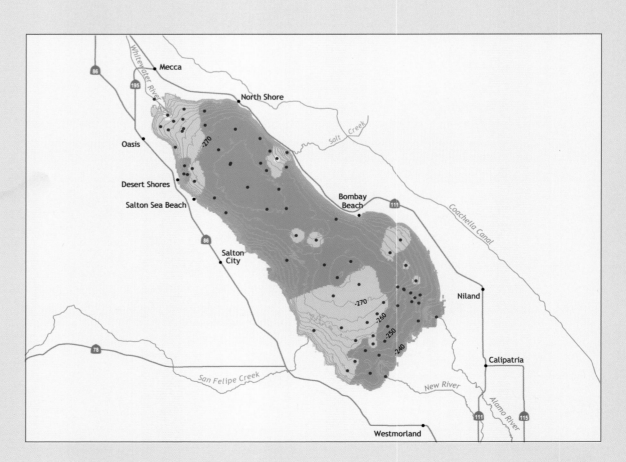

Zinc

milligrams per kilogram (mg/kg), dry weight

150 mg/kg ——— ERL
42 mg/kg
0 mg/kg

The highest concentrations of zinc are found at the mouths of Whitewater River and Salt Creek.

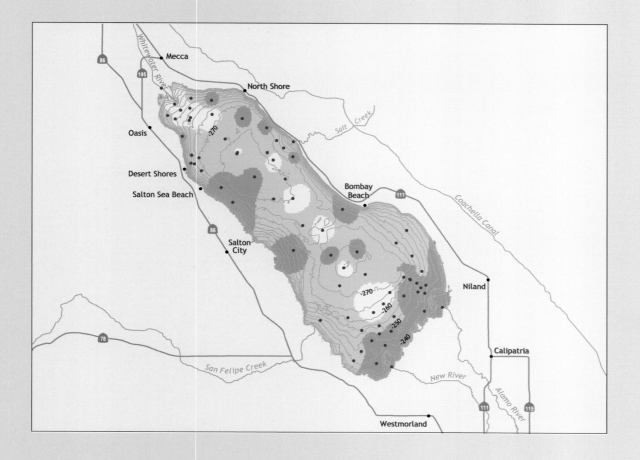

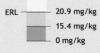

Nickel

milligrams per kilogram (mg/kg), dry weight

ERL —— 20.9 mg/kg
15.4 mg/kg
0 mg/kg

Nickel is found in the greatest concentrations near the mouth of the Whitewater River and in the deepest parts of the Sea.

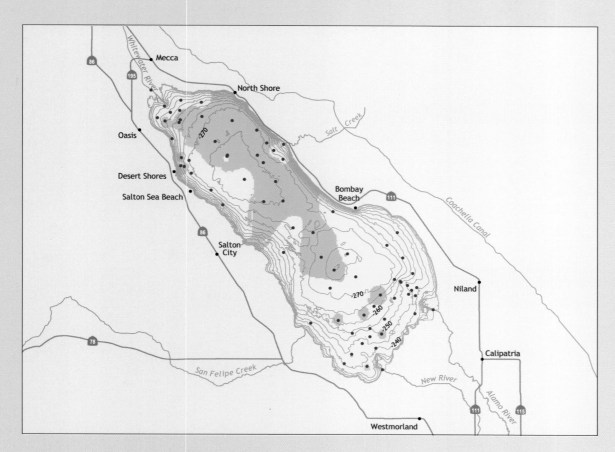

Cadmium

milligrams per kilogram (mg/kg), dry weight

3.0 mg/kg
ERL —— 1.2 mg/kg
0 mg/kg

The greatest concentrations of cadmium are found near the deepest parts of the Sea.

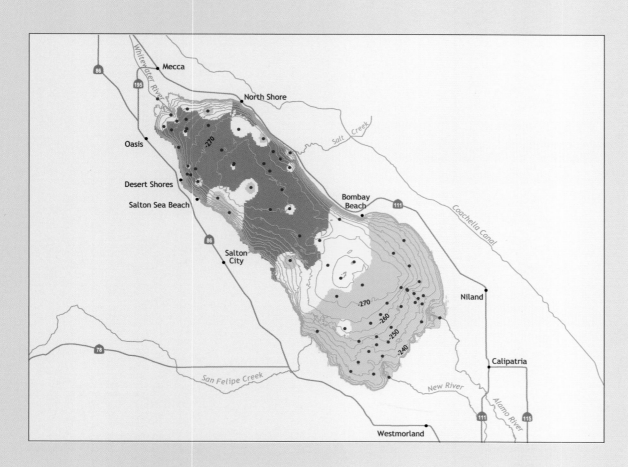

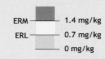

Selenium

milligrams per kilogram (mg/kg), dry weight

ERM —— 1.4 mg/kg
ERL —— 0.7 mg/kg
0 mg/kg

Selenium is concentrated in the northern portion of the Sea, and is of the greatest concern among the inorganic contaminants.

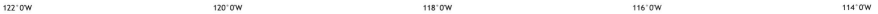
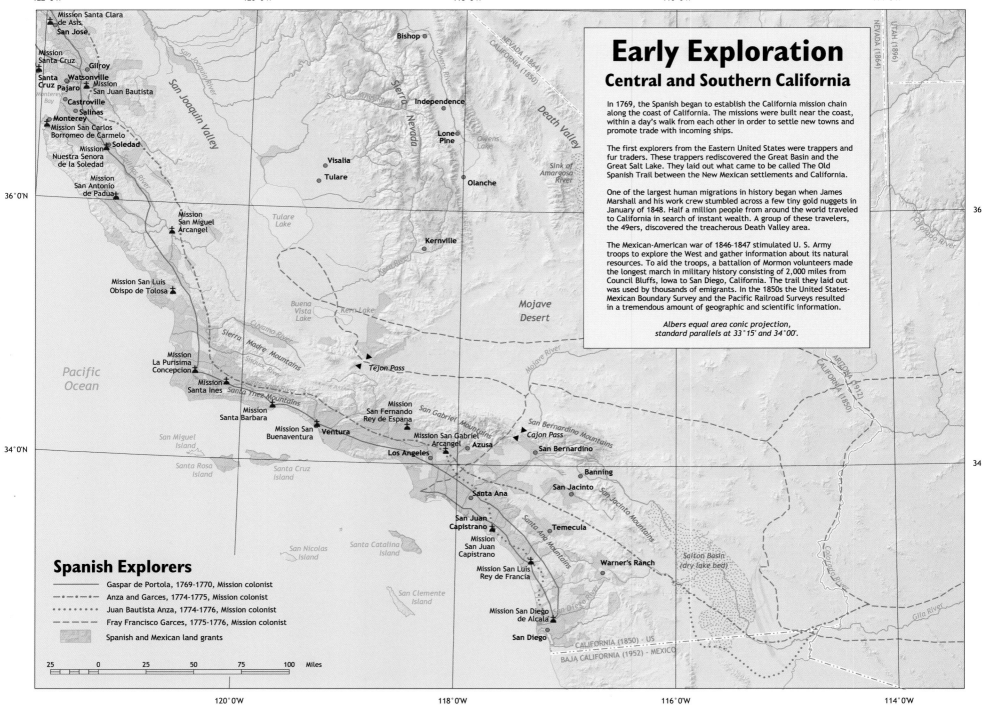
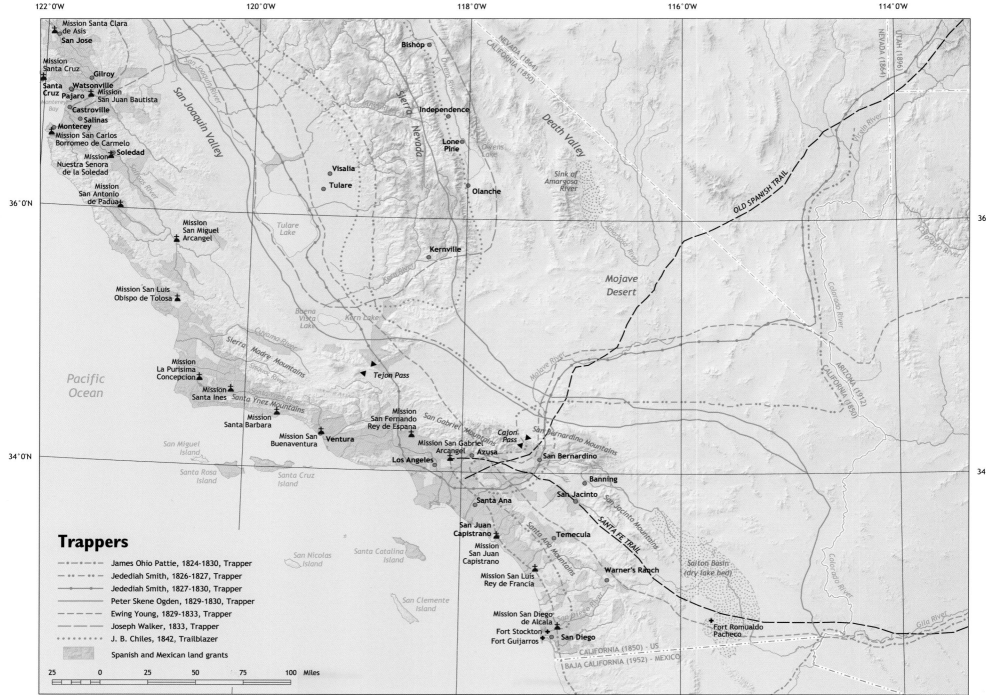

Gold Rush map (top)

122°0'W   120°0'W   118°0'W   116°0'W   114°0'W

Mission Santa Clara de Asis
San Jose
Mission Santa Cruz
Santa Cruz
Gilroy
Pajaro
Watsonville
Mission San Juan Bautista
Castroville
Monterey Bay
Salinas
Monterey
Mission San Carlos Borromeo de Carmelo
Mission Nuestra Senora de la Soledad
Soledad
Mission San Antonio de Padua
Mission San Miguel Arcangel
Mission San Luis Obispo de Tolosa

Bishop
Fort Miller
Independence
Lone Pine
Owens Lake
Visalia
Tulare
Olanche
Tulare Lake
Kernville
Sink of Amargosa River

Death Valley

San Joaquin Valley
Sierra Nevada

Mojave Desert

Pacific Ocean

Buena Vista Lake
Kern Lake
Sierra Madre Mountains
Fort Tejon
Tejon Pass
Mission La Purisima Concepcion
Mission Santa Ines
Santa Ynez Mountains
Mission Santa Barbara
Mission San Buenaventura
Ventura
Mission San Fernando Rey de Espana
Mission San Gabriel Arcangel
Azusa
Los Angeles
Fort San Bernardino
San Gabriel Mountains
San Bernardino Mountains
Cajon Pass
San Bernardino
Banning
San Jacinto
Santa Ana
San Juan Capistrano
Mission San Juan Capistrano
Santa Ang Mountains
Temecula
San Jacinto Mountains
Warner's Ranch
Salton Basin (dry lake bed)
Mission San Luis Rey de Francia
Mission San Diego de Alcala
San Diego
Fort Rosencrans
Fort Yuma

MORMON BATTALION TRAIL
Mojave River

San Miguel Island
Santa Rosa Island
Santa Cruz Island
San Nicolas Island
Santa Catalina Island
San Clemente Island

NEVADA (1864)
CALIFORNIA (1850)
NEVADA (1864)
ARIZONA
CALIFORNIA (1912)
UTAH (1896)
Colorado River
Gila River
CALIFORNIA (1850) - US
BAJA CALIFORNIA (1952) - MEXICO

Area enlarged in maps below
OREGON IDAHO NEVADA UTAH CALIFORNIA ARIZONA MEXICO Pacific Ocean

Gold Rush

— Death Valley 49ers, 1849, Gold Rush
▓ Spanish and Mexican land grants

25 0 25 50 75 100 Miles

Surveyors map (bottom)

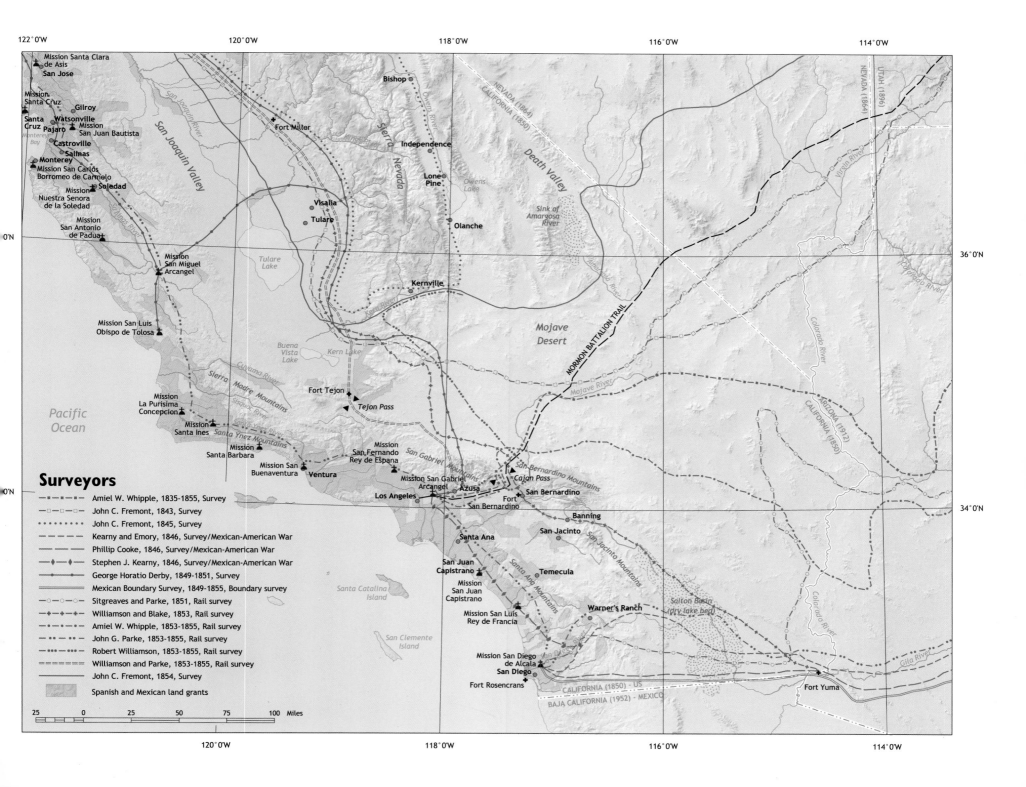

122°0'W   120°0'W   118°0'W   116°0'W   114°0'W

Surveyors

—•— Amiel W. Whipple, 1835-1855, Survey
—□— John C. Fremont, 1843, Survey
······ John C. Fremont, 1845, Survey
— — — Kearny and Emory, 1846, Survey/Mexican-American War
——— Phillip Cooke, 1846, Survey/Mexican-American War
—◆— Stephen J. Kearny, 1846, Survey/Mexican-American War
—•— George Horatio Derby, 1849-1851, Survey
——— Mexican Boundary Survey, 1849-1855, Boundary survey
—○— Sitgreaves and Parke, 1851, Rail survey
—□— Williamson and Blake, 1853, Rail survey
—•— Amiel W. Whipple, 1853-1855, Rail survey
—••— John G. Parke, 1853-1855, Rail survey
—•••— Robert Williamson, 1853-1855, Rail survey
—•— Williamson and Parke, 1853-1855, Rail survey
——— John C. Fremont, 1854, Survey
▓ Spanish and Mexican land grants

25 0 25 50 75 100 Miles

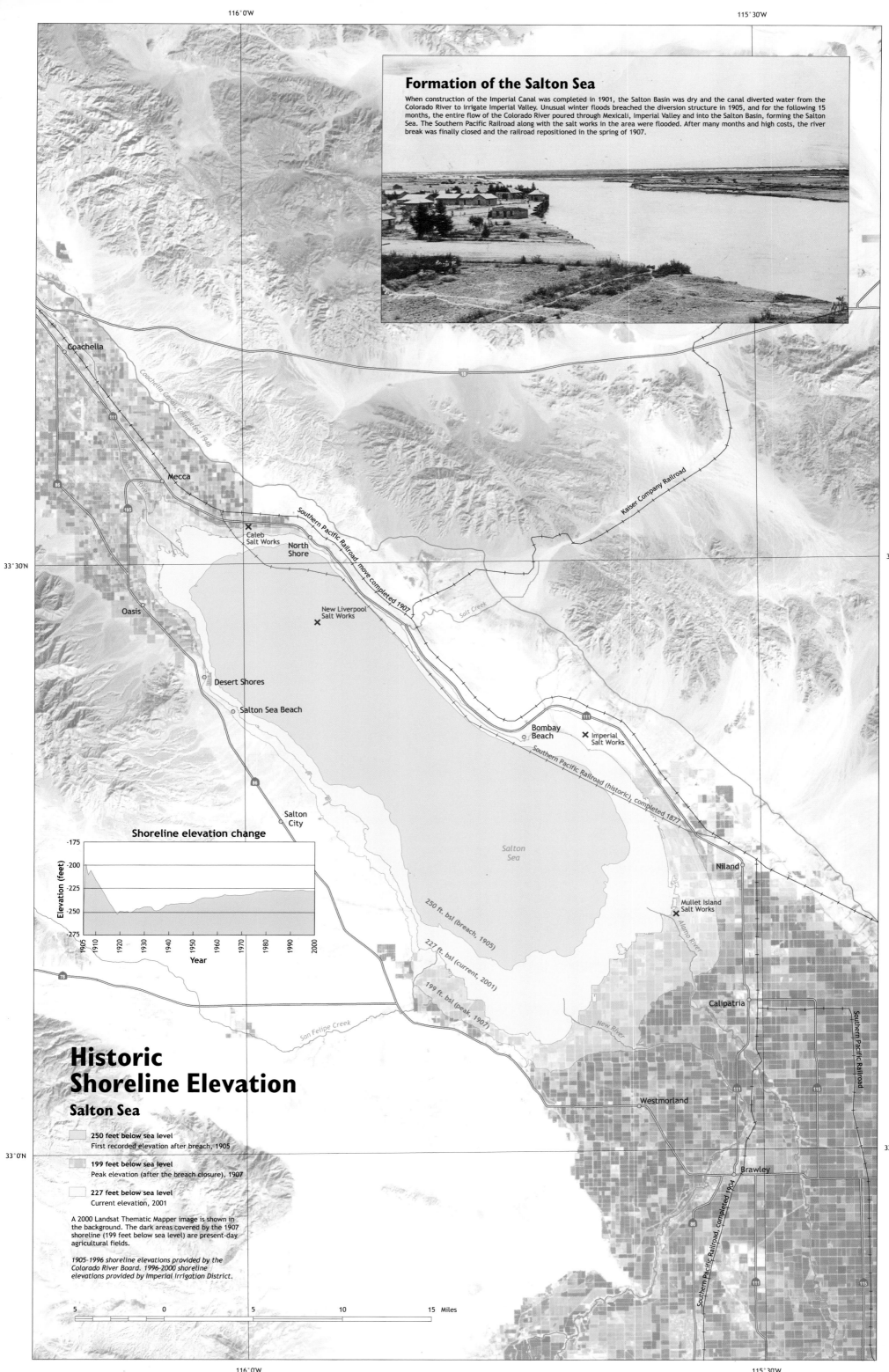

Formation of the Salton Sea

When construction of the Imperial Canal was completed in 1901, the Salton Basin was dry and the canal diverted water from the Colorado River to irrigate Imperial Valley. Unusual winter floods breached the diversion structure in 1905, and for the following 15 months, the entire flow of the Colorado River poured through Mexicali, Imperial Valley and into the Salton Basin, forming the Salton Sea. The Southern Pacific Railroad along with the salt works in the area were flooded. After many months and high costs, the river break was finally closed and the railroad repositioned in the spring of 1907.

Shoreline elevation change

(graph: Elevation (feet) vs. Year, 1905–2000)

250 ft. bsl (breach, 1905)

227 ft. bsl (current, 2001)

199 ft. bsl (peak, 1907)

Historic Shoreline Elevation

Salton Sea

250 feet below sea level
First recorded elevation after breach, 1905

199 feet below sea level
Peak elevation (after the breach closure), 1907

227 feet below sea level
Current elevation, 2001

A 2000 Landsat Thematic Mapper image is shown in the background. The dark areas covered by the 1907 shoreline (199 feet below sea level) are present-day agricultural fields.

1905-1996 shoreline elevations provided by the Colorado River Board. 1996–2000 shoreline elevations provided by Imperial Irrigation District.

Map labels: Coachella, Mecca, Oasis, Caleb Salt Works, North Shore, New Liverpool Salt Works, Desert Shores, Salton Sea Beach, Salton City, Bombay Beach, Imperial Salt Works, Niland, Mullet Island Salt Works, Calipatria, Westmorland, Brawley, Salton Sea, Salt Creek, San Felipe Creek, New River, Alamo River, Coachella Canal completed 1948, Southern Pacific Railroad move completed 1907, Kaiser Company Railroad, Southern Pacific Railroad (historic), completed 1877, Southern Pacific Railroad completed 1904, Southern Pacific Railroad

Comparative land use areas within the Salton Sea Basin

Cropland and pasture
506,607 acres

48 %

48 %

All others
520,734 acres

4 %

Orchards, groves, vineyards and nurseries
38,862 acres

Coachella valley agricultural development

Value of agricultural products (millions of dollars)

1200
1000
800
600
400
200
0

1910 1920 1930 1940 1950 1960 1970 1980 1990 2000

Year

Imperial valley agricultural development

Value of agricultural products (millions of dollars)

1200
1000
800
600
400
200
0

1910 1920 1930 1940 1950 1960 1970 1980 1990 2000

Year

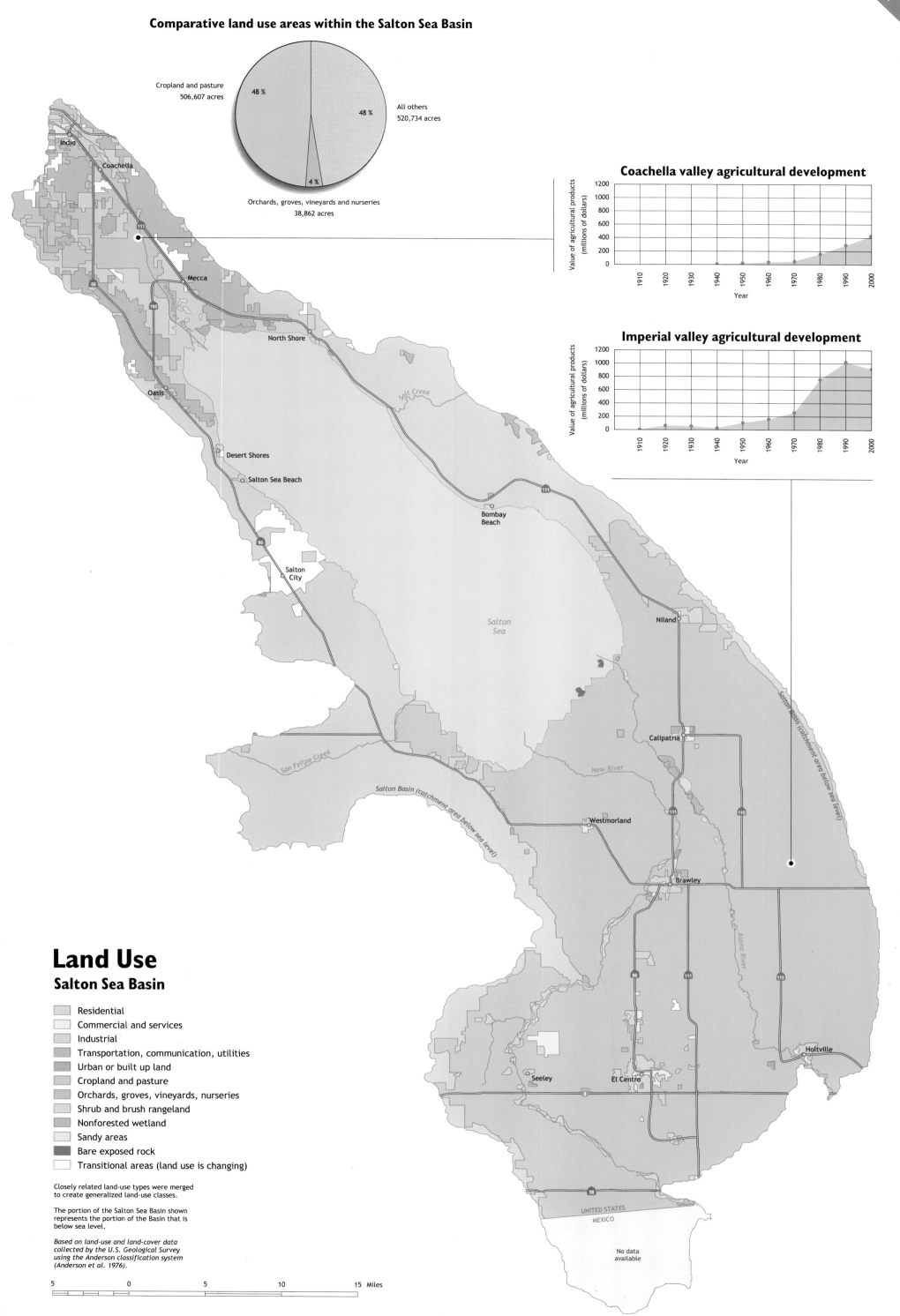

Indio
Coachella
Mecca
North Shore
Oasis
Desert Shores
Salton Sea Beach
Bombay Beach
Salton City
Salt Creek
Salton Sea
Niland
Calipatria
San Felipe Creek
New River
Salton Basin (catchment area below sea level)
Westmorland
Brawley
Alamo River
Seeley
El Centro
Holtville
UNITED STATES
MEXICO
No data available

Land Use
Salton Sea Basin

- Residential
- Commercial and services
- Industrial
- Transportation, communication, utilities
- Urban or built up land
- Cropland and pasture
- Orchards, groves, vineyards, nurseries
- Shrub and brush rangeland
- Nonforested wetland
- Sandy areas
- Bare exposed rock
- Transitional areas (land use is changing)

Closely related land-use types were merged
to create generalized land-use classes.

The portion of the Salton Sea Basin shown
represents the portion of the Basin that is
below sea level.

*Based on land-use and land-cover data
collected by the U.S. Geological Survey
using the Anderson classification system
(Anderson et al. 1976).*

5 0 5 10 15 Miles

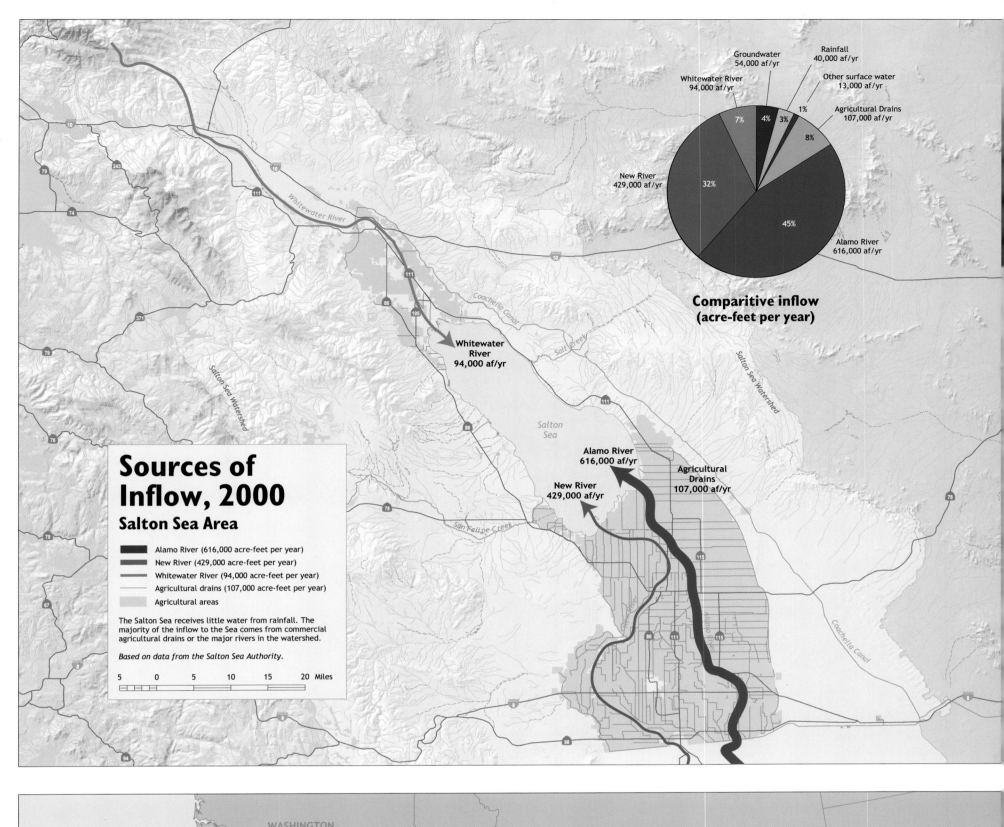

Sources of Inflow, 2000

Salton Sea Area

- ■ Alamo River (616,000 acre-feet per year)
- ■ New River (429,000 acre-feet per year)
- ■ Whitewater River (94,000 acre-feet per year)
- Agricultural drains (107,000 acre-feet per year)
- ▨ Agricultural areas

The Salton Sea receives little water from rainfall. The majority of the inflow to the Sea comes from commercial agricultural drains or the major rivers in the watershed.

Based on data from the Salton Sea Authority.

5 0 5 10 15 20 Miles

**Comparitive inflow
(acre-feet per year)**

Groundwater 54,000 af/yr — 4%
Rainfall 40,000 af/yr — 3%
Whitewater River 94,000 af/yr — 7%
Other surface water 13,000 af/yr — 1%
Agricultural Drains 107,000 af/yr — 8%
New River 429,000 af/yr — 32%
Alamo River 616,000 af/yr — 45%

Whitewater River 94,000 af/yr

Alamo River 616,000 af/yr

New River 429,000 af/yr

Agricultural Drains 107,000 af/yr

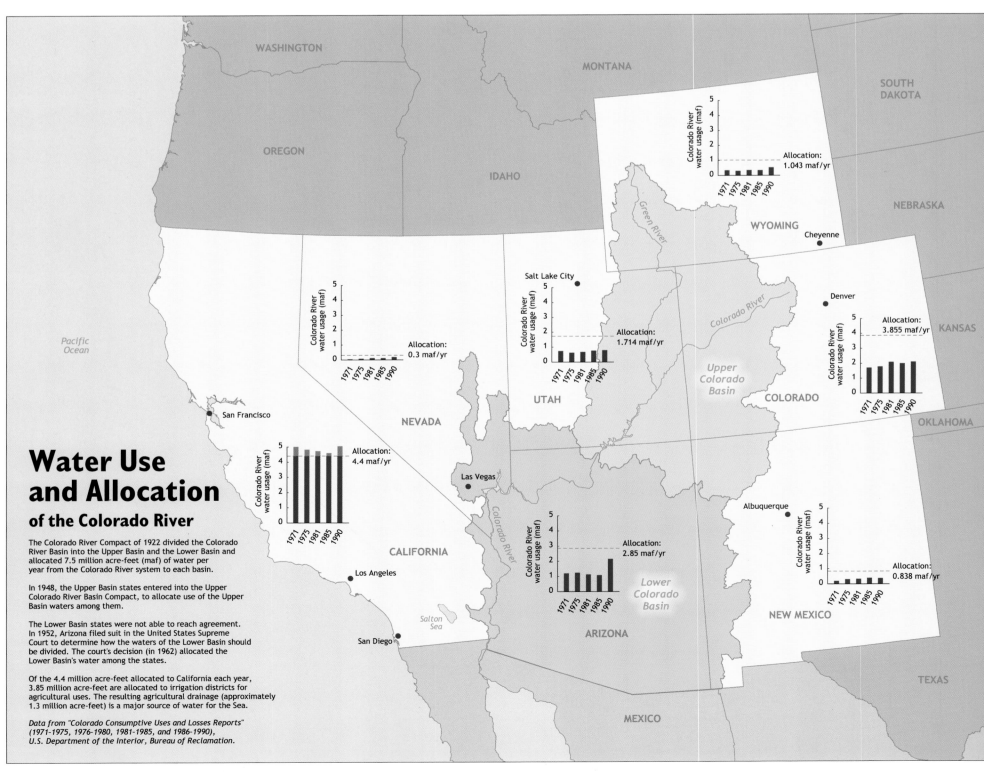

Water Use and Allocation

of the Colorado River

The Colorado River Compact of 1922 divided the Colorado River Basin into the Upper Basin and the Lower Basin and allocated 7.5 million acre-feet (maf) of water per year from the Colorado River system to each basin.

In 1948, the Upper Basin states entered into the Upper Colorado River Basin Compact, to allocate use of the Upper Basin waters among them.

The Lower Basin states were not able to reach agreement. In 1952, Arizona filed suit in the United States Supreme Court to determine how the waters of the Lower Basin should be divided. The court's decision (in 1962) allocated the Lower Basin's water among the states.

Of the 4.4 million acre-feet allocated to California each year, 3.85 million acre-feet are allocated to irrigation districts for agricultural uses. The resulting agricultural drainage (approximately 1.3 million acre-feet) is a major source of water for the Sea.

Data from "Colorado Consumptive Uses and Losses Reports" (1971-1975, 1976-1980, 1981-1985, and 1986-1990), U.S. Department of the Interior, Bureau of Reclamation.

Allocation: 1.043 maf/yr (Wyoming)
Allocation: 0.3 maf/yr (Nevada)
Allocation: 1.714 maf/yr (Utah)
Allocation: 3.855 maf/yr (Colorado)
Allocation: 4.4 maf/yr (California)
Allocation: 2.85 maf/yr (Arizona)
Allocation: 0.838 maf/yr (New Mexico)

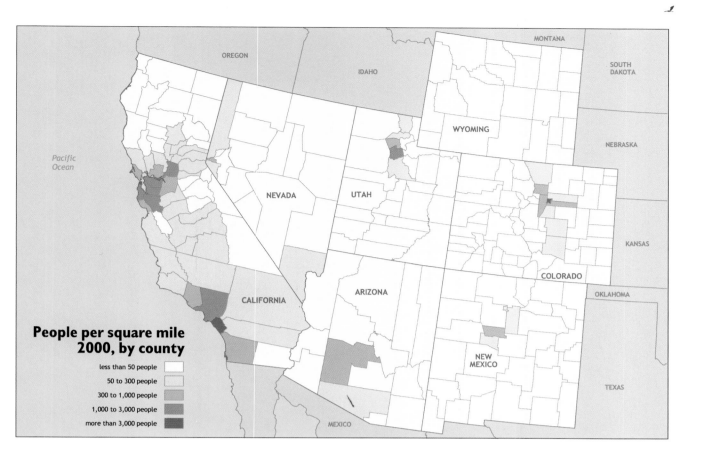

People per square mile 2000, by county

- less than 50 people
- 50 to 300 people
- 300 to 1,000 people
- 1,000 to 3,000 people
- more than 3,000 people

Population

Southwestern United States

Data provided by the Population Estimates Program of the U. S. Census Bureau.

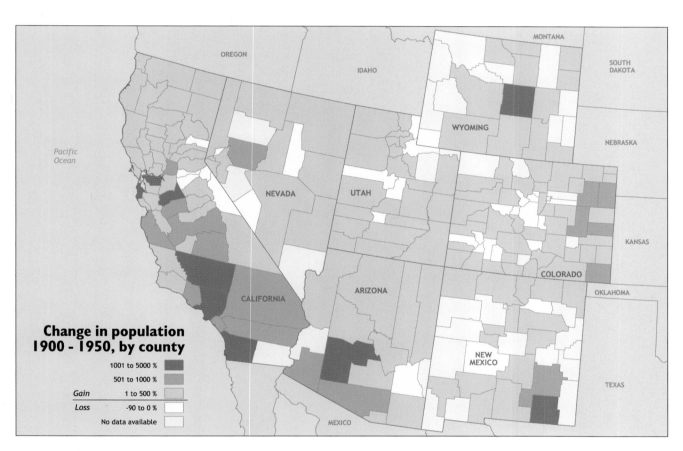

Change in population 1900 - 1950, by county

- 1001 to 5000 %
- 501 to 1000 %
- *Gain* 1 to 500 %
- *Loss* -90 to 0 %
- No data available

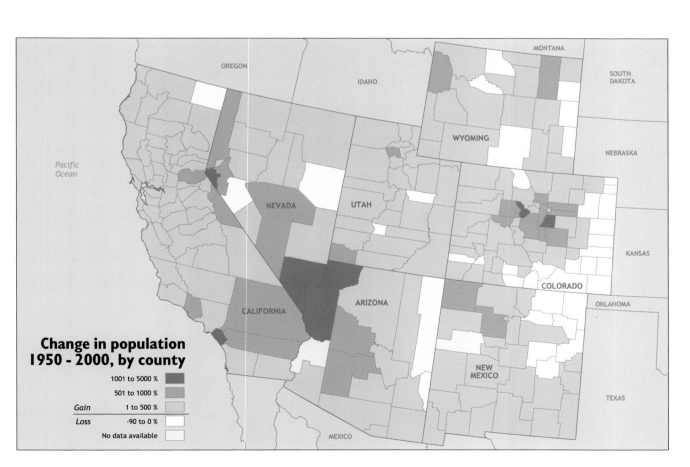

Change in population 1950 - 2000, by county

- 1001 to 5000 %
- 501 to 1000 %
- *Gain* 1 to 500 %
- *Loss* -90 to 0 %
- No data available

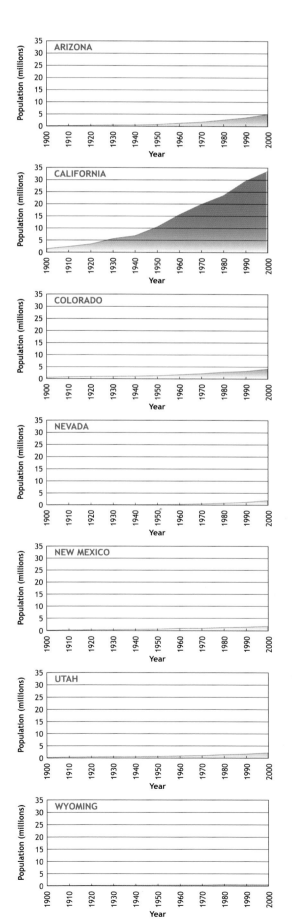

Population Density, Gender, and Age Structure by Census Tract, 1990

Southern California

Data provided by the Population Estimates Program of the U. S. Census Bureau.

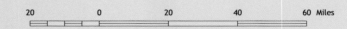

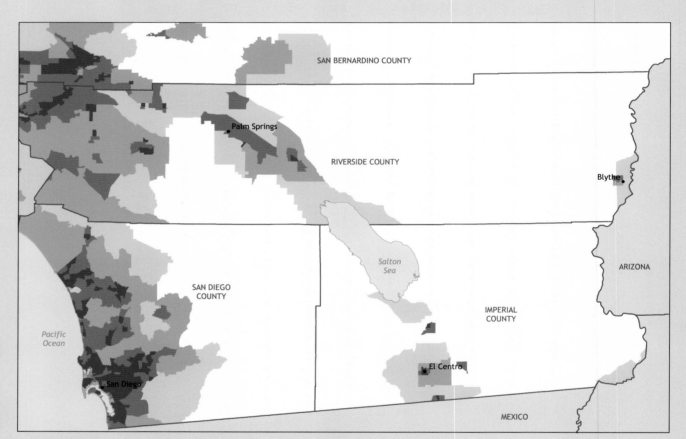

People per square mile

less than 20 people	
20 to 100	
100 to 500	
500 to 3,000	
more than 3,000 people	

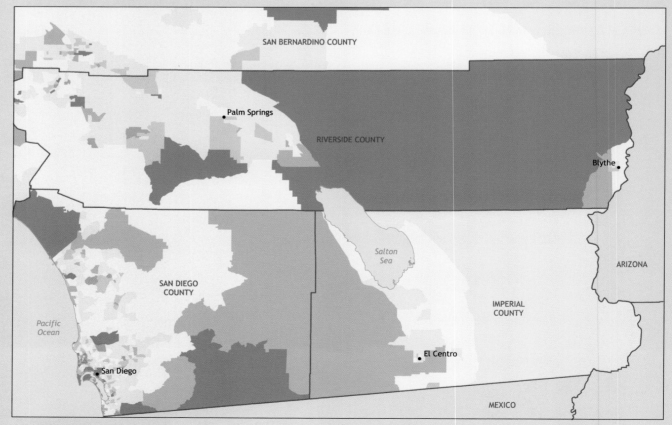

Percentage of the population who are male

	less than 46%
higher percentage of females	46 to 48%
	48 to 50%
higher percentage of males	50 to 52%
	52 to 54%
	greater than 54%

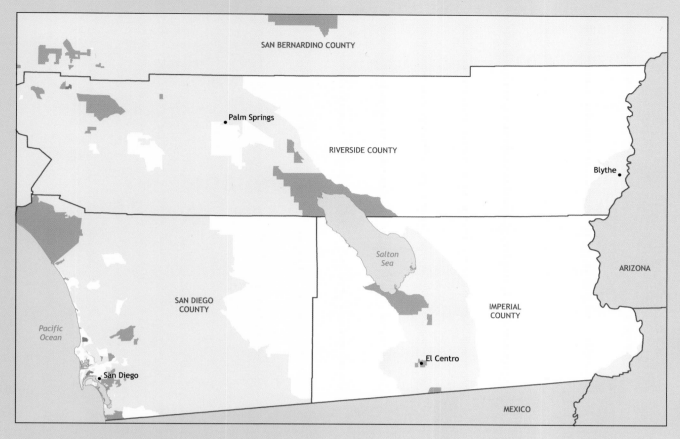

Percentage of the population aged 20 and younger

- less than 20%
- 20 to 40%
- 40 to 60%
- more than 60%

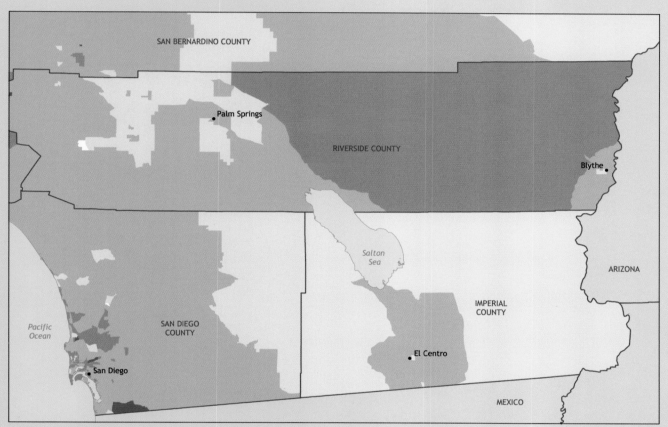

Percentage of the population aged 21 to 54

- less than 20%
- 20 to 40%
- 40 to 60%
- 60 to 80%
- greater than 80%

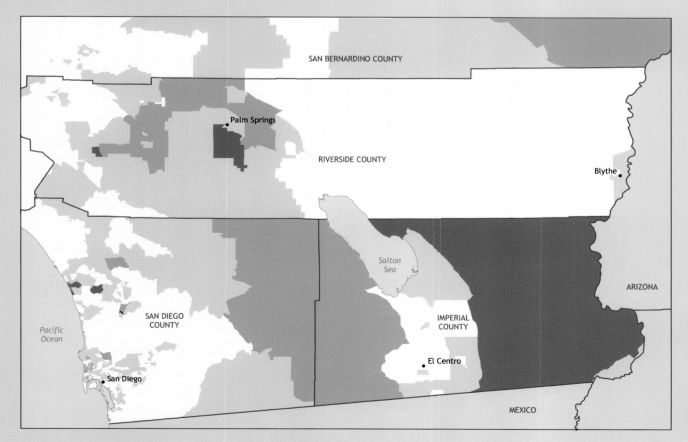

Percentage of the population aged 55 and older

- less than 20%
- 20 to 40%
- 40 to 60%
- 60 to 80%
- greater than 80%

Income, Education, and
Housing Patterns by Census Tract, 1990

Southern California

*Data provided by the Population Estimates
Program of the U. S. Census Bureau.*

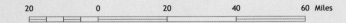

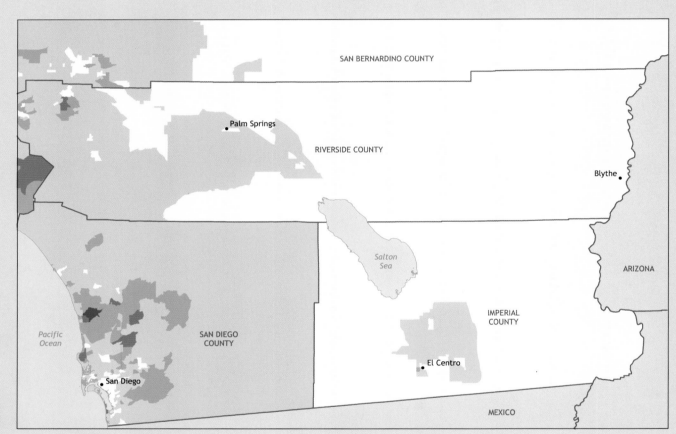

Median annual household income

- less than $25,000
- $25,000 to $50,000
- $50,000 to $75,000
- $75,000 to $100,000
- greater than $100,000

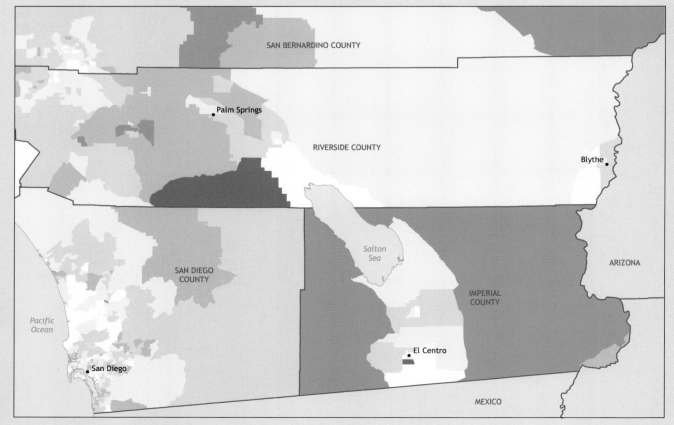

**Percentage of people
who graduated from high school**

- less than 10%
- 10 to 15%
- 15 to 20%
- 20 to 25%
- 25 to 30%
- greater than 30%

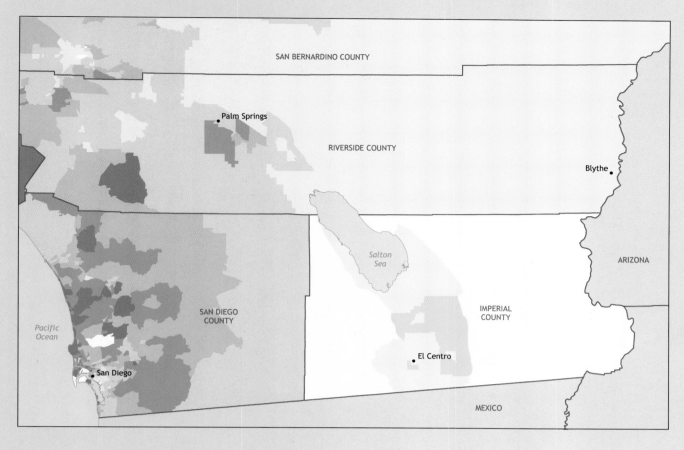

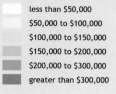

Median property value

- less than $50,000
- $50,000 to $100,000
- $100,000 to $150,000
- $150,000 to $200,000
- $200,000 to $300,000
- greater than $300,000

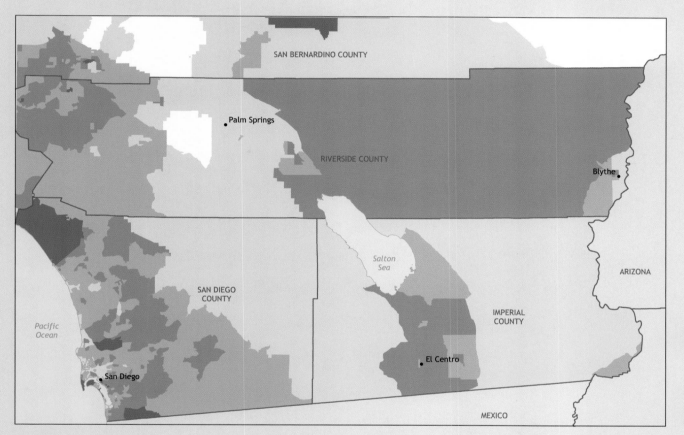

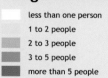

Average number of people living in each home

- less than one person
- 1 to 2 people
- 2 to 3 people
- 3 to 5 people
- more than 5 people

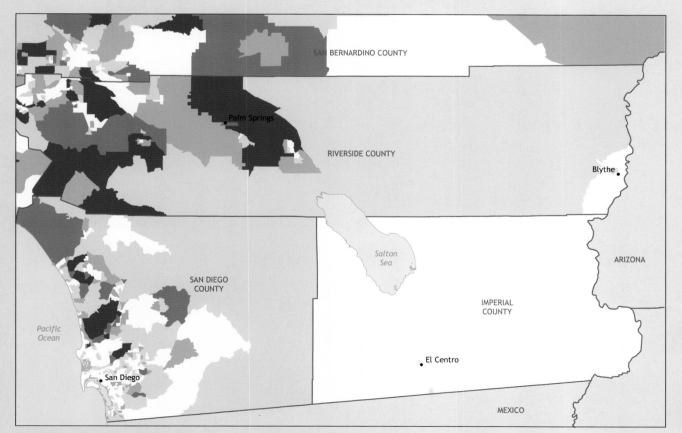

Number of homes built after 1970

- less than 1,000 homes
- 1,000 to 2,000
- 2,000 to 3,000
- 3,000 to 4,000
- more than 4,000 homes

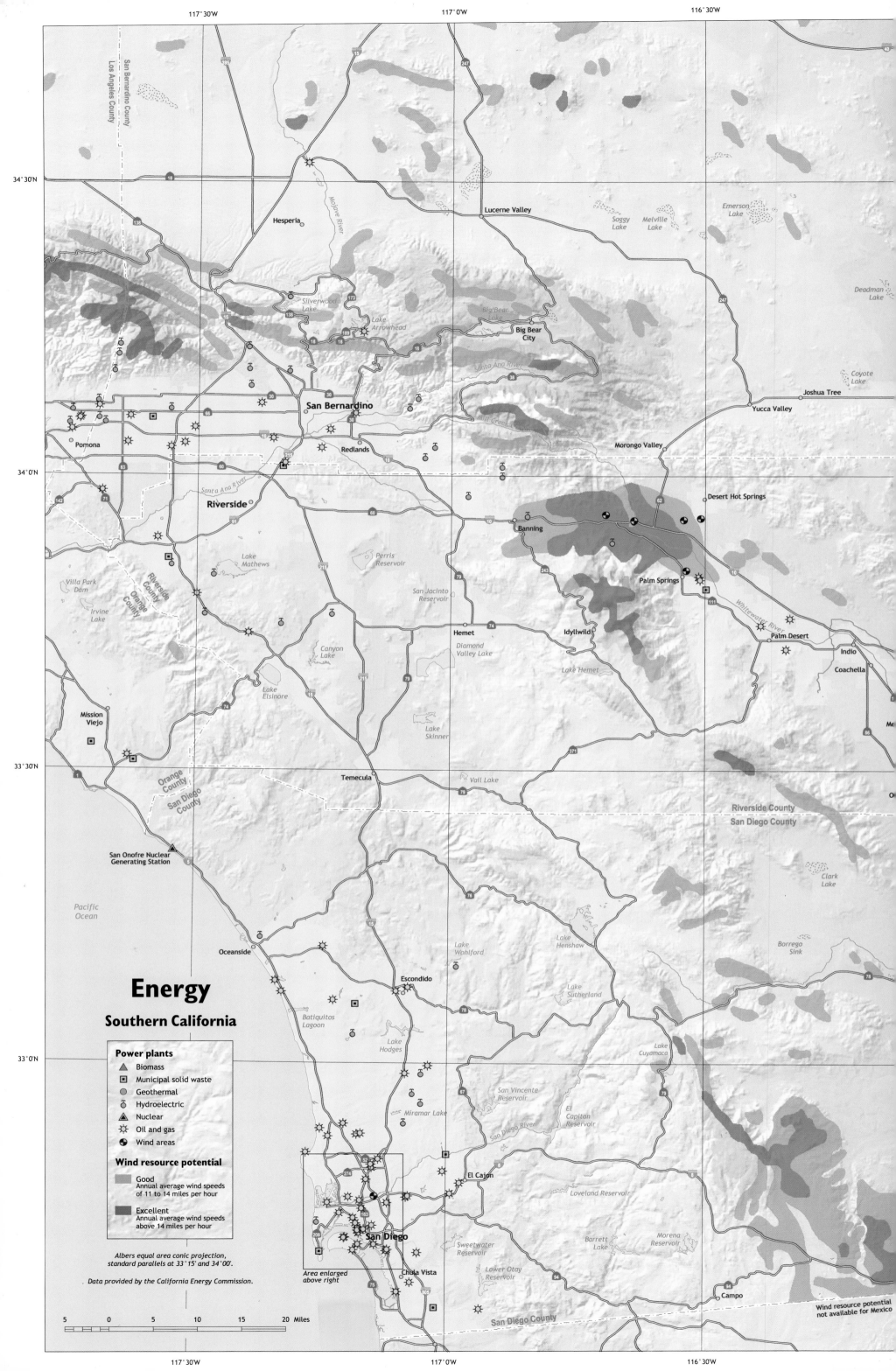

Energy

Southern California

Power plants
- ▲ Biomass
- ▣ Municipal solid waste
- ● Geothermal
- ◔ Hydroelectric
- ▲ Nuclear
- ☼ Oil and gas
- ◍ Wind areas

Wind resource potential

Good
Annual average wind speeds
of 11 to 14 miles per hour

Excellent
Annual average wind speeds
above 14 miles per hour

Albers equal area conic projection,
standard parallels at 33°15' and 34°00'.

Data provided by the California Energy Commission.

Area enlarged
above right

5   0   5   10   15   20 Miles

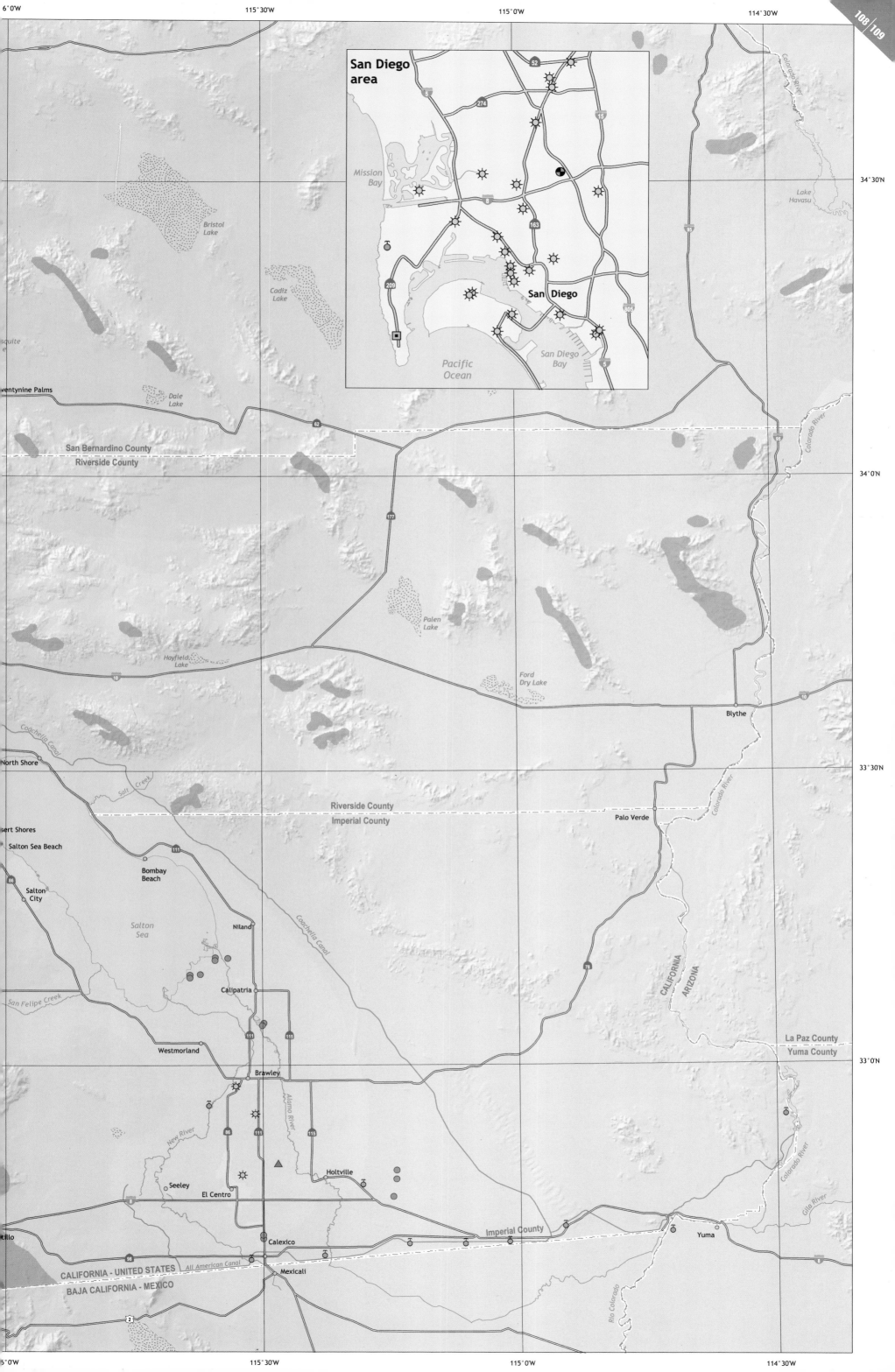

6°0'W 115°30'W 115°0'W 114°30'W

34°30'N

San Diego area

Mission Bay

San Diego

Pacific Ocean

San Diego Bay

Bristol Lake

Cadiz Lake

Lake Havasu

quite e

Twentynine Palms

Dale Lake

San Bernardino County
Riverside County

34°0'N

Palen Lake

Hayfield Lake

Ford Dry Lake

Blythe

North Shore

33°30'N

Riverside County
Imperial County

Palo Verde

sert Shores

Salton Sea Beach

Bombay Beach

Salton City

Salton Sea

Niland

Calipatria

San Felipe Creek

Coachella Canal

CALIFORNIA
ARIZONA

Westmorland

La Paz County
Yuma County

33°0'N

Brawley

Alamo River

New River

Seeley

Holtville

El Centro

Calexico

CALIFORNIA - UNITED STATES   All American Canal

BAJA CALIFORNIA - MEXICO

Mexicali

Yuma

Colorado River

Gila River

Rio Colorado

Coachella Canal

Soft Creek

6°0'W 115°30'W 115°0'W 114°30'W

115°30'W
115°0'W

Desert Center Landfill
(Eagle Mountain)

Desert Center Airport

Facilities
Salton Sea Area

♪ University

H Hospital

☼ Prison

▲ Municipal solid
waste facility

✈ Airport

*Data developed by the Stephen P. Teale
Data Center, GIS Technology Center.*

Chiriaco Summit
Airport

Ironwood State Prison

Chuckawalla Valley
State Prison

33°30'N

Hot Spa Cut and Fill Site

Thiery Creek

Niland Cut
and Fill Site

Bombay
Beach

Niland

Calipatria
Municipal
Airport

Calipatria

Calipatria
State Prison

Palo Verde
Cut and Fill Site

Westmorland

Brawley
Disposal Site

33°0'N

Brawley Municipal Airport

Brawley

Pioneers
Memorial
Hospital

Holtville Disposal Site

Coachella Canal

Imperial Waste Site

Centinela
State Prison

Holtville Airport

Imperial County
Airport

Republic Imperial Landfill

El Centro
Naval Air Facility

Imperial
Valley
College

Holtville

Seeley

El Centro Regional
Medical Center

El Centro

115°30'W
115°0'W

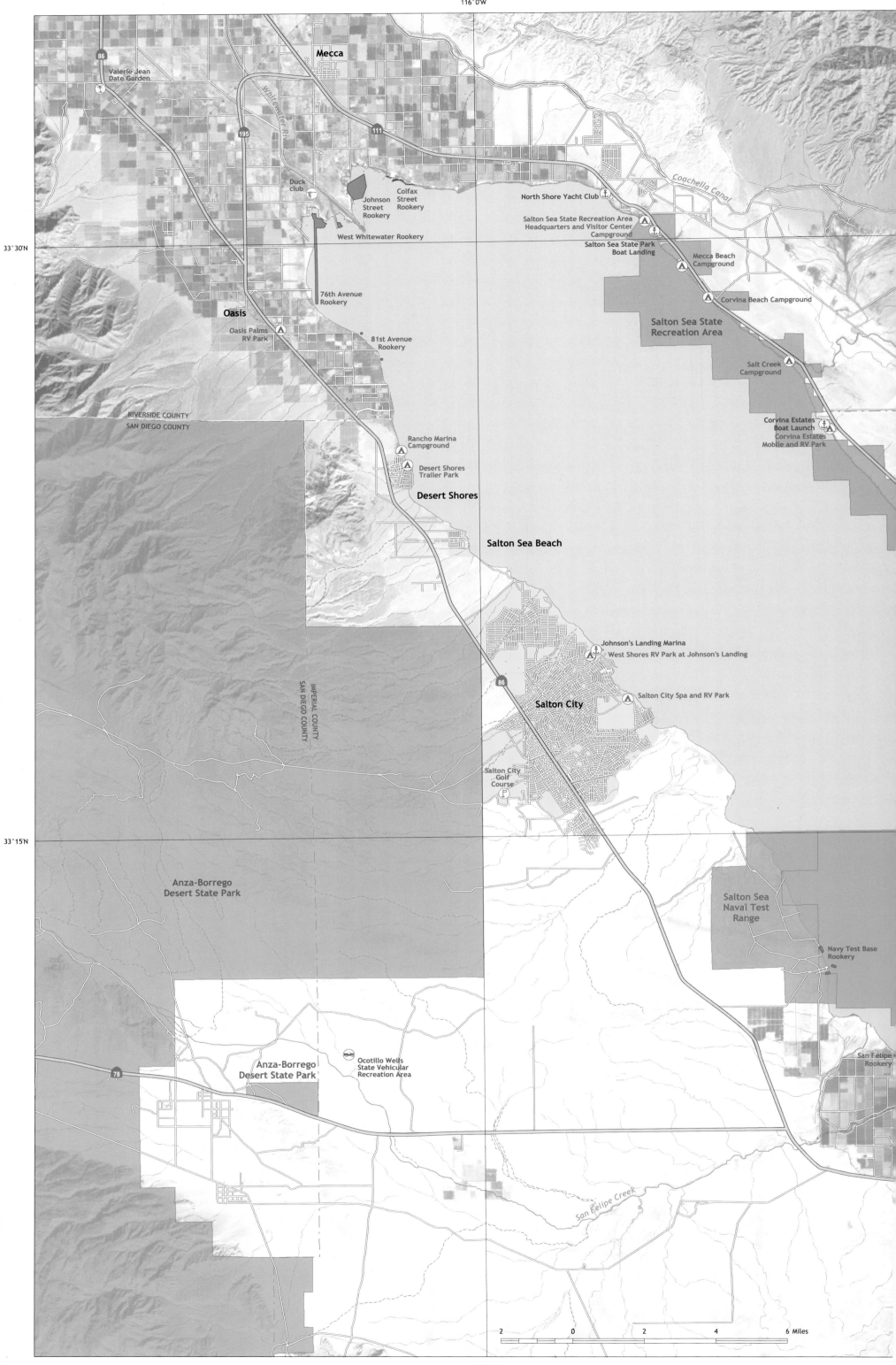

Mecca

Valerie-Jean
Date Garden

Whitewater Rv.

86

195

111

Duck
club

Johnson
Street
Rookery

Colfax
Street
Rookery

West Whitewater Rookery

Coachella Canal

North Shore Yacht Club

Salton Sea State Recreation Area
Headquarters and Visitor Center
Campground

Salton Sea State Park
Boat Landing

Mecca Beach
Campground

Corvina Beach Campground

33°30'N

76th Avenue
Rookery

Oasis

Oasis Palms
RV Park

81st Avenue
Rookery

Salton Sea State
Recreation Area

Salt Creek
Campground

RIVERSIDE COUNTY
SAN DIEGO COUNTY

Corvina Estates
Boat Launch
Corvina Estates
Mobile and RV Park

Rancho Marina
Campground

Desert Shores
Trailer Park

Desert Shores

Salton Sea Beach

IMPERIAL COUNTY
SAN DIEGO COUNTY

Johnson's Landing Marina
West Shores RV Park at Johnson's Landing

86

Salton City Spa and RV Park

Salton City

Salton City
Golf Course

P

33°15'N

Anza-Borrego
Desert State Park

Salton Sea
Naval Test
Range

Navy Test Base
Rookery

Anza-Borrego
Desert State Park

78

Ocotillo Wells
State Vehicular
Recreation Area

San Felipe
Rookery

San Felipe Creek

2   0   2   4   6 Miles

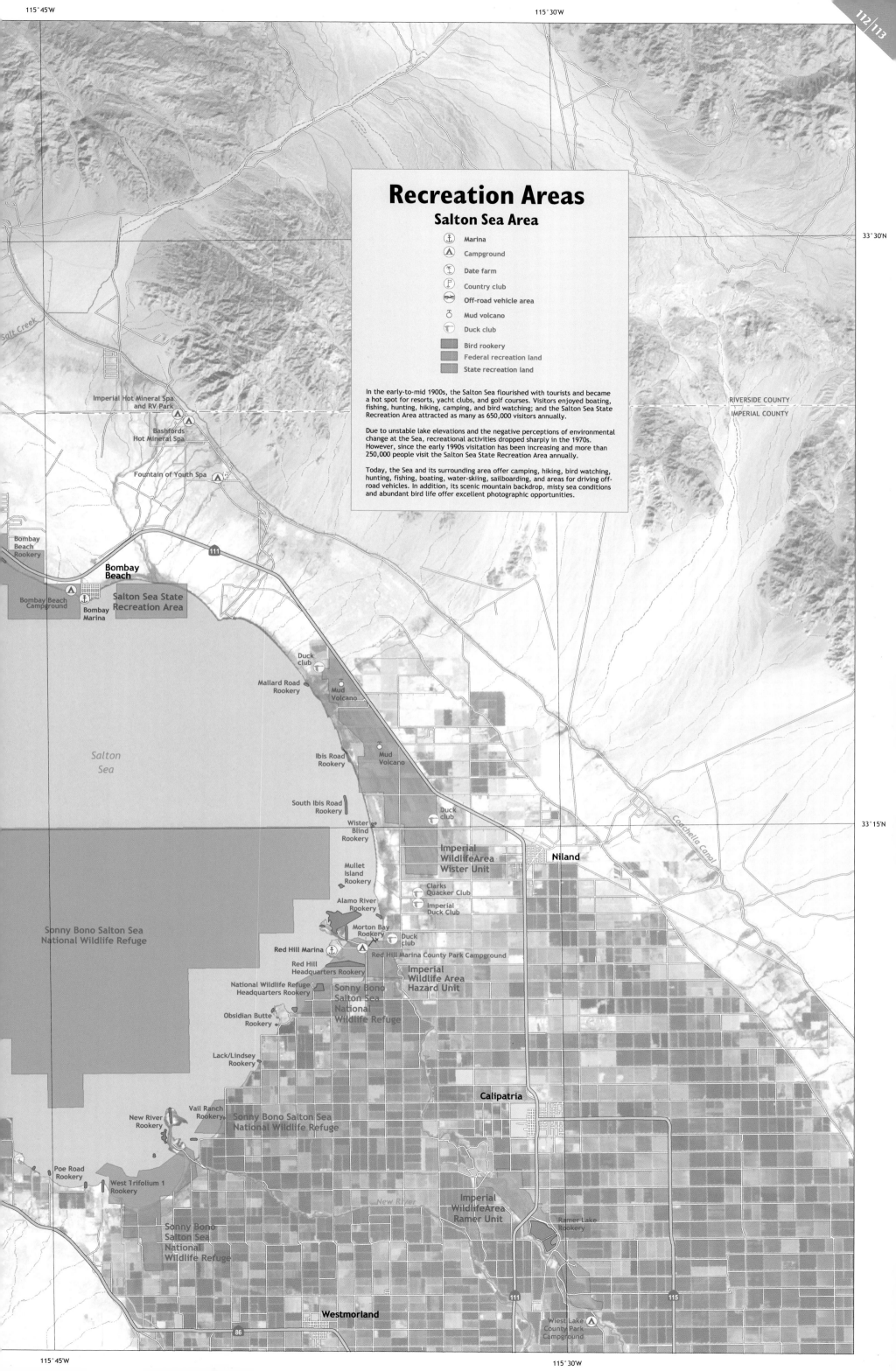

Recreation Areas
Salton Sea Area

⚓ Marina

Ⓐ Campground

⌖ Date farm

Ⓟ Country club

⊘ Off-road vehicle area

○ Mud volcano

⏚ Duck club

▮ Bird rookery

▮ Federal recreation land

▮ State recreation land

In the early-to-mid 1900s, the Salton Sea flourished with tourists and became a hot spot for resorts, yacht clubs, and golf courses. Visitors enjoyed boating, fishing, hunting, hiking, camping, and bird watching; and the Salton Sea State Recreation Area attracted as many as 650,000 visitors annually.

Due to unstable lake elevations and the negative perceptions of environmental change at the Sea, recreational activities dropped sharply in the 1970s. However, since the early 1990s visitation has been increasing and more than 250,000 people visit the Salton Sea State Recreation Area annually.

Today, the Sea and its surrounding area offer camping, hiking, bird watching, hunting, fishing, boating, water-skiing, sailboarding, and areas for driving off-road vehicles. In addition, its scenic mountain backdrop, misty sea conditions and abundant bird life offer excellent photographic opportunities.

115°45'W

115°30'W

33°30'N

RIVERSIDE COUNTY
IMPERIAL COUNTY

Salt Creek

Imperial Hot Mineral Spa and RV Park

Bashfords Hot Mineral Spa

Fountain of Youth Spa

Bombay Beach Rookery

Bombay Beach

Bombay Beach Campground

Bombay Marina

Salton Sea State Recreation Area

111

Duck club

Mallard Road Rookery

Mud Volcano

Salton Sea

Ibis Road Rookery

Mud Volcano

South Ibis Road Rookery

Duck club

Wister Goose Blind Rookery

Imperial Wildlife Area Wister Unit

Niland

33°15'N

Corchella Canal

Mullet Island Rookery

Clarks Quacker Club

Imperial Duck Club

Alamo River Rookery

Morton Bay Rookery

Duck club

Red Hill Marina

Red Hill Marina County Park Campground

Red Hill Headquarters Rookery

Sonny Bono Salton Sea National Wildlife Refuge

Imperial Wildlife Area Hazard Unit

National Wildlife Refuge Headquarters Rookery

Sonny Bono Salton Sea National Wildlife Refuge

Obsidian Butte Rookery

Lack/Lindsey Rookery

Calipatria

Vail Ranch Rookery

New River Rookery

Sonny Bono Salton Sea National Wildlife Refuge

Poe Road Rookery

West Trifolium 1 Rookery

New River

Imperial Wildlife Area Ramer Unit

Sonny Bono Salton Sea National Wildlife Refuge

Ramer Lake Rookery

Westmorland

86

111

115

Wiest Lake County Park Campground

115°45'W

115°30'W

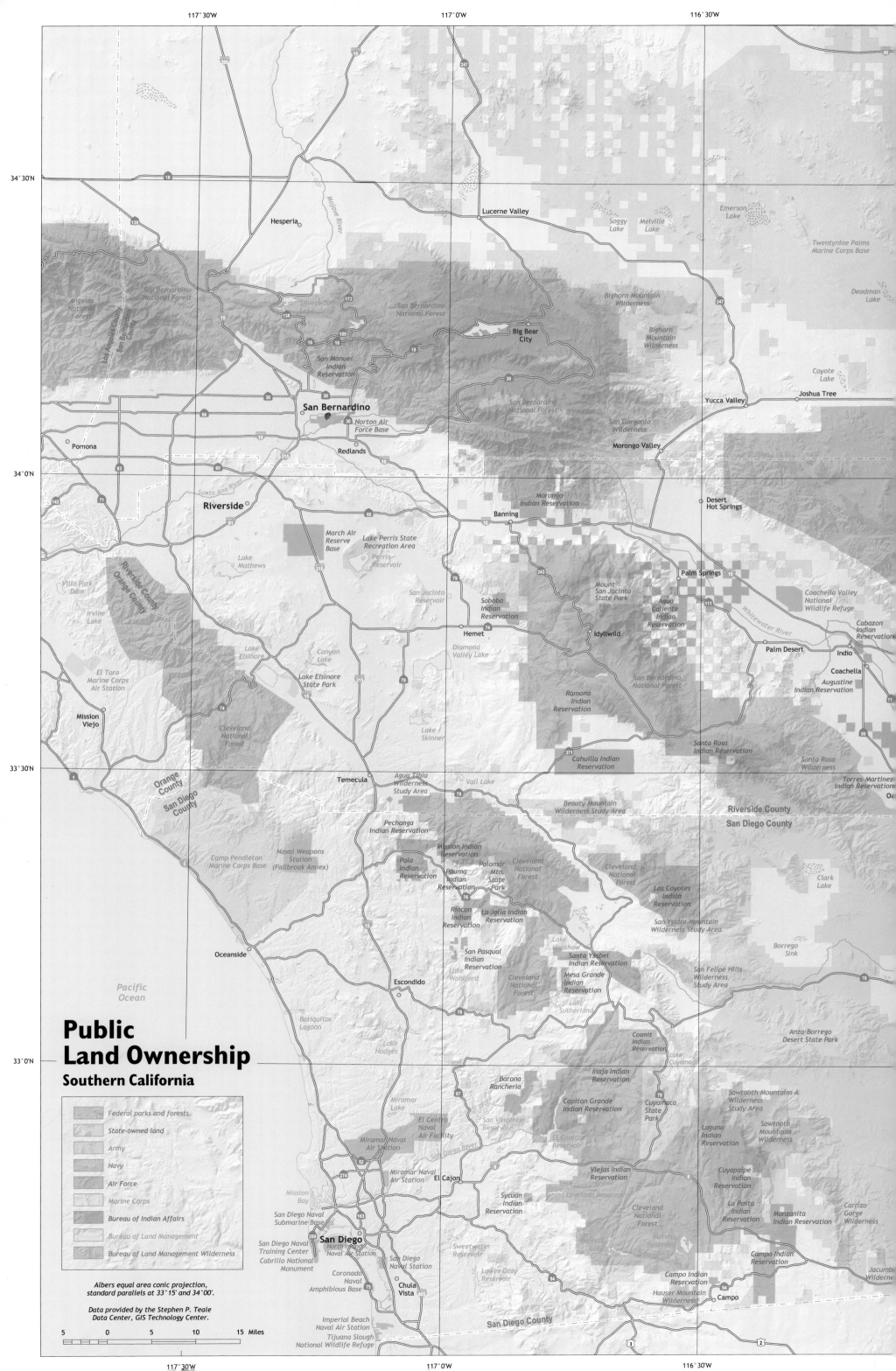

116°0'W   115°30'W   115°0'W   114°30'W

34°30'N

34°0'N

33°30'N

33°0'N

Lake Havasu National Wildlife Refuge

Lake Havasu

Chemehuevi Indian Reservation

Whipple Mountains Wilderness

Turtle Mountains Wilderness

Old Woman Mountains Wilderness

Bristol Lake

Cadiz Dunes Wilderness

Cadiz Lake

Danby Lake

Cleghorn Lakes Wilderness

Sheephole Valley Wilderness

...tynine Palms ...ne Corps Base

...entynine Palms

...entynine Palms ...ian Reservation

Dale Lake

San Bernardino County
Riverside County

177

Riverside Mountains Wilderness

Palen/McCoy Wilderness

Rice Valley Wilderness

Colorado River Indian Reservation

Big Maria Mountains Wilderness

Joshua Tree National Park

Palen/McCoy Wilderness

Palen Lake

Hayfield Lake

Ford Dry Lake

10

Mecca Hills Wilderness

Orocopia Mountains Wilderness

Orocopia Mountains Wilderness

Coachella Canal

North Shore

Chuckwalla Mountains Wilderness

Blythe

CALIFORNIA   ARIZONA

Colorado River

Salt...

Riverside County
Imperial County

Little Chuckwalla Mountains Wilderness

...esert Shores

Salton Sea Beach

Salton Sea State Recreation Area

111

Palo Verde

Palo Verde Mountains Wilderness

Cibola National Forest

Yuma Proving Ground

Bombay Beach

86

Salton City

Salton Sea

Salton Sea Naval Test Range

Imperial Wildlife Area Wister Unit

Chocolate Mountains Naval Aerial Gunnery Range

Niland

Sonny Bono Salton Sea National Wildlife Refuge

Imperial Wildlife Area Hazard Unit

Sonny Bono Salton Sea National Wildlife Refuge

78

Trigo Mountains Wilderness

Calipatria

Imperial Wildlife Area Ramer Unit

Sonny Bono Salton Sea National Wildlife Refuge

111   115

Indian Pass Wilderness

Imperial National Wildlife Refuge

Westmorland

North Algodones Dunes Wilderness

La Paz Co.
Yuma Co.

Picacho State Recreation Area

33°0'N

...reek

...tains ...ness

Brawley

El Centro Naval Auxiliary Air Station

New River

Alamo River

Coachella Canal

Picacho Peak Wilderness

Little Picacho Wilderness

Martinez Lake

Colorado River

Wilderness Study Area

86   111   115

El Centro Naval Auxiliary Air Station

Seeley

Holtville

Fort Yuma Indian Reservation

El Centro

New River

8

Gila River

...otillo

...cumba ...derness

Calexico

Yuma

CALIFORNIA - UNITED STATES

BAJA CALIFORNIA - MEXICO

98

All American Canal

Mexicali

Imperial County

Rio Colorado

Cocopah Indian Reservation

Yuma Marine Corps Air Station

Barry M. Goldwater Air Force Range

2

Laguna Salada

2

116°0'W   115°30'W   115°0'W   114°30'W

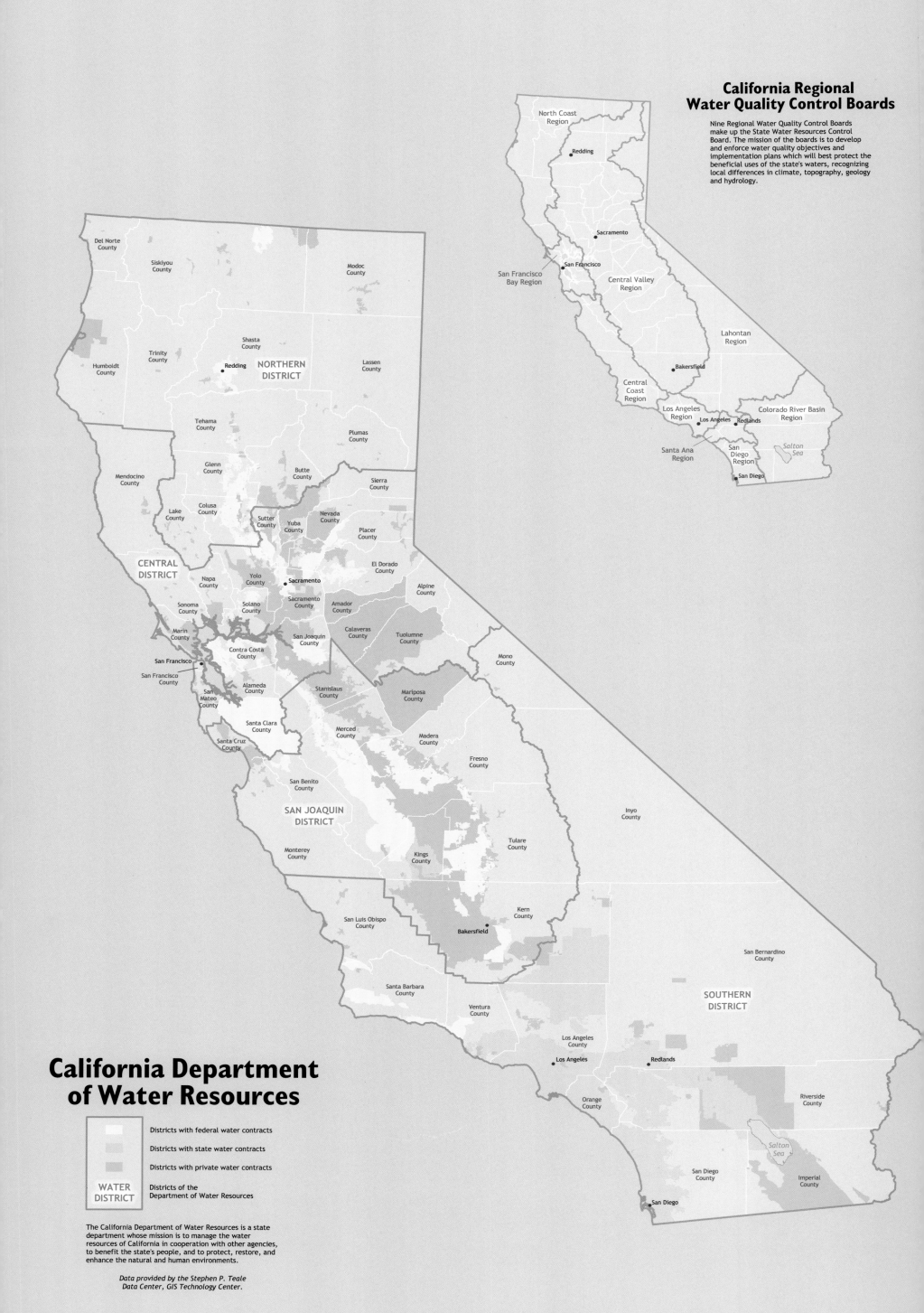

California Regional Water Quality Control Boards

Nine Regional Water Quality Control Boards make up the State Water Resources Control Board. The mission of the boards is to develop and enforce water quality objectives and implementation plans which will best protect the beneficial uses of the state's waters, recognizing local differences in climate, topography, geology and hydrology.

North Coast Region
Redding
Sacramento
San Francisco Bay Region
San Francisco
Central Valley Region
Lahontan Region
Central Coast Region
Bakersfield
Los Angeles Region
Los Angeles
Redlands
Colorado River Basin Region
Santa Ana Region
San Diego Region
San Diego
Salton Sea

Del Norte County
Siskiyou County
Modoc County
Trinity County
Shasta County
Lassen County
Redding
NORTHERN DISTRICT
Humboldt County
Tehama County
Plumas County
Mendocino County
Glenn County
Butte County
Sierra County
Lake County
Colusa County
Nevada County
Sutter County
Yuba County
Placer County
CENTRAL DISTRICT
Napa County
Yolo County
El Dorado County
Sacramento
Alpine County
Sonoma County
Solano County
Sacramento County
Amador County
Marin County
Calaveras County
Tuolumne County
San Joaquin County
Contra Costa County
Mono County
San Francisco
San Francisco County
Stanislaus County
Mariposa County
Alameda County
San Mateo County
Santa Clara County
Merced County
Madera County
Santa Cruz County
San Benito County
Fresno County
Inyo County
SAN JOAQUIN DISTRICT
Monterey County
Kings County
Tulare County
San Luis Obispo County
Kern County
Bakersfield
San Bernardino County
Santa Barbara County
SOUTHERN DISTRICT
Ventura County
Los Angeles County
Riverside County
Los Angeles
Redlands
Orange County
Salton Sea
San Diego County
Imperial County
San Diego

California Department of Water Resources

Districts with federal water contracts

Districts with state water contracts

Districts with private water contracts

WATER DISTRICT
Districts of the Department of Water Resources

The California Department of Water Resources is a state department whose mission is to manage the water resources of California in cooperation with other agencies, to benefit the state's people, and to protect, restore, and enhance the natural and human environments.

Data provided by the Stephen P. Teale Data Center, GIS Technology Center.

California State Responsibility Areas for Fire Protection

State Responsibility Areas (shown in brown) are areas where the California Department of Forestry and Fire Prevention has a legal responsibility to provide fire protection for wildland fires. The California Department of Forestry and Fire Prevention does not have responsibility for densely populated areas, incorporated cities, agricultural lands, or lands administered by the federal government.

Data provided by the Stephen P. Teale Data Center, GIS Technology Center.

State
Senate
Districts

The State Senate and State Assembly
together form the legislative branch of
the California government. The State
Senate is composed of 40 senators
elected for four-year terms.

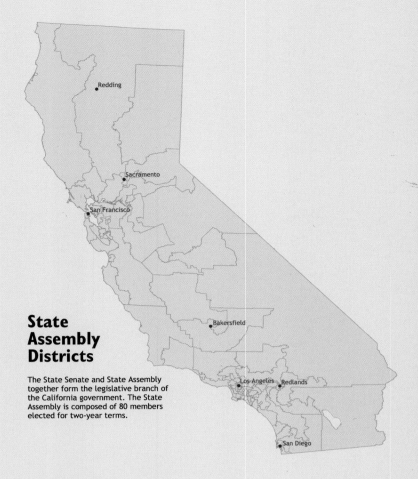

State
Assembly
Districts

The State Senate and State Assembly
together form the legislative branch of
the California government. The State
Assembly is composed of 80 members
elected for two-year terms.

Counties

California
Legislative Boundaries

Results of 2001 Redistricting

Political party

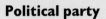

Democrat

Republican

*Data provided by the Stephen P. Teale
Data Center, GIS Technology Center.*

Federal
Congressional
Districts

The Federal Congress is the legislative
branch of the federal government
responsible for making the laws that
govern the nation.

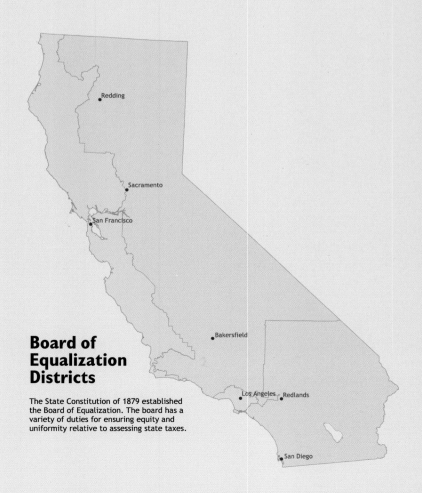

Board of
Equalization
Districts

The State Constitution of 1879 established
the Board of Equalization. The board has a
variety of duties for ensuring equity and
uniformity relative to assessing state taxes.

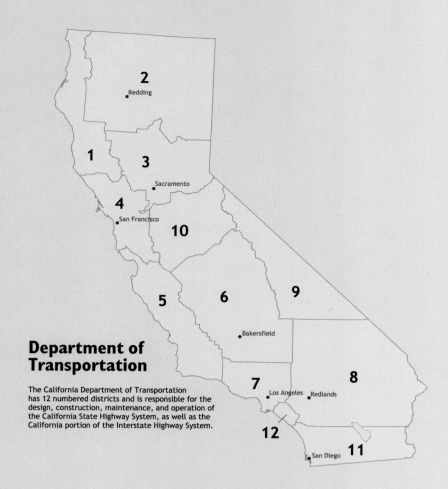

Department of Transportation

The California Department of Transportation has 12 numbered districts and is responsible for the design, construction, maintenance, and operation of the California State Highway System, as well as the California portion of the Interstate Highway System.

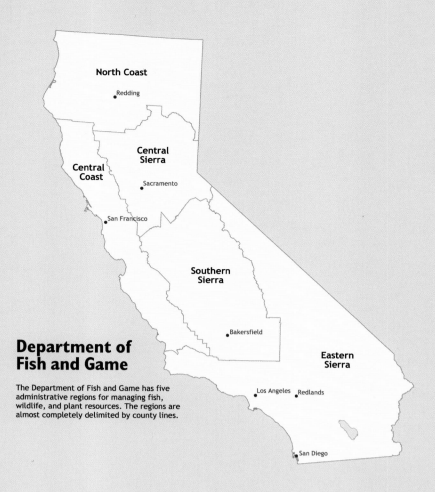

Department of Fish and Game

The Department of Fish and Game has five administrative regions for managing fish, wildlife, and plant resources. The regions are almost completely delimited by county lines.

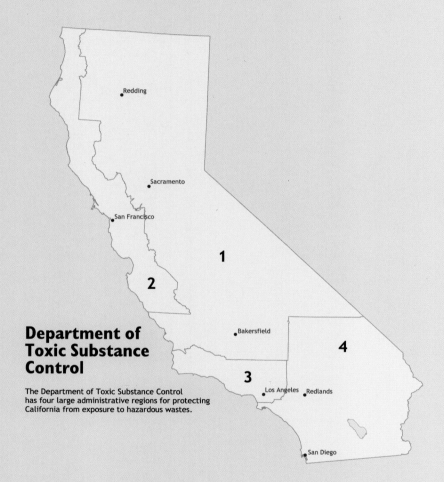

Department of Toxic Substance Control

The Department of Toxic Substance Control has four large administrative regions for protecting California from exposure to hazardous wastes.

California Administrative Boundaries

Data provided by the Stephen P. Teale Data Center, GIS Technology Center.

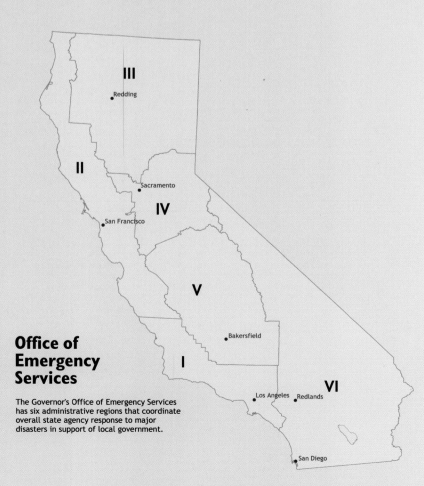

Office of Emergency Services

The Governor's Office of Emergency Services has six administrative regions that coordinate overall state agency response to major disasters in support of local government.

California Air Resources Board

California is divided into 15 regional air basins for managing the state's air resources. Areas within each air basin share the same air masses and are expected to have similar ambient air quality.

Index

Italicized page references denote illustrative content including photos, diagrams, charts, graphs, illustrations, and maps.

Bibliography

Research materials related to the Salton Sea exist in many forms from expert testimonial to electronic statistical data on water supply, and the material continues to grow. This bibliography has consequently been limited to the works used to create this volume. Those readers wishing learn more should visit The Redlands Institute — Salton Sea Database Program Web site at http://institute.redlands.edu/salton.

Introduction

de Buys, W. & Meyers, J. (1999). *Salt dreams: Land and water in low-down California* (1st ed.). Albuquerque, NM: University of New Mexico Press.

Meinig, D. (1978). *The Interpretation of ordinary landscapes*. Oxford: Oxford University Press.

Physical Geography

Abbott, P. L. (Ed.). (1979). *Geological excursions in the Southern California area*. San Diego, CA: San Diego State University Department of Geological Sciences.

Adams, J. M., & Faure, H. (1995). *Global atlas of palaeovegetation since the last glacial maximum*. Quaternary Environments Network. Retrieved from: http://www.soton.ac.uk/~jims/namerica.html.

Babcock, E. A. (1974). Geology of the northeast margin of the Salton trough, Salton Sea, California. *Geological Society of America Bulletin*, 85, 321-322. Boulder, CO: Geological Society of America.

Benson, L. (1969). *The native cacti of California*. Stanford, CA: Stanford University Press.

California Bureau of Land Management. (2000). *Imperial Sand Dunes: BLM Recreation & Wilderness Area*. Retrieved from: http://www.desertusa.com/sandhills/sandhillsorg.html.

California Department of Conservation Division of Mines and Geology (n. d.) *Geology and mineral resources of Imperial County, California*, (County Report 7), Sacramento, CA: California Department of Conservation Division of Mines and Geology.

California Department of Water Resources. (2001). *Imperial CIMIS data*. Retrieved from: http://www.dpla.water.ca.gov/cgi-bin/cimis/cimis/data/get_data.

California Regional Water Quality Control Board & State Water Resources Control Board. (1994). *Water quality control plan: Colorado River basin - Region 7*. (Sacramento, CA): State Water Resources Control Board.

Christopherson, R. W. (1994). *Geosystems: An introduction to physical geography* (2nd ed.). Englewood Cliffs, NJ: MacMillan College Publishing Company.

Coachella Valley Water District. (2000). *Coachella Valley draft water management plan*. Montgomery Watson.

Cohen, M. J., Morrison, J. I., & Glenn, E. P. (1999). *Haven or hazard: The ecology and future of the Salton Sea*. Oakland, CA: Pacific Institute.

Cole, K. (2001). *Packrat middens*. USGS Forest and Rangeland Ecosystem Science Center, Colorado Plateau Field Station. Retrieved from: http://www.usgs.nau.edu/Methods/middens.html.

Columbia Encyclopedia. (2000). *Encyclopedia.com: Mojave Desert* (6th). Retrieved from: http://www.encyclopedia.com/articles/08617.html.

Corona, F. V., & Sabins, F. F. (1993). *The San Andreas fault of the Salton trough region, California, as expressed on remote sensing data*. San Bernardino County Museum Association.

Dainer, J. S. (Webmaster). (1999). *Lower Colorado River*. Retrieved from: http://www.sci.sdsu.edu/salton/Lower_Colorado_River.html.

Earthquakes, active faults, and geothermal areas in the Imperial Valley, California. (1975). *Science*, 188, 1.

Emmel, T. C., & Emmel, J. F. (1973). *The butterflies of Southern California*. Los Angeles, CA: Anderson, Ritchie and Simon.

ESRI. (1999). *ESRI data & maps*, [CD-Rom]. Redlands, CA: ESRI, Inc.

Fuis, G. S., & Kohler, W. M. (1984). *Crustal structure and tectonics of the Imperial Valley region, California*. Menlo Park, CA: U. S. Geological Survey.

Geothermal Education Office. (1997). *United States*. Retrieved from: http://geothermal.marin.org/map/usa.html.

Godfrey, B. (1999). *State climate services for Idaho*. State Climate Services, Biological & Agricultural Engineering Department, University of Idaho. Retrieved from: http://snow.ag.uidaho.edu/Clim_Map.

Grabau, A. W. (1920). *Geology of the non-metallic mineral deposits other than silicates (first ed., Vol. 1 Principles of Salt Deposition)*. New York: McGraw-Hill Book Company, Inc.

Greeley, R., Spudis, P. D., Papson, R.P., & Wormer, M.B. (Eds.). (1978). *Aeolian features of Southern California: A comparative planetary geology guidebook*. Washington, D. C.: U. S. Government Printing Office.

Hely, A. G., & Peck, E. L. (1964). *Precipitation, runoff and water loss in the lower Colorado River—Salton Sea area* (Professional Paper 486-B). Washington, D. C.: U. S. Department of the Interior and the U. S. Weather Bureau.

Jameson, E. W. J., & Peeters, H. J. (1988). *California mammals*. Berkeley, CA: University of California Press.

Krantz, T. P. (1994). *A phytogeography of the San Bernardino Mountains, San Bernardino County, California*. Unpublished Doctoral dissertation, University of California Berkeley.

Larsen, S. & Reilinger, R. (1991). Age constraints for the present fault configuration in the Imperial Valley, California: Evidence for northwestward propagation of the Gulf of California rift system. *Journal of Geophysical Research*, 96 (No. B6), 10,339-310,346.

MacDonald, G. M. (n.d.) *Ice ages, packrats and ancient trees: Climatic environmental change in the Salton Sea region and Colorado River basin (Draft 2)*. Los Angeles, CA: University of California, Los Angeles.

McDougall, K., Poore, R., & Matti, J. (1999). Age and paleoenvironment of the Imperial formation near San Gorgonio Pass, Southern California. *Journal of Foraminiferal Research*, 29(1), 4-25.

McKibben, M. (1993). The salton trough rift. *SBCMA Spec. Publ*. 93- 1, 76- 80.

McNab, W. H., & Avers, P. E. (1996). *Chapter 40: Ecological subregions of the United States*. U.S.D.A. Forest Service. Retrieved from: http://www.fs.fed.us/land/pubs/ecoregions/ch40.html.

Merifield, P. M., & Lamar, D. L. (1975). *Faults on Skylab imagery of the Salton Sea trough area, Southern California (Vol. Part 4)*. Santa Monica, CA: California Earth Sciences Corp.

Merriam, C. H. (1898). Life zones and crop zones of the United States: *U. S. D. A. Biological Survey Bulletin*. Washington, D. C.: United States Government Printing Office.

Miller, D. M. (2000) *Geology and seismicity of the Salton Basin*. 2000 Salton Sea Science Symposium.

National Climate Data Center (n. d.). *San Diego monthly precipitation*. Reno, NV: Western Regional Climate Center.

National Climate Data Center (n. d.). *San Diego monthly temperature*. Reno, NV: Western Regional Climate Center.

National Geographic Society. (1999). *Atlas of the World (7th ed.)*, Washington, D. C.: National Geographic Society.

National Park Service. (2001). *Mojave National Preserve: North American deserts*. Retrieved from: http://www.nps.gov/moja/mojadena.htm.

National Weather Service. (2001). *Annual average precipitation of Southern California period: 1961-1990*. Retrieved from: http://www.nws.mbay.net/CA_SOUTH.GIF.

Northern Arizona University. (2000). *Biotic communities of the Colorado plateau*. Colorado Plateau Land Use History of North America. Northern Arizona University. Retrieved from: http://www.cpluhna.nau.edu/Biota/merriam.htm.

Ohio Department of Natural Resource, Division of Geological Survey (1999). *Lake Erie geology*. Glenn Larson. Retrieved from: http://www.ohiodnr.com/geosurvey/lakeeerie/lakeerie.htm.

Plagens, M. J. (2001). *Sonoran Desert naturalist*, Retrieved from: http://members.aol.com/Melasoma/index.html.

Powell, C. L. (1993). *Macrofossils from the imperial formation in the Ocotillo Wells State Vehicle Recreation Area, Imperial and San Diego Counties, California* (open file report 93- 562). Menlo Park, CA: U. S. Geological Survey.

Powell, C. L. (1995). *Paleontology and significance of the Imperial formation at Garnet Hill, Riverside County, California* (open-file report 95- 489). Menlo Park, CA: U. S. Geological Survey.

Powell, C. L. (1997). *A record of the inarticulate brachiopod glottidia from the ancestral Gulf of California (miocene to pliocene Imperial formation), Southern California* (open-file report 97- 538). Menlo Park, CA: U.S. Geological Survey.

Powell, C. L., & Stevens, D. (2000). *Age and paleoenvironmental significance of mega-invertebrates from the " San Pedro" formation in the Coyote Hills, Fullerton and Buena Park, Orange County, Southern California* (open-file report 00-319). Menlo Park, CA: U. S. Geological Survey.

Rand McNally & Delf, B. (ill.). (1993). *Picture atlas of the world* (rev. ed.). Chicago, IL: Rand McNally.

Rymer, M. J., Powell, C. L., & Wojcicki, A. S. (1995). *Late miocene stratigraphic and paleographic setting of Garnet Hill in the northwestern Salton trough, Southern California Vol. 79*.

Salton Sea Authority. (2001). *Sea notes: a newsletter of the Salton Sea Restoration Project*. La Quinta, CA: Salton Sea Authority.

Savage, J. C., Prescott, W. H., Lisowski, M., & King, N. (1979). Deformation across the Salton trough, California, 1973-1977. *Journal of Geophysical Research*, 84, 3069. Washington, D. C.: American Geophysical Union.

Singer, E. (1998). *Geology of the Imperial Valley California: A monograph*. Eugene Singer. Retrieved from: http://www.aloha.net/~esinger/homegeol.

Smith, T., & Chisholm, L. (1997). *Geomorphic provinces*. California Department of Conservation, Division of Mines & Geology. Retrieved from: http://www.consrv.ca.gov/dmg/pubs/notes/36/index.htm.

Stebbins, R. C. (1966). *A field guide to western reptiles and amphibians*. Boston: Houghton Mifflin Company.

Stewart, B. (1997). *Common butterflies of California*. Patagonia, AZ: West Coast Lady Press.

Takhtajan, A. (1986). *Floristic regions of the world*. Berkeley, CA: University of California Press.

Tucker, A. B., Feldmann, R. M., & Powell, C. L. (1994). *Speocarcinus berglundi N. SP. (Decapoda: Brachyura), a new crab from the Imperial formation (late miocene-late pliocene) of Southern California*. *Journal of Paleontology*, 68(4), 800- 807. Tulsa, OK.: Society of Economic Paleontologists and Mineralogists.

United States Census Bureau. (2002). *Topologically integrated geographic encoding and referencing system*. Retrieved from: http://www.census.gov/geo/www/tiger/index.html.

U. S. Geological Survey. (1997). *Global 30-arc-second elevation data set*. U. S. Geological Survey. Retrieved from: http://edc.usgs.gov/glis/hyper/guide/gtopo_30.

U. S. Geological Survey. (1999). *Shrinking Farallon plate*. Retrieved from: http://pubs.usgs.gov/publications/text/Farallon.html.

U. S. Geological Survey. (1999). *Transform boundaries*. Retrieved from:http://pubs.usgs.gov/publications/text/understanding.html.

U. S. Geological Survey. (2000). *California earthquake history 1769 - present*. Retrieved from: http://pasadena.wr.usgs.gov/cahist_eqs.html.

U. S. Geological Survey. (2000). *Landsat enhanced thematic mapper*, [CD-Rom]. Washington, D. C.: U. S. Geological Survey, Eros Data Center.

U. S. Geological Survey. (2000). *Water resources in California project description: Measurement and analysis of potential land subsidence in Coachella*. Retrieved from: http://ca.water.usgs.gov/projects00/ca517.html.

U. S. Geological Survey. (2001). *Calendar year streamflow statistics for the nation*. Retrieved from: http://waterdata.usgs.gov/nwis/annual.

U. S. Geological Survey National Park Service. (2001). *Geologic provinces of the United States*. Retrieved from: http://geology.wr.usgs.gov/docs/usgsnps/province/province.html.

Vaughan, T. W. (1906). *The reef-coral fauna of Carrizo Creek, Imperial County, California, and its significance* (Prof. Paper). Washington, D. C.: US Government Printing Office.

Veirs, S. D. J., & Opler, P. A. (1998). *California.*
Retrieved from: http://biology.usgs.gov/s+t/SNT/noframe/ca162.htm.

Wells, S. G., Connell, S., & Martin, J. J. (1993). Geomorphic and soil stratigraphic evaluation of a faulted alluvial sequence, eastern Coachella Valley, California. *SBCMA Spec. Publ.* 93-1, 39-49.

Western Regional Climate Center. (2000). *Imperial, California (044223): Period of record monthly climate summary 7/1/1948- 7/31/2000.* Retrieved from: wrcc@dri.edu.

Western Regional Climate Center. (2000). *Southern California climate summaries.*
Retrieved from: http://www.wrcc.dri.edu/summary/climsmsca.html.

Western Regional Climate Center. (2001). *Yuma Citrus Station, Arizona.*
Retrieved from: http://www.wrcc.dri.edu/cgi-bin/cliF30.pl?azyucs.

Woodward, S. (1996). *Merriam's life zones.*
Retrieved from: http://www.radford.edu/~swoodwar/CLASSES/GEOG235/lifezone/merriam.html.

World Meteorological Organization. (2001). *WMO statement on the status of the global climate in 2000.* Geneva, Switzerland.

Zabriskie, J.G. (1979). *Plants of Deep Canyon and the central Coachella Valley, California.* Riverside, CA: Philip L. Boyd Deep Canyon Desert Research Center, University of California, Riverside.

Cultural History

Agricultural Commissioner. (1991). *1990 Agricultural crop & livestock report, Imperial Valley.* Imperial.

Agua Caliente Band of Cahuilla Indians. *Agua Caliente tribal history.*
Retrieved from: http://www.aguacaliente.org/acthis.html.

American Farm Bureau Federation & Chenango County Farm Bureau. (2000). *Chenango County Farm Bureau: Events in agriculture history.* Chenango County Farm Bureau.
Retrieved from: http://www.norwich.net/~fb/aghistry.htm.

American Geographical Society. (1933). *Map of The Colorado Delta region.* San Diego State University Center for Inland Waters. Retrieved from: http://www.sci.sdsu.edu/salton/CoRDeltaFull.JPEG.

Arizona Department of Water Resources. (1999). *Third management plan for Tucson active management area 2000-2010.* Phoenix, AZ Arizona Department of Water Resources.

Association of California Water Agencies. (2000). *Water facts: Colorado River.*
Retrieved from: http://www.acwanet.com/waterfacts/colorado.html.

Bazdarich, M. J. Water economics and the Salton Sea (n. d.). *Inland Empire Review, vol. 7,* 6. Riverside, CA: Inland Empire Economic Databank and Forecasting Center, Graduate School of Management, University of California, Riverside.

Bean, L. J. (1978). Cahuilla. In W. C. Sturtevant (Ed.). *Handbook of North American Indians* (Vol. 8, pp. 575 - 587). Washington, D. C.: Smithsonian Institution.

Bean, L. J., & Saubel, K. S. (1972). *Temalpakh (from the Earth): Cahuilla Indian knowledge and usage of plants.* Morongo Indian Reservation, CA: Malki Museum Press.

Bean, L. J., & Shipek, F. C. (1978). Luiseño. In W. C. Sturtevant (Ed.). *Handbook of North American Indians* (Vol. 8, pp. 550 - 563). Washington, D. C.: Smithsonian Institute.

Bean, L. J., & Smith, C. R. (1978). Cupeño. In W. C. Sturtevant (Ed.). *Handbook of North American Indians* (Vol. 8 California, pp. 588 - 591). Washington, D. C.: Smithsonian Institution.

Bean, L. J., & Smith, C. R. (1978). Gabrieleño. In W. C. Sturtevant (Ed.). *Handbook of North American Indians* (Vol. 8, pp. 538 - 549). Washington, D. C.: Smithsonian Institution.

Bean, L. J., & Smith, C. R. (1978). Serrano. In W. C. Sturtevant (Ed.). *Handbook of North American Indians* (Vol. 8, pp. 570 - 574). Washington, D. C.: Smithsonian Institution.

Bee, R. L. (1983). Quechan. In W. C. Sturtevant (Ed.). *Handbook of North American Indian* (Vol. 10, pp. 86 - 98). Washington, D. C.: Smithsonian Institute.

Beidelman, K. (n. d.) *Native American living conditions and history by region.* Karen Beidelman.
Retrieved from: http://php.iupui.edu/~kmbeidel/webquest/NAlivcon.htm.

Birdsall, S. L. (2000). *Imperial County Agricultural Commissioner's 1999 agricultural crop and livestock report.* Imperial, CA: Agricultural Commission.

Black, G. F. (1985). The Salton Sea sport fishery Region Five informational bulletin (bulletin 0010-5-1985). Sacramento, CA: State of California The Resources Agency Department of Fish and Game.

Blake, W. (1857). *Report of explorations in California for railroad routes, to connect with the routes near the 35th and 32nd parallels of north latitude, by Lieutenant R. S. Williamson.* Geological report.

Boettcher, S., & Trinklein, M. (1997). *The Gold Rush: Discovery.* PBS Online.
Retrieved from: http://www.isu.edu/~trinmich/discovery.html.

Bogdan, S. (2000, Nov/Dec 2000). The birth of a valley. *Valley Grower,* 25-29. El Centro, CA: M. V. Productions.

Bogert, M. F. M. The History of Palm Springs: An Indian beginning. *Palm Springs First Hundred Years* (pp. 4).

Bolton, H. E. (c. 1916). *Spanish exploration in the Southwest 1542-1706.* New York: Charles Scribner's Sons.

Bolton, H. E. (c. 1930, 1966). *Anza's California expeditions, volume 1: An Outpost of empire* (Vol. 1). New York: Russell & Russell.

Bombardier, T. (n. d.) *Estimated annual water use.* San Diego, CA: San Diego County Water Authority.

Cabazon Band of Mission Indians. (8/14/01). *Who we are.*
Retrieved from: http://www.cabazonindians.com/who.html.

California Bureau of Land Management. (2001). *Old Plank Road BLM recreation & wilderness area.* Digital West Media, Inc. Retrieved from: http://www.desertusa.com/sandhills/plankrd.html.

California Environmental Resources Evaluation System. (8/13/99). *State historical landmarks Imperial County.* Retrieved from: http://www.ceres.ca.gov/geo_area/counties/Imperial/landmarks.html.

California Historical Society. *Riverside County historical agencies.* California Historical Society.
Retrieved from: http://www.calhist.org/Support_Info/CHAs.htmld /CHA-Riverside.html.

California State Department of Finance. *Historical census population of places, towns, and cities in California, 1850-1990,* Demographic Research Unit.
Retrieved from: http://www.dof.ca.gov/HTML/DEMOGRAP/histtext.htm.

Central Arizona Project. *Historic timeline.* Retrieved from: http:www.cap-az.com/about/history/timeline.

Chenango County Farm Bureau. *Significant events in agricultural history.*
Retrieved from: http://www.norwich.net/~fb/aghistry.htm.

CIC Research, I. (1989). *The Economic importance of the Salton Sea sportfishery.*
Retrieved from: http://www.sci.sdsu.edu/salton/EconImpSSSportfishery3.htm.

City of Los Angeles Water Services (n. d.). *Major aqueduct systems serving Southern California.*
Retrieved from: http://www.ladwp.com/water/supply/aqua.htm.

City of Los Angeles Water Services (n. d.). *Metropolitan Water District of Southern California.* Retrieved from: http://www.ladwp.com/water/supply/MWD/index.htm.

City of Los Angeles Water Services (n. d.). *Water supply fact sheet.*
Retrieved from: http://www.ladwp.com/water/supply/facts/index.htm.

Cleland, J. H., York, A., & Johnson, A (n. d.). *The tides of history: Modeling Native American use of recessional shorelines.* San Diego, CA: KEA Environmental, Inc. Retrieved from: http://www.esri.com/library/userconf/proc00/professional/papers/PAP377/p.377.htm.

Coachella Valley Water District (n. d.). *Coachella Valley Water District, District boundary and ET map.* Coachella Valley, CA: Coachella Valley Water District.

Coachella Valley Water District. (1999). *Annual review 1999.* Coachella Valley, CA: Coachella Valley Water District.

Coachella Valley Water District. (2000). *Coachella Valley draft water management plan.* Coachella Valley, CA: Coachella Valley Water District.

Colorado River Board of California. (1992). *Report to the California Legislature on the current conditions of the Salton Sea and the potential impacts of water transfers.* Palm Desert, CA: Water Quality Control Board.

Colorado River Board of California. (2000). *California's Colorado River water use plan (DRAFT).* Palm Desert, CA: Colorado River Water Quality Control Board.

Colorado River Board of California. (2000). *Colorado River Board of California.*
Retrieved from: http://ceres.ca.gov/crb.

Colorado River Water Users Association. *California Colorado River profile.* Colorado River Water Users Association. Retrieved from: http://crwua.mwd.dst.ca.us/ca/crwua_ca.htm.

Colorado River Water Users Association. *Colorado River at a glance: Colorado River profile.* Colorado River Water Users Association. Retrieved from: http://crwua.mwd.dst.ca.us/tcr/crwua_tc.htm.

Colorado River Water Users Association. *Law of the river: The Colorado River compact.* Colorado River Water Users Association. Retrieved from: http://crwua.mwd.dst.ca.us/lor/crwua_lor.htm.

Colorado River Water Users Association. *Urban use along the river.* Colorado River Water Users Association. Retrieved from: Amrivers.localweb.com/20-6.html.

Davis, J. T. *Trade routes and economic exchange among the Indians of California.*
Retrieved from: http://www.snowcrest.net/geography/trade/caltrade.htm.

deBuys, W., & Myers, J. (1999). *Salt dreams: Land and water in low-down California* (1st ed.). Albuquerque, NM: University of New Mexico Press.

Department of Parks and Recreation, & Area, Salton Sea State Recreation Area. Department of Water Resources, Division of Planning and Local Assistance. (1994). *Bulletin 160-93, The California water plan update, October 1994.* Retrieved from: http://rubicon.water.ca.gov/vlcwp/tbls/t6-4.html; http://rubicon.water.ca.gov/vlcwp/tbls/t6-5.html.

Department of Water Resources, Division of Planning and Local Assistance (1998). *California water plan update bulletin 160-98.* Sacramento, CA: California Department of Water Resources.

El Centro Chamber of Commerce & Visitors Bureau (n. d.). *History.* Conveyor Group.
Retrieved from: http://www.elcentrochamber.com/history.htm.

Encyclopedia Britannica. (n. d.). *Chemehuevi.*
Retrieved from: http://www.britannica.com/eb/article?eu=127686.

Encyclopedia Britannica. (n.d.). *Chumash.* Retrieved from: http://www.britannica.com/eb/article?eu=84710.

Encyclopedia Britannica. (n.d.). *Diegueño.* Retrieved from: http://www.britannica.com/eb/article?eu=30874.

Encyclopedia Britannica. (n.d.). *Gabrieleño.* Retrieved from: http://www.britannica.com/eb/article?eu=36441.

Encyclopedia Britannica. (n.d.). *Luiseño.* Retrieved from: http://www.britannica.com/eb/article?eu=50505.

Encyclopedia Britannica. (n.d.). *Serrano.* Retrieved from: http://www.britannica.com/eb/article?eu=68594.

Encyclopedia Britannica. (n.d.). *Yuman.* Retrieved from: http://www.britannica.com/eb/article?eu=80245.

Encyclopedia Britannica. (2001). *Cahuilla.* Retrieved from: http://www.britannica.com/eb/article?eu=18840.

ESRI. (1993). *Digital chart of the world for use with ARC/INFO software,* [CD-Rom]. Redlands, CA: ESRI, Inc.

ESRI. (1999). *ESRI data & maps,* [CD-Rom]. Redlands, CA: ESRI, Inc.

Fridmann, M. (1998). *The Salton Sea restoration project: Opportunities and challenges history.* Marcy Fridmann. Retrieved from: http://www.lc.usbr.gov/~g2000/ssbro.html.

Gold Bug. (c1992). *1885 map of California with alphabetical list of towns & counties.* Alamo, CA: The Gold Bug Historic Map Reproductions.

Green River Basin Advisory Group. (1973). *The Wyoming framework water plan.* Green River, WY: Green River Basin Advisory Group.

H., S. (2001, 2/1/01). *Jedediah Smith Strong and his life.* Tigard-Tualatin School District.
Retrieved from: http://www.ttsd.k12.or.us/schools/cft/html/Explorers/Jedediah.html.

Hague, H. (1978). *The road to California: The search for a southern overland route 1540-1848* (Vol. XI). Glendale, CA: Arthur H Clark Co.

Harrigan, B. A. (1951). *Annual report for the year ending December 31, 1950.* El Centro, CA: Imperial County Department of Agriculture.

Heizer, R. F. (Ed.). (1978). *California* (Vol. 8). Washington, D. C.: Smithsonian Institution.

Hodgson, S. F. *Oil & Gas in California.* Sacramento, CA: California Department of Conservation Division of Oil & Gas.

Holms, B. (1996). *Lake Cahuilla II.* Retrieved from: http://www.geocities.com /MotorCity/2801/961c3.html.

Horovitz, S. (1997). *The Fishernet Magazine California's Salton Sea.* Steve Woolbert (publisher). Retrieved from: http://www.thefishernet.com/saltonsea.htm.

Hughes, A. *John Wesley Powell.* (n. d.) John Wesley Powell River History Museum.
Retrieved from: http://www.surweb.org/surweb/tour/jwp/jwpowell.htm.

Imperial County. (n. d.) *Imperial County agriculture.*
Retrieved from: http://commserv.ucdavis.edu/CEImperial/overview.htm.

Imperial County Board of Trade. (1931). *Imperial County, California 1930 statistics.* El Centro, CA: Imperial County Board of Trade.

Imperial County Board of Trade. (1941). *Imperial County, California 1940 statistics.* El Centro, CA: Imperial County Board of Trade.

Imperial County Office of the Agricultural Commissioner. (1961). *Agricultural crop report County of Imperial -1960-.* El Centro, CA: Imperial County Office of the Agricultural Commissioner.

Imperial County Office of the Agricultural Commissioner. (1981). *Imperial County agriculture 1980.* El Centro, CA: Office of the Agricultural Commissioner.

Imperial County Publicity Commission (n. d.). *Increase in live stock, crop acreages and property values in Imperial County.* El Centro, CA: Imperial County Publicity Commission.

Imperial Irrigation District (n. d.). *1999 annual report Imperial Irrigation District.*
Retrieved from: http://www.iid.com.

Imperial Irrigation District (n. d.). *History: How we started.*
Retrieved from: http://www.iid.com/aboutiid/history-how.html.

Imperial Irrigation District. (n. d.). *IID background facts & figures.*
Retrieved from: http://www.iid.com/aboutiid/iidbackground-facts.html.

Imperial Irrigation District (n. d.). *Water transfer agreement.*
Retrieved from: http://www.iid.com/water/transfer.html.

Imperial Irrigation District. (1998). *Fact sheet: Imperial Valley agriculture 1998.* El Centro, CA: Imperial Irrigation District.

Imperial Irrigation District. (1998). *Irrigation services agriculture.*
Retrieved from: http://www.iid.com/water/irr-agriculture.html.

Imperial Irrigation District. (2000). *Fact sheet: Water conservation.* El Centro, CA: Imperial Irrigation District.

Imperial Irrigation District. (2000). *Imperial County 1999 agricultural crop and livestock report.* El Centro, CA: Imperial Irrigation District.

Imperial Valley Historical Society. (2000). *A History of the Imperial Valley part 1-5.* Pioneers Museum & Cultural Center of the Imperial Valley.
Retrieved from: http://www.imperial.cc.ca.us/pioneers/HISTORY.htm.

Internet Public Library (n. d.). *Native American authors: Browsing by tribe: Cahuilla Tribe.*
Retrieved from: http://www.ipl.org/cgi/ref/native/browse.pl/t8.

John Wesley Powell Memorial Museum (n. d.). *John Wesley Powell Memorial Museum: Major John Wesley Powell.* CyberSpaces. Retrieved from: http://www.powellmuseum.org/MajorPowell.html.

John Wesley Powell Memorial Museum. (n. d.) *Powell expedition maps.*
Retrieved from: http://www.powellmuseum.org/Gallery/Maps.html.

Juaneño Band of Mission Indians Acjachemem Nation. (1999). *Juaneño Band of Mission Indians Acjachemem Nation fact sheet.* Retrieved from: http://sun3.lib.uci.edu/~m2martin/juanfact.html.

Kimball, D. (1995). *Shapes and uses of California Indian basketry.* University of California Berkeley Museum Informatics Project, California Indian Library Collections Project.
Retrieved from: http://www.mip.berkeley.edu/cilc/basket.html.

Koluvek, P. K. (n. d.). *Irrigation and drainage practices in the Colorado River Basin of California.* El Centro, CA: (unpublished report) United States Soil Conservation Service.

Laflin, P. (1995). *The Salton Sea: California's overlooked treasure.* Indio, CA: The Periscope, Coachella Valley Historical Society.

Laylander, D. (1997). The Last days of Lake Cahuilla: The Elmore Site. *Pacific Coast Archaeological Society Quarterly,* 1-138. Costa Mesa, CA: Pacific Coast Archaeological Society.

Library of Congress. (2000). *Table of contents for reports of explorations and survey to ascertain the most practicable and economical route for a railroad from the Mississippi River to the Pacific Ocean* (Vol. 5). Washington, D. C.: Beverly Tucker.

Little, I. (1982). *Imperial Valley historical markers.* Holtville, CA: Holtville Printers.

Luomala, K. (1978). Tipai-Ipai. In W. C. Sturtevant (Ed.). *Handbook of North American Indian* (Vol. 8, pp. 592 - 609). Washington, D. C.: Smithsonian Institute.

MacKichan, K. A., & Kammerer, J. C. (1961). *Estimated use of water in the United States, 1960.* Washington, D. C.

McBride, D. (n.d.). *Early California history.* Donald McBride.
Retrieved from: http://www.geocities.com/dtmcbride/tahoe/cal-hist.html.

McClure, D. (2000). *Water quality laws history (Vol. 2000).* Palm Desert, CA: Colorado River Water Quality Control Board.

Metropolitan Water District of Southern California (n. d.). *Supply/demand comparison 2000 UWMP vs. MWD's forcast.* San Diego, CA: Metropolitan Water District of Los Angeles.

Metropolitan Water District of Southern California. (2001). *Historical water sales* (Chart). San Diego, CA: Metropolitan Water District of Southern California.

Murray, C. R. (1968). *Estimated use of water in the United States, 1965.* Washington D. C.: U. S. Geological Survey.

Murray, C. R., & Reeves, E. B. (1977). *Estimated use of water in the United States, 1975.* Washington D. C.: U. S. Geological Survey.

National Parks Service Heritage Trails Task Force. (1993). *Juan Bautista De Anza national historic trail: Appendix C - Imperial County*. Retrieved from: http://www.nps.gov/juba/plan/appc-imperial.htm.

Nevada Division of Water Planning. (1999). *Nevada state water plan summary*. Department of Conservation and Natural Resources.

New Mexico State Engineer. (2001). *New Mexico Office of the State Engineer Interstate Stream Commission*. Retrieved from: http://www.seo.state.nm.us.

Pacific Institute. (2000). *Missing water: The flows and uses of water in the Colorado River border region*. Oakland, CA: Pacific Institute.

Peppin, N. (n. d.). *A River too far: The Past and future of the arid west*. Reno, NV: Nevada Humanities Committee.

Pick, J. B. (2000). *Border economics: Demographic impacts on the urban environment and sustainable development of Imperial County* (proposal). Redlands, CA: University of Redlands.

Pioneers Museum & Cultural Center of the Imperial Valley. (1997). *Imperial Valley Historical Society*. E.R. Caldwell. Retrieved from: http://www.imperial.cc.ca.us/pioneers.

Pontius, D. (1997). *Colorado River basin study* (Final Report). Tucson, AZ: SWCA, Inc. Environmental Consultants.

Prentiss, D. E. (1995). *Lost treasures in the desert*.
Retrieved from: http://www.geog.ucsb.edu/~dylan/history.htm.

Public Broadcasting System. (n. d.). *The American experience: Lost in the Grand Canyon, The Powell expedition*. Alexandra, VA: Public Broadcasting System.
Retrieved from: http://www.pbs.org/wgbh/amex/canyon/filmmore/reference/primary/desertnews.html.

Public Broadcasting System. (n.d.). *Water fights*.
Retrieved from: http://www.pbs.org/wgbh/amex/canyon/peopleevents/pandeAMEX07.html.

Rand McNally and Company. (map). (1900, c1904). *California & Nevada*. Chicago, IL: Rand McNally and Company.

Regents of the University of California. (1997). *Counting California, agriculture and natural resources, farms and farming: California's agricultural commodities: Commodity ranking, acreage, production, value, crop harvest seasons, and leading producing counties, 1997*. Riverside, CA: Regents of the University of California. Retrieved from: http://countingcalifornia.cdlib.org/matrix/c64.html.

Reisner, M., & Bates, S (n. d.). *Overtapped oasis: Reform or revolution for western water*. Washington,D. C.: Island Press.

Ribokas, B. (1994-2000). *Grand Canyon explorer: The Powell expedition*.
Retrieved from: http://www.kaibab.org/powell/powexp.htm.

Rupert Costo Chair in American Indian History Webmaster. (n.d.). *Historic lands of the Cahuilla*. University of California Riverside College of Humanities, Arts & Social Sciences.
Retrieved from: http://www.chass.ucr.edu/costo/page8.html.

Salton Sea Authority. (n. d.). *Fish and wildlife: Sea facts. Historical chronology*.
Retrieved from: http://saltonsea.ca.gov/histchron.htm.

Salton Sea Authority. (n. d.). *Recreation: Sea facts*. La Quinta, CA: Salton Sea Authority.

Salton Sea Authority. (2000). *Agriculture and the sea*. Retrieved from: http://www.saltonsea.ca.gov/ag.htm.

Salton Sea Authority. (2000). *Economic development and the sea*. KG WebWorks.
Retrieved from: http://www.saltonsea.ca.gov/econdev.htm.

Salton Sea Authority, U.S. Department of Interior, Bureau of Reclamation, & Tetra Tech, Inc. (2000). *Draft Salton Sea restoration project: Environmental impact statement, environmental impact report*. La Quinta, CA: Salton Sea Authority.

Salton Sea State Recreation Area. (1999). *Salton Sea 101*. Steve Horvitz.
Retrieved from: http://www.saltonseainfo.com/SS101/ss101.html.

San Diego Historical Society. (n. d.). *San Diego County*. San Diego, CA: San Diego Historical Society.

San Diego State University. (n. d.). *California Indians and their reservations: An Online dictionary (D-L)*. Retrieved from: http://libweb.sdsu.edu/sub_libs/pwhite/calinddictdl.html.

Sato, P. (n.d.). *The Cahuilla Indians*. P Sato Web Design.
Retrieved from: http://www.jurupa.com/history/cahuilla.html.

Signor, J. R. (n.d.). *The railroad in the Salton Sink*. Pasadena, CA: Southern Pacific Historical and Technical Society.

Singer, E. (n.d.). *Geology of the Imperial Valley California: A monograph*.
Retrieved from: http://www.aloha.net/~esinger/homegeol.

Solley, W. B. (1997). *Estimates of water use in the western United States in 1990 and water-use trends 1960- 90*. Reston, Virginia, VA: U. S. Geological Survey.

Solley, W. B., Chase, E. B., & Mann, W. B. (1983). *Estimated use of water in the United States in 1980*. Denver, CO: U. S. Geological Survey.

Southern California Association of Governments. (n.d.). *County population projections*. Sacramento, CA: Southern California Association of Governments.

Southern Pacific. (n.d.). *Southern Pacific Railroad*. Retrieved from: http://www.linecamp.com/museums/americanwest/western_clu.../southern_pacific_railroad.htm.

State of California. (2000). *The California spatial information library*. State of California.
Retrieved from: http://www.gis.ca.gov/data_index.epl.

State of California Employment Development Department. (2000). *California agricultural bulletin*. Sacramento, CA: Employment Development Department.

Stewart, K. M. (1983). Mohave. In W. C. Sturtevant (Ed.). *Handbook of North American Indians* (Vol. 10, pp. 55 - 70). Washington, D. C.: Smithsonian Institute.

Stoner, J. D. (1978). *Water-quality indices for specific water uses*. Denver, CO: U. S. Geological Survey.

Swajian, A. &, Colorado River Basin Regional Water Quality Control Board (1969). *Identification and evaluation of federal, state, and local interests in Salton Sea, California*.

Tokita, J. (1999). *150 Years of California's water history*.
Retrieved from: http://www.dwr.water.ca.gov/DWRNews/fall99/150yr.html.

Tostrud, M. B. (1997). *The Salton Sea, 1906-1996, computed and measured salinities and water levels*. Glendale, CA: Colorado River Board of California.

Tout, O. B. (1931). *The First thirty years being an account of the principle events in the history of Imperial Valley Southern California, U. S. A.* Imperial, CA: Imperial County Historical Society.

U. S. Census Bureau. (n.d.). *Projections of the total population of states: 1995- 2025*. Washington D. C.: Bureau of Census.

U. S. Census Bureau. (1995). *Arizona: Population of counties by decennial census, 1900 to 1990*. Richard L. Forstall. Retrieved from: http://www.census.gov/population/cencounts/az190090.txt.

U. S. Census Bureau. (1995). *California: Population of counties by decennial census, 1900 to 1990*. Richard L. Forstall. Retrieved from: http://www.census.gov/population/cencounts/ca190090.txt.

U. S. Census Bureau. (1995). *Colorado: Population of counties by decennial census, 1900 to 1990*. Richard L. Forstall. Retrieved from: http://www.census.gov/population/cencounts/co190090.txt.

U. S. Census Bureau. (1995). *Nevada: Population of counties by decennial census, 1900 to 1990*. Richard L. Forstall. Retrieved from: http://www.census.gov/population/cencounts/nv190090.txt.

U. S. Census Bureau. (1995). *New Mexico: Population of counties by decennial census, 1900 to 1990*. Richard L. Forstall. Retrieved from: http://www.census.gov/population/cencounts/nm190090.txt.

U. S. Census Bureau. (1995). *Utah: Population of counties by decennial census, 1900 to 1990*. Richard L. Forstall. Retrieved from: http://www.census.gov/population/cencounts/ut190090.txt.

U. S. Census Bureau. (1995). *Wyoming: population of counties by decennial census, 1900 to 1990*. Richard L. Forstall. Retrieved from: http://www.census.gov/population/cencounts/wy190090.txt.

U. S. Census Bureau. (2000). *Resident population of the United States*: Population Division. (Washington D. C.): Bureau of Census.

U. S. Census Bureau. (2002). *Selected historical census data*. Population Division.
Retrieved from: http://www.census.gov/population/www/censusdata/hiscendata.html.

U. S. Department of the Interior. (2001). *National atlas of the United States: Map layers warehouse*. Retrieved from: http://www.nationalatlas.gov/atlasftp.html.

U. S. Department of the Interior, Bureau of Reclamation. (n.d.). *Colorado River system: Consumptive uses and losses report 1976-1980*. Denver, CO: Bureau of Reclamation.

U. S. Department of the Interior, Bureau of Reclamation (1975). *Colorado River system consumptive uses and losses report 1971-1975*. Denver, CO: Bureau of Reclamation.

U. S. Department of the Interior, Bureau of Reclamation (1991). *Colorado River system consumptive uses and losses report 1981-1985*. Denver, CO: Bureau of Reclamation.

U. S. Department of the Interior, Bureau of Reclamation (1998). *Colorado River system consumptive uses and losses report 1986-1990*. Denver, CO: Bureau of Reclamation.

U. S. Department of the Interior Bureau of Reclamation (2000). *Lower Colorado River accounting system 1999 report executive summary*. Denver, CO: Bureau of Reclamation.

U. S. Department of the Interior, Bureau of Reclamation (2001). *History of early major diversions on the Lower Colorado River*. Colleen Dwyer. Retrieved from: http://www.lc.usbr.gov.

U. S. Department of the Interior, Bureau of Reclamation (2001). *Colorado River water use, acre-feet*. Boulder Canyon Operations Office. Retrieved from: http://www.lc.usbr.gov/~g4000/use.txt.

U. S. Environmental Protection Agency. (1998). *California Indian reservations, California tribal lands*. Retrieved from: http://www.epa.gov/Region9/cross_pr/indian/mapca.html.

U. S. Geological Survey. (n.d.). *Accounting for consumptive use of Lower Colorado River water in Arizona, California, Nevada, and Utah*. Retrieved from: http://az.water.usgs.gov/factsheets/fs94-74/FS94-074.html.

U. S. Geological Survey (Cartographer). (1915, c1992). *1915 Railroad maps: California, the Shasta coast, and Southern Pacific routes*.

U. S. Geological Survey. (1990). *Estimated use of water in the U. S. in 1990 conversion factors*. Denver, CO: U. S. Geological Survey.

U. S. Geological Survey. (1999). *Trends in water use, 1950-1990*.
Retrieved from: http://ga.water.usgs.gov/edu/tables/totrendbar.html.

U. S. Geological Survey. (2000). *USGS water resources data report - California introduction*.
Retrieved from: http://www.ca.water.usgs.gov/data/text/intro.html.

U. S. Geological Survey. (2000). *Water-use information for California*.
Retrieved from: http://ca.water.usgs.gov/projects/ca007.html.

University of California, Berkeley Department of Anthropology. (1978). Aboriginal environments of Coachella Valley. In University of California Archaeological Research Facility (Ed.). *Late Prehistoric Human Ecology at Lake Cahuilla: Coachella Valley, California* (Vol. 38, pp. 19- 21). Berkeley, CA: University of California Berkeley, Department of Anthropology.

University of California, Berkeley Department of Anthropology. (1978). The return to desert conditions. In University of California Archaeological Research Facility (Ed.). *Late Prehistoric Human Ecology at Lake Cahuilla: Coachella Valley, California* (Vol. 38, pp. 109- 125). Berkeley, CA: University of California Berkeley, Department of Anthropology.

University of Northern Texas. (1998). *John Wesley Powell 1834 - 1902*.
Retrieved from: http://www.library.unt.edu/gpo/powell/powell.htm.

Urban Water Management Plan, City of Los Angeles, Department of Water and Power (2000). *Historical and projected water use and population*. Los Angeles, CA: Department of Water and Power.

Utah Division of Water Resources. (2001). Population and water use trends and projections, *Utah's Water Resources: Planning for the Future*. Logan, UT: Utah Water Research Laboratory.

Valley of Imperial Development Alliance. *Dairy consultant-Imperial County*.
Retrieved from: http://www.moohere.com/jobs.html.

ver Planck, W. E. (1958). *Salt in California* (Bulletin 175). San Francisco, CA: Department of Natural Resources.

Wade, Jon P. G. (2001). *State Water Use Projections*.
Retrieved from: http://cem.uor.edu/salton/rfi/rfiRequest.

Water Education Foundation. *Water education foundation*. Retrieved from: http://www.water-ed.org.

Waters, M. R. (1983). Late Holocene lacustrine chronology and archaeology of ancient Lake Cahuilla, California. *Quaternary Research, 19*, 373-387.

White, P. (2001). *California Indians*. San Diego State University.
Retrieved from: http://infodome.sdsu.edu/research/guides/calindians/calind.shtml.

Wilke, P. J. (n. d.). Prehistoric weir fishing on recessional shorelines of Lake Cahuilla, Salton Basin, Southeastern California. In E. P. Pister (Ed.). *Proceedings of the Desert Fishes Council* (Vol. 11).

Wilke, P. J. (1975). *The Cahuilla Indians of the Colorado Desert: Ethnohistory and prehistory*. Ramona, CA: Ballena Press.

Wilke, P. J. (1978). *Late prehistoric human ecology at Lake Cahuilla Coachella Valley, California*. Berkeley, CA.

Winter, T. C. (1982). *Bibliography of U. S. Geological Survey studies of lakes and reservoirs- The First 100 years*. Denver, CO: U. S. Geological Survey.

Wyoming Water Development Commission. (7/26/01). *Wyoming state water plan*.
Retrieved from: http://waterplan.state.wy.us/.

The Sea Today

Bloxham, M. (n. d.). *Salinity modeling on the back of an envelope*. University of Redlands.
Retrieved from: http://newton.uor.edu/FacultyFolder/Bloxham/salton/pages/index.html.

California Department of Water Resources. (1994). Colorado River hydrologic region. *Bulletin 160-98: California Water Plan* (Vol. 2 chapter 9, pp. 25).

California Regional Water Quality Control Board, & State Water Resources Control Board. (1994). *Water quality control plan: Colorado River basin - Region 7*.

California Tahoe Conservancy. (1997). *California Tahoe Conservancy progress report: Tahoe — A treasure and challenge*. State of California. Retrieved from: http://www.tahoecons.ca.gov/library/progrep/treasure.html.

Coachella Valley Water District. (2000). *Coachella Valley draft water management plan*. Montgomery Watson.

Cook, C., Huston, D., Orlob, G., & Schladow, G. (1997). *Animation of hypothetical two-dimensional hydrodynamic model results*. Retrieved from: http://www.engr.ucdavis.edu/~wremg/Salton_Sea/2-d_animation.html.

Cook, C., Huston, D., Orlob, G., & Schladow, G. (1997). *Historic perspective*.
Retrieved from: http://www.engr.ucdavis.edu/~wremg/Salton_Sea/introduction.html.

Cook, C., Huston, D., Orlob, G., & Schladow, G. (1997). *Historical elevation of the Salton Sea*. Retrieved from: http://www.engr.ucdavis.edu/~wremg/Salton_Sea/elevation.html.

Cook, C. B., Orlob, G. T., Huston, D., & Schladow, G. (n. d.). *Field monitoring and hydrodynamic modeling of the Salton Sea, CA*. UC Davis. Retrieved from: http://www.engr.ucdavis.edu/~wremg/Salton_Sea/IAHR97_paper.html.

Cook, C. B., Orlob, G. T., Huston, D., & Schladow, G. (1996). *Two- and three-dimensional hydrodynamic modeling of the Salton Sea, California*.
Retrieved from: http://www.engr.ucdavis.edu/~wremg/Salton_Sea /WC96_paper.htm.

Corona, F. V., & Floyd F Sabins, J. (n. d.). The San Andreas Fault of the Salton Trough region, California, as expressed on remote sensing data. *SBCMA Special Pubication. 93-1*, 69-75.

Dainer, J. S. (Webmaster). *Lower Colorado River*.
Retrieved from: http://www.sci.sdsu.edu/salton/Lower_Colorado_River.html.

ESRI. (1993). *Digital chart of the world for use with ARC/INFO software*, [CD-Rom]. Redlands, CA: ESRI.

ESRI. (1999). *ESRI data & maps*, [CD-Rom]. Redlands, CA: ESRI, Inc.

Fuller, K., Harvey Shear, P. D., & Wittig, J. (1995). *The Great Lakes, An environmental atlas and resource book Chapter 2: Natural processes in the Great Lakes* (3rd ed.). U. S. Environmental Protection Agency Great Lakes National Program Office Government of Canada.
Retrieved from: http://www.epa.gov/glnpo/atlas/glat-ch2.html.

Geothermal Education Office. (1997). *GEO: Geothermal Education Office*.
Retrieved from: http://geothermal.marin.org/map/usa.html.

Gormley, P. (n. d.). *Analysis of phosphorous in fertilizer*.
Retrieved from: http://chem.lapeer.org/Chem2Docs/PhosphateAnal.html.

Gwynn, J. W. (n. d.). *Commonly asked questions about Utah's Great Salt Lake and ancient Lake Bonneville*. Utah Geological Survey — Public Information Series.
Retrieved from: http://geology.utah.gov/online/PI-39/PI39PG3.HTM.

Hely, A. G., Hughes, G. H., & Irelan, B. (1966). *Hydrologic regimen of Salton Sea, California* (Geological Survey Professional Paper 486- C). Washington D. C.: U. S. Department of the Interior.

Holdren, C., Robertson, D., Amrhein, C., Elder, J., Schroeder, R., Schladow, G., McKellar, H., & Gersberg, R. (2000). *Eutrophic conditions at the Salton Sea*. La Quinta, CA: Salton Sea Authority.

Holdren, G. C. (1999). *Chemical and physical analyses of the Salton Sea, California* (Literature review). Denver, CO: U. S. Bureau of Reclamation.

Holdren, G. C. (2001). *Salton Sea chemistry data*. In S. Huynen (Ed.). Denver, CO: U. S. Bureau of Reclamation Ecological Research and Investigations Group.

Holdren, G. C., & Montano, A. (n. d.). *Chemical/physical limnology of the Salton Sea*. Denver, CO: U. S. Bureau of Reclamation.

Holdren, G. C., & Montano, A. M. (n. d.). *Chemistry of the Salton Sea, California* [Powerpoint Presentation]. Denver, CO: U. S. Bureau of Reclamation Ecological Research and Investigations Group.

Hoong, C. (2001). *Facts about Lake Tahoe*, USGS Western Geographic Science Center Lake Tahoe data clearinghouse. Retrieved from: http://tahoe.usgs.gov/facts.html.

Hurlbert, S. (2000). *Report 18*. Institute of Applied Agriculture. *The Impact of phosphorus on aquatic life: Eutrophication*. University of Maryland. Retrieved from: http://www.agnr.umd.edu/users/agron/nutrient/Factshee/Phosphorus/Eutrop.html.

Interhemispheric Resource Center. (1999). *Borderlines 52*.
Retrieved from: http://www.irconline.org/borderline/1999/b152tab.html.

International Lake Environment Committee (n. d.). *World lakes database – Survey of the state of world lakes, Data summary – Laguna de Bay (Lake Bay).* International Lake Environment Committee. Retrieved from: http://www.ilec.or.jp/database/asi/dasi13.html.

International Lake Environment Committee (n. d.). *World lakes database – Survey of the state of world lakes, Data summary – Lake Victoria.* International Lake Environment Committee. Retrieved from: http://www.ilec.or.jp/database/afr/dafr05.html.

International Lake Environment Committee. (2001). *International Lake Environment Committee, World Lakes Database, Lake Tahoe.* International Lake Environment Committee. Retrieved from: http://www.ilec.or.jp/database/nam/nam-02.html.

Kelley, R. L., & Nye, R. L. (1984). *Historical perspective on salinity and drainage problems in California: California Agriculture.*

LFR Levine - Fricke Inc. (1999). *Synthesis document of current information on the sediment physical characteristics and contaminants at the Salton Sea, Riverside, and Imperial Counties, California.* Prepared for Salton Sea Authority.

Lipton, D. S., Leventhal, R. D., Beadle, S. C., Hamann, M. E., & Vogl, R. (n. d.). *Environmental reconnaissance of the Salton Sea: Sediment contaminants.* Levine-Fricke. Retrieved from: http://cem.uor.edu/salton/recon/Sediment.cfm.

Mandaville, S. M. (n.d.). *Saline lakes.* Retrieved from: http://www.chebucto.ns.ca/Science/SWCS/saline1.html.

Niiler, E. (2001). *Border River is also sewage drain.* Retrieved from: http://www.msnbc.com.

Ohio Department of Natural Resource, Division of Geological Survey. (1999). *Lake Erie geology.* Glenn Larson. Retrieved from: http://www.ohiodnr.com/geosurvey/lakeeerie/lakeerie.htm.

Penn State University. (n.d.). *Effects on communities and ecosystems.* Retrieved from: http://www.personal.psu.edu.

Powell, C. L. (1995). *Paleontology and significance of the Imperial Formation at Garnet Hill, Riverside County, California* (open-file report 95- 489). Menlo Park, CA: U. S. Geological Survey.

Salton Sea Authority. (n.d.). *Sea myths & realities.* Retrieved from: http://www.saltonsea.ca.gov/myths.htm.

Salton Sea Authority. (n.d.). *Water quality sea facts.* La Quinta, CA: Salton Sea Authority.

Salton Sea Authority. (2000). *About the Salton Sea: The sea's vital statistics.* Retrieved from: http://www.saltonsea.ca.gov/thesea.html.

Salton Sea Authority, U. S. Department of Interior, Bureau of Reclamation & Tetra Tech, I. (2002). *Draft Salton Sea restoration project: Environmental impact statement, environmental impact report.* La Quinta, CA: Salton Sea Authority.

Salton Sea Database Program. (1998). *Salton Sea Database Program bibliographic report: Sedimentology.* Redlands, CA: University of Redlands.

Schroeder, R. (2000). *Facts about nutrient dynamics in the Salton Basin.* 2000 Salton Sea Science Symposium.

Schroeder, R. A., & Orem, W. H. (2000). *Nutrient dynamics in the Salton Basin – Implication from calcium, uranium, molybdenum, and selenium.*

Seese, W. S., & Daub, G. H. (1972). *Basic chemistry* (7th ed.). Englewood Cliffs, NJ: Prentice-Hall.

Setmire, J. G., & Schroeder, R. A. *Selenium and salinity concerns in the Salton Sea area of California.* In J. William T Frankenberger & R. A. Engberg (Eds.), *Environmental Chemistry of Selenium.* New York: Marcel Dekker, Inc.

Sims, D. R. C. (1997, 3/11/97). *Water atlas of Utah: Terminal lake systems: The Great Salt Lake.* Utah Water Research Laboratory. Retrieved from: http://www.engineering.usu.edu/uwrl/atlas/ch6/ch6overview.html.

Swan, B. K., Watts, J. M., Tiffany, M. A., & Hurlbert, S. H. (1999). *Thermal, mixing, and oxygen regimes of the Salton Sea, 1997-1999.*

Takhtajan, A. (1986). *Floristic regions of the world.* Berkely, CA: University of California Press.

Tostrud, M. B. (1997). *The Salton Sea, 1906-1996, Computed and measured salinities and water levels.* Colorado River Board of California.

U. S. Department of Agriculture, F. S., Humboldt-Toiyabe National Forest. (n.d.). *Lake Tahoe Facts.* Retrieved from: http://www.fs.fed.us/htnf/laketaho.htm.

U. S. Department of the Interior, Bureau of Reclamation (1997). *Salton Sea 1995 hydrographic GPS survey.* Washington D. C.: U. S. Department of the Interior, Bureau of Reclamation.

U. S. Department of the Interior, Bureau of Reclamation (2001). *Salton Sea inflows.* Washington D. C.: U. S. Department of the Interior, Bureau of Reclamation.

U. S. Geological Survey – *Index for the 1996 California hydrologic data report.* Retrieved from: http://ca.water.usgs.gov/data/96.

U. S. Geological Survey. (1999). *1999 California hydrologic data report Alamo River near Niland, CA.* Retrieved from: http://water.wr.usgs.gov/data/99/volume1.pdf.

U. S. Geological Survey. (1999). *1999 California hydrologic data report New River near Westmorland, CA.* Retrieved from: http://water.wr.usgs.gov/data/99/volume1.pdf.

U. S. Geological Survey. (1999). *1999 California hydrologic data report Salt Creek near Mecca, CA.* Retrieved from: http://water.wr.usgs.gov/data/99/volume1.pdf.

U. S. Geological Survey. (1999). *1999 California hydrologic data report Whitewater River near Mecca, CA.* Retrieved from: http://water.wr.usgs.gov/data/99/volume1.pdf.

U. S. Geological Survey. (2000). *California earthquake history 1769 – present.* Retrieved from: http://pasadena.wr.usgs.gov/cahist_eqs.html.

U. S. Geological Survey. (2000). *Water Resources in California project description: Measurement and analysis of potential land subsistence in Coachella.* Retrieved from: http://ca.water.usgs.gov/projects00/ca517.html.

U. S. Geological Survey. (2002). *Facts about Lake Tahoe.* Connie Hoong, Lake Tahoe Data Clearinghouse, Western Geographic Science Center. Retrieved from: http://tahoe.usgs.gov/facts.html.

United Nations Environment Programme. (n.d.). *Eutrophication.* Retrieved from: http://www.grida.no/soeno97/eutro/eutro.htm.

United Nations Environment Programme. (n.d.). *Newsletter and technical publications: Planning and management of lakes and reservoirs: An Integrated approach to eutrophication.* Retrieved from: http://www.unep.or.jp/ietc/Publications/TechPublications/TechPub-11/1-1.asp.

Veirs, S. D. J., & Opler, P. A. (n.d.). *California.* Retrieved from: http://biology.usgs.gov /s+t/SNT/noframe/ca162.htm.

Vogl, R. A., Henry, R. N., & Lipton, D. S. (n.d.). *Characteristics and contaminants of the Salton Sea sediments.* LFR Levine-Fricke.

Watts, J. M., Swan, B. K., Tiffany, M. A., & Hurlbert, S. H. (1999). *Progress report 1: Temperature, dissolved oxygen, pH, ammonia, and light penetration.*

Watts, J. M., Swan, B. K., Tiffany, M. A., & Hurlbert, S. H. (2000). *Progress Report 18: Thermal, mixing, and oxygen regimes of the Salton Sea, 1997-1999.*

Ecology of the Salton Sea

Barnum, D. (2001). *Importance of migratory/breeding habitat in terms of quality, quantity, temporally and spatially, Biotic communities of the Colorado Plateau.* Retrieved from: http://www.cpluhna.nau.edu/Biota/merriam.htm.

Boschung, H. T. (1997). *National audubon society field guide to North American fishes, whales, and dolphins.* New York: Knopf.

Cambridge University. (1991). *The Cambridge encyclopedia of ornithology.* Cambridge, NY: The Press Syndicate of the University of Cambridge.

Cohen, M. J., Morrison, J. I., & Glenn, E. P. (1999). *Haven or hazard: The ecology of the Salton Sea.* Oakland, CA: Pacific Institute.

Costa-Pierce, B. (n.d.). *Fish and fisheries of the Salton Sea.* Mississippi-Alabama Sea Grant Consortium.

Costa-Pierce, B. A., & Riedel, R. (2000). *Final report: Fish biology and fisheries ecology of the Salton Sea.*

Defenders of Wildlife Salton Sea Position Statement. (2001). *The Ecological realities of the Salton Sea.* Retrieved from: http://www.sci.sdsu.edu/DOWPositionSaltonSea.html.

Eisler, R. (1985). *Selenium hazards to fish, wildlife, and invertebrates: A Synoptic review* (Biological Report 85(1.5)). U. S. Department of the Interior Fish and Wildlife Service.

Eisler, R. (1986). *Chromium hazards to fish, wildlife, and invertebrates: A Synoptic review* (Biological Report 85(1.6)). U. S. Department of the Interior Fish and Wildlife Service.

Farrand, John. (1988). *Western birds.* New York: McGraw Hill.

Friend, M. (2000). *Avian disease at the Salton Sea.* Salton Sea Science Subcommittee. 2000 Salton Sea Science Symposium.

Gilliard, E. T. (1958). *Living birds of the world.* Garden City, NY: Doubleday & Company, Inc.

Horovitz, S. (1997). *The Fishernet magazine California's Salton Sea.* Steve Woolbert (publisher). Retrieved from: http://www.thefishernet.com/saltonsea.htm.

Institute of Applied Agriculture. *The Impact of phosphorus on aquatic life: eutrophication.* University of Maryland. Retrieved from: http://www.agnr.umd.edu/users/agron/nutrient/Factshee/Phosphorus/Eutrop.html.

International Lake Environment Committee. (1999). *International Lake Environment Committee Foundation for sustainable management of world lakes and reservoirs.* Retrieved from: http://www.ilec.or.jp/databse/index/idx-lakes.html.

Johnsgard, P. A. (1975). *Waterfowl of North America.* Bloomington, IN: Indiana University Press.

Karr, B. *Fishing Salton Sea.* La Quinta, CA: Salton Sea Authority.

Krantz, T. P. (1994). *A Phytogeography of the San Bernardino Mountains, San Bernardino County, California.* Unpublished Doctoral dissertation, University of California Berkeley.

Mandaville, S. M. (1998). *Saline lakes of the World.* International Lake Environment Committee Foundation for Sustainable Management of World Lakes & Reservoirs. Retrieved from: http://www.chebucto.ns.ca/Science/SWCS/saline1.html; http://www.ilec.or.jp/database/nam/dnam02.html.

Mattison, C. (1996). *Rattler!: A natural history of rattlesnakes.* New York: Blandford.

Mehrtens, J. M. (1987). *Living snakes of the world in color.* New York: Sterling.

Merriam, C. H. (1898). Life zones and crop zones of the United States. *U. S. D. A. Biological Survey Bulletin.* Washington, D. C.: U. S. Government Printing Office.

Mitsch, W. J., & Gosselink, J. G. (1993). *Wetlands* (2nd ed.). New York: Van Nostrand Reinhold.

Montgomery, S. J. (n.d.). *Yuma Clapper Rails at the Salton Sea.* SJM Biological Consultants.

National Geographic Society. (1981). *National Geographic book of mammals, V 1&2.* Washington, D. C.: The Society

National Geographic. (1987). *Field guide to the birds of North America* (3rd ed.). Washington, D. C.: National Geographic.

Patten, M. A., McCaskie, G., & Unitt, P. (n.d.). *Birds of the Salton Sea: Status, biogeography, and ecology.* Penn State University webmaster. *Effects on communities and ecosystems.* Retrieved from: http://www.personal.psu.edu.

Radtke, D. B., Kepner, W. G., & Effertz, R. J. (1988). *Reconnaissance investigation of water quality, bottom sediment, and biota associated with irrigation drainage in the Lower Colorado River Valley, Arizona, California, and Nevada, 1986-87* (Water Resources Investigation Report 88-4002 88-4002). Tucson, AZ: U. S. Geological Survey.

Richards, A. J. (1990). *Seabirds of the northern hemisphere.* New York: Gallery Books.

Robbins, C. S., Bruun, B., Zim, H. S., & Singer, A. (1966). *A Guide to field identification: Birds of North America.* New York: Golden Press.

Salton Sea Authority. (2000). *Fishing at the Salton Sea.* KG WebWorks. Retrieved from: http://www.saltonsea.ca.gov/fishing.htm.

Schroeder, R. (2000). *Facts about nutrient dynamics in the Salton Basin.* In R. Schroeder (Ed.). Retrieved from: http://cem.uor.edu/salton/rfi/rfiRequest.

Setmire, J. (n.d.). *Selenium in water, sediment, and transplanted Corbicula in irrigation drainage and wildlife use of drains in the Imperial Valley, California 1994-1995.* Denver, CO: U. S. Geological Survey.

Shuford, W. D., Warnock, N., Molina, K. C., Mulrooney, B., & Black, A. E. (2000). *Avifauna of the Salton Sea: Abundance, distribution, and annual phenology* (Final Report EPA Contract No. R826552-01-0 to the Salton Sea Authority). Point Reyes Bird Observatory.

State of California. (2000). *The California spatial information library.* State of California. Retrieved from: http://www.gis.ca.gov/data_index.epl.

Sutton, R. (2001). *Summary of pupfish and historical background.* Denver, CO: U. S. Department of the Interior.

Takhtajan, A. (1986). Floristic regions of the world. 171-178. Berkeley, CA: University of California Press.

Terres, J. K. (1980). *The Audubon Society encyclopedia of North American birds* (1st ed.). New York: Alfred A. Knopf, Inc.

Tucker, A. B., Feldmann, R. M., & Powell, C. L. (1994). Speocarcinus berglundi n. sp. (Decapoda: brachyura), A New crab from the Imperial Formation (Late Miocene- Late Pliocene) of Southern California. *Journal of Paleontology,* 68(4), 800-807.

United Nations Environment Programme. (n.d.). *Eutrophication.* Retrieved from: http://www.grida.no/soeno97/eutro/eutro.htm.

U. S. Fish and Wildlife Service. (n.d.). *An approach to address losses of fish and wildlife habitat at the Salton Sea* (Mitigation Approach).

U. S. Fish and Wildlife Service. (n.d.). *Target species to address fish and wildlife goals.* Washington, D. C.: United States Fish and Wildlife Service.

U. S. Geological Survey. (2000). *Water resources in California project description: Measurement and analysis of potential land subsistence in Coachella.* Retrieved from: http://ca.water.usgs.gov/projects00/ca517.html.

Veirs, S. D. J., & Opler, P. A. (n.d.). *California.* Retrieved from: http://biology.usgs.gov/s+t/SNT/noframe/ca162.htm.

Woodward, S. (1996). *Merriam's life zones.* Retrieved from: http://www.runet.edu/~swoodwar/CLASSES/GEOG235/lifezone/merriam.html.

Yuhas, R. H. (1996, 7/10/97). *Loss of wetlands in the Southwestern United States.* Retrieved from: http://goechange.er.usgs.gov.

Maps

California Department of Conservation, Division of Oil, Gas, and Geothermal Resources. (2001). *Maps.* Retrieved from: http://www.consrv.ca.gov/dog/publications/map_b.htm.

California Department of Fish and Game, Wildlife & Data Analysis Branch. (2001). *California wildlife habitat relationship.* Retrieved from: http://www.dfg.ca.gov/whdab/html/cwhr.html.

California Energy Commission. (2001). *California on-line energy maps.* State of California. Retrieved from: http://www.energy.ca.gov/maps/index.html.

California Integrated Waste Management Board. (2001). *Solid waste information system (SWIS) database.* Retrieved from: http://www.ciwmb.ca.gov/SWIS.

Daly, C., & Taylor, G. (1998). *Climate mapping with PRISM.* Oregon State University, Spatial Climate Analysis Service. Retrieved from: http://www.ocs.orst.edu/prism.

Davis, L. (2001). *National state soil geographic (STATSGO) database.* UDSA-NRCS Soil Survey Division. Retrieved from: http://www.ftw.nrcs.usda.gov/stat_data.html.

Dwyer, C. (2002). *Bureau of Reclamation lower Colorado regional office.* United States Department of the Interior, Bureau of Reclamation. Retrieved from: http://www.lc.usbr.gov.

ESRI. (2001). *ESRI GIS & mapping software.* Retrieved from: http://www.esri.com/index.html.

LFR Levine-Fricke. (2001). *LFR Levine-Fricke.* Retrieved from: http://www.lfr.com/mainpage/mainpage4c.html.

Southern California Seismic Network. (2001). *Index of ftp/catalogs/SCSN.* U. S. Geological Survey. Retrieved from: http://www.scecdc.scec.org/ftp/catalogs/SCSN.

Stephen P. Teale Data Center. (2000). *Teale.* State of California. Retrieved from: http://www.teale.ca.gov.

The Redlands Institute. (2001). *Salton Sea database program.* Redlands, CA: University of Redlands. Retrieved from: http://www.institute.redlands.edu.

The University of Texas at Austin. (2001). *Perry-Castaneda Library map collection: Historical maps of the United States.* Austin,TX: General Libraries, The University of Texas at Austin. Retrieved from: http://www.lib.utexas.edu/maps/histus.html.

U. S. Department of the Interior. (1997). *Map layers warehouse: The national atlas of the United States of America.* Retrieved from: http://www.nationalatlas.gov/atlasftp.html.

U. S. Fish and Wildlife Service. (2002). *U. S. Fish and Wildlife Service: Conserving the nature of America.* Retrieved from: http://www.fws.gov.

U. S. Geological Survey. (2001). *Minerals Availability System/Minerals Industry Location System (MAS/MILS) database.* Retrieved from: http://www.usgs.gov.

U. S. Geological Survey. (2002). *List of spatial data sets for water.* Retrieved from: http://water.usgs.gov/lookup/getgislist.

U. S. Geological Survey Western Earth Surface Processes Team & National Park Service. (2000). *Geologic provinces of the Untied States: Records of an active earth.* Retrieved from: http://www2.nature.nps.gov/grd/usgsnps/province/province.html.

United States Census Bureau. (2002). *Topologically integrated geographic encoding and referencing system.* Retrieved from: http://www.census.gov.

Image Credits

The following photographs and illustrations are reprinted by permission. All rights are reserved by the copyright holders. Permission to reproduce these photographs and illustrations should be obtained directly from the copyright holders listed below:

Area Information Steward

Bulldozer, PhotoDisc V31 Environmental Concerns #BU000227. *Capital Building*, Nick Burka, istockphoto.com. *GPS Surveyor*, ESRI. *Library stacks*, PhotoDisc V107 School Life #AA039598. *Monitoring*, ESRI. *Protesters*, Bruce Livingston, istockphoto.com. *Researcher*, PhotoDisc V18 Health & Medicine #ST000997.

Salton Sea Database Program

Data: Funk, Digital Vision #237029. *Equipment*, Daniel Tang, istockphoto.com. *Group picture*, PhotoDisc V69 Meetings & Groups #AA001451. *Rolled map*, PhotoDisc DT03 Maps & Navigation #TR007464. *Software package*, ESRI.

Making the Atlas

Data inventory, ESRI.

Physical Geography

Bigelow Beargrass, photograph by Virginia Moore, California Academy of Sciences. *Blue Palo Verde*; *Joshua Tree*; and *Creosote* photographs by Charles Webber, California Academy of Sciences. *California Juniper*; *Whipple Yucca*; *Pygmy Cedar*; and *Mormon Tea*, photographs © Br. Alfred Brousseau, Saint Mary's College. *Catclaw*, photograph by Douglas Barbe. *Composite Brittlebush Image*, photographs by Gerald and Buff Corsi, California Academy of Sciences, and © Br. Alfred Brousseau, Saint Mary's College. *Composite Packrat* photographs, U. S. Geological Society U. S. Geological Survey / photos by Cole, Ken & W. G. Spaulding. *Desert Lavender* and *White Bursage*, photographs by Larry Blakely. *Mojave Sage*, photograph by Tom Schweich 2000, http://www.schweich.com. *Ragged Rock Flower*, photograph by G.F. Hrusa. *Tree-ring Dating*, PhotoDisc Environmental Concerns, vol. 31, 1996.

Cultural History

33 Frontage Rd., Highway 86 Salton City 1997, photograph by Chris Landis in *In Search of Eldorado: The Salton Sea*, 2000. *Agriculture field*, photographs PhotoDisk, vol. 31, Environmental Concerns, 1996. *Basket, pottery*, and *Gourd Rattles*, photographs of artifacts on display at Malki Museum, Inc., used with permission from Malki Museum, Inc. *Beau Geste movie poster*, Copyright 2002 by Univerisal Studios, courtesy of Univerisal Studios Publishing Rights, a Division of Universal Studios Licensing Inc. All rights reserved. *Bird*, photograph by Shuzo Yoshihara. *Modern Cahuilla dancers*, photograph used with permission from Malki Museum, Inc. *Canal lining*, photograph by Marcus Diederich. *Cahuilla House (Kish)*, James, George Wharton. *Through Ramona's Country.* Composite art: *Cahuilla man, Cahuilla woman, Four children sitting, Train, Group of men, Rail workers, Compass*, and *Boy fishing*; photographs of *Cahuilla man, Cahuilla woman, Four children sitting, Rail workers, Train*, and *Group of men* courtesy of Coachella Valley Historical Society; *Compass*, PhotoDisk, Maps and Navigation, vol. 3, 1999; *Boys fishing*, photograph by Bill Gay. Composite digital raster images: **Santa Ana** (33116-A1), **Salton Sea** (33114-A1), **San Diego** (32116-A1), **El Centro** (32 114-A1), U. S. Geologic Survey. *Dam*, U. S. Bureau of Reclamation / photograph by Kelly Conner. *Figure 10. - Wreck at Disaster Falls* from *Exploration of the Colorado River of the West and its tributaries: Explored in 1869, 1870, 1871, and 1872 under the direction of the Secretary of the Smithsonian Institution*, Washington, D.C.: Government Printing Office, 1875, University of North Texas Libraries, Government Documents Collection. *Fig. 59-Sketch map showing the engineering operations undertaken to close the openings in the western bank of the Colorado River, June, 1905, to February, 1907, Scale 1:42,240*, based on map by C.E. Tait, 60th Congr., 1st Sess., Senate Doc. No. 246, Washington, 1908 in Sykes, Godfrey (1937), *The Colorado Delta*, American Geographical Society Special Publication No. 19, edited by W. L. G. Joerg, Kennikat Press, New York, pg 113. *Fig. 62- Map showing the recession of the shoreline at the southeastern end of Salton Sea 1907-1923, Scale 1:253,440* in Sykes, Godfrey (1937), *The Colorado Delta*, American Geographical Society Special Publication No. 19, edited by W. L. G. Joerg, Kennikat Press, New York, pg 118. *First IID Board of Directors*, photograph used by permission of Imperial Irrigation District. *Fishkill*, U. S. Fish & Wildlife Service, Sonny Bono Salton Sea National Wildlife Refuge. *Flood*, photograph courtesy of Coachella Valley Historical Society. *Flooded homes*, photographs courtesy of Coachella Valley Historical Society. *Floods - 1906 Calexico waterfall*, photograph used by permission of Imperial Irrigation District. *Floods - 1906 Southern Pacific station at Mexicalli*, photograph used by permission of Imperial Irrigation District. *Floods - train on tracks over river*, photograph used by permission of Imperial Irrigation District. *Fruit*, PhotoDisc Fitness & Well-Being. *Gold nuggets*, PhotoDisc. *Group of men standing*, photograph courtesy of Coachella Valley Historical Society. *Historic California mission*, photograph from Keystone-Mast Collection UCR/California Museum of Photography, University of California at Riverside. *Historic canal*, photograph courtesy of Coachella Valley Historical Society. *Historic desert landscape*, photograph courtesy of Coachella Valley Historical Society. *Historic fruit stand*, photograph courtesy of Coachella Valley Historical Society. *Historic hand plow*, photograph of artifact on display at the Coachella Valley Historical Society Museum, courtesy of Coachella Valley Historical Society. *Historic market scene*, photograph courtesy of Coachella Valley Historical Society. *Historic people - two men talking, one on horseback*, photograph used by permission of Imperial Irrigation District. *Historic storefront with people standing*, photograph courtesy of Coachella Valley Historical Society. *Legal Documents*, PhotoDisc image #BU003209. *Lot auction - 1904 groundbreaking ceremony*, photograph used by permission of Imperial Irrigation District. *Map of California to accompany printed agreement of S.O. Houghton as to the rights of the Southern Pacific Railroad Company of California to government lands under Acts of Congress passed July 27, 1866 and March 3, 1871 made before the committee of the judiciary for the Senate and House of Reps. in May 1876, Scale 1:2,090,880*, G. W. & C. B. Colton & Company, Library of Congress Geography and Map Division. *Map of the Trans-Mississippi of the United States during the period of the American fur trade as conducted from St. Louis between the years 1807 and 1843*, in Chittenden, H. M., (S.1.) 1902, *History of the Fur Trade of the Far West*, vol. 3, Library of Congress, Geography and Map Division. *New 11x17 map of California*, in *Atlas of the World*, Rand McNally, 1895, Color Landform Atlas of the United States, http://fermi.jhuapl.edu/states. *Pelican*, photograph by Shuzo Yoshihara. *People bird watching*, photograph by Shuzo Yoshihara. *Rector & Griffin real estate sign*, photograph courtesy of Coachella Valley Historical Society. *Salt works*, photograph courtesy of Coachella Valley Historical Society. *Salton City "500" World's Richest Power Boat Race*, poster courtesy of Coachella Valley Historical Society. *Salton Sea boating - boy with fish*, photograph used by permission of Imperial Irrigation District. *Speed boat race*, photograph courtesy of Coachella Valley Historical Society. *Speed boat*, photograph courtesy of Coachella Valley Historical Society. *Reconnaissance Map of the Salton Sink, California*, E. M. Douglas, R. B. Marshall, W. Carvel Hal, Scale 1:500,000, 1908, U. S. Geologic Survey. *Train trestle*, photograph courtesy of Coachella Valley Historical Society. *The Union Pacific system of railroad and steamship lines, 1900*, Scale 1:6,000,000, Chicago, 1900, Library of Congress Geography and Map Division. *Various postcards*, courtesy of Coachella Valley Historical Society.

Limnology - The Sea Today

Bird die off, U. S. Fish & Wildlife Service, Sonny Bono Salton Sea National Wildlife Refuge. *Fish kill*, U.S. Fish & Wildlife Service, Sonny Bono Salton Sea National Wildlife Refuge. *Microrganisms*, PhotoDisc vol. 31 Environmental Concerns 1996. *Mountain and sea landscape*, photograph by Marcus Diederich. *Pelican*, photograph by Shuzo Yoshihara. *Primary producers/electron microscope organisms*, photograph printed with permission of San Diego State University, Center for Inland Waters, Principle Investigator Dr. Stuart H. Hurlbert. *Sunset*, photograph by Shuzo Yoshihara. *View of lake*, photograph by Dr. Milton Friend.

Ecology

Microscopic life, photograph printed with permission of San Diego State University, Center for Inland Waters, Principle Investigator Dr. Stuart H. Hurlbert. *Migrating birds*, photograph by Shuzo Yoshihara. *Fish die off*, U. S. Fish & Wildlife Service, Sonny Bono Salton Sea National Wildlife Refuge. *Fish scales*, U. S. Fish & Wildlife Service, Sonny Bono Salton Sea National Wildlife Refuge. *Birds*, photographs by Shuzo Yoshihara. *Microscopic view of food chain*, photograph printed with permission of San Diego State University, Center for Inland Waters, Principle Investigator Dr. Stuart H. Hurlbert.

Future of the Salton Sea

Flooded speed sign, photograph by Bill Gates Photography.

Maps

Mountain terrain land cover, photographs by Dr. Timothy Krantz. *Natural vegetation*, photographs by Dr. Timothy Krantz. *Bird banding*, U. S. Geological Society U. S. Geological Survey / photos by John Tautin. *Imperial Canal floods*, photograph used by permission of Imperial Irrigation District.

The Redlands Institute
Mark Sorensen, Redlands Institute Director

Salton Sea Database Program
Timothy Krantz, Salton Sea Database Program Principal Investigator
Stephen Hoover, Atlas Project Manager
Marcus Diederich, Editor and Project Technical Manager
Melissa Brenneman, Cartographic Manager

Content Research and Writing
Kenneth Althiser, Content Research
Pamela Arroues, Content Research
Patrick Egle, Content Research
Dina Guthrie, Content Research
Sabine Huynen, Content Research and Writing
Eric Kenas, Content Research
Debra Kreske, Content Research
Michael Karman, ESRI, Writing
Jacquie Lesch, Content Research
Lisa Lewis, Content Research

Information Collection and Cataloging
Lisa Lewis, Coordinator, Information Collection
Kenneth Althiser, Information Collection
Sabine Huynen, Information Collection
Patrick Egle, Information Collection
Jacqueline Lesch, Coordinator, Information Catalog
Pamela Arroues, Information Catalog
Alexandria Rackerby, Intern, Information Catalog

GIS Production
Kenneth Althiser, Data Analysis and Preparation
Richard Inman, Data Analysis and Preparation
Frank Davenport, Intern, Data Analysis
Peter Ma, Intern, Data Analysis
Eric Kenas, Data Preparation
Lisa Lewis, Data Preparation

Cartographic Production
Edith Punt, ESRI, Cartography
Richard Inman, Cartography
Frank Davenport, Intern, Cartography
Peter Ma, Intern, Cartography
Ayako Oyako, RI International Intern, Cartography
Elianne Loya, Intern, Cartography

Project Administration and Support
Dina Guthrie, Office Administration
Beth Eiland, Grant Administration
Helen Morey, Grant Administration
Patrick Egle, Project Tracking
Giovani Napoletano, Project Tracking
Erika Edwards, Office Support
Janurary Gregov, Intern, Office Support

Computing Infrastructure
Clay Collins, Programming and System Support
Steven Paplanus, Programming and System Support
Robert Sporrong, Systems Administration

Graphic Design and Production
Robert Rose, Art Director, Designer
Wendy Atil, Designer
Michael Brown, Designer
Scott Goto, Illustrator
Robert Rusnak, Designer

Lead Agency - Atlas Review
Milton Friend, Salton Sea Science Sub-Committee
Executive Director & Salton Sea Science Office Chief Scientist
Tom Kirk, Salton Sea Authority Executive Director
Bill Steele, Salton Sea Program Manager
Michael Walker, Salton Sea Project Manager

Atlas Review
Michael Cohen, Pacific Institute Senior Research Associate

Content Contributors
Doug Barnum, Bird Diversity & Migration
Christopher Cook, Limnology
Christopher Holdren, Limnology
Steve Horvitz, Development
Patricia Laflin, Cultural History
Glen McDonald, Paleo Climate
Richard Minnich, Climate
Roy Schroeder, Limnology
James Setmire, Limnology
Michael Rymer, Geology
Michael Walker, Controlled River & Economy of Water

Special Thanks
Doug Barnum
Barry Costa-Pierce
Karen Kemp
Jonathan Matti
Michael Patten
Ralf Riedel
Eugene Singer
Jonathan Singer
Ron Sutton

Environmental Systems Research Institute (ESRI, Inc.)

ESRI Press
Christian Harder, ESRI Press Manager
Edith Punt, Atlas Project Manager
Steve Hegle, Distribution Manager

Print Production
Cliff Crabbe, Print Coordinator
Michael Hyatt, Production Consultant
Jennifer Johnston, Production Consultant

Editorial Review
Gary Amdahl, Editor
Michael Karman, Editor
Tiffany Wilkerson, Copy Editor